COAL WARS

COAL WARS

Unions, Strikes, and Violence
in Depression-Era Central Washington

DAVID BULLOCK

WSU
PRESS

Washington State University
Pullman, Washington

Washington State University Press
PO Box 645910
Pullman, Washington 99164-5910
Phone: 800-354-7360
Fax: 509-335-8568
Email: wsupress@wsu.edu
Website: wsupress.wsu.edu

Library of Congress Cataloging-in-Publication Data

Bullock, David, 1954-
   Coal wars : unions, strikes, and violence in depression-era central Washington / David Bullock.
       pages cm
   Includes bibliographical references and index.
   ISBN 978-0-87422-325-5 (alk. paper)
1. Strikes and lockouts—Washington (State) 2. Strikes and lockouts—Coal min-ing—Washington (State) 3. Coal miners—Washington (State) 4. Labor disputes—Washington (State) I. Title.
   HD5325.M615B85 2014
   331.892'82233409797509043--dc23

                                                                            2014017377

Contents

Illustrations

Preface and Dedication

The struggle for recognition of a new labor union—the Western Miners Union of America—in a remote community of coal miners in central Washington State in the 1930s is the story of America's struggle to rebuild the nation's economy in the depths of the worst economic crisis the United States has ever faced. It is the story of the struggle to bring fair wages and safe conditions to workers who risked their lives to fuel the wheels of national progress, the struggle of local leaders who stood against powerful federal and labor interests.

But it is also the story of simple, hard-working families, transplanted far from relatives, homes, and familiar customs, seeking the promise of work and a better life for their children, pulled into a conflict that they did not fully understand and acting to protect their families, their jobs, and their lives.

My grandfather, Herman Swanson, was one of those miners. He died eight years before I was born. I knew nothing of his life in mining. Visiting his grave in Roslyn, Washington, I have wondered about his life. My quest brought me to the story of the Western Miners Union.

Herman's daughter, my mother Hannah, wrote a personal history that included childhood memories of Roslyn. That history has provided a rich context of life in Roslyn in the 1930s. Herman's son, my uncle Clarence, also shared with me, through numerous hikes and stories, his love of the mountains and the history of the land. Family events and conversations in this book have been created to aid the narrative and are noted in italic type. All other information was obtained from documented sources and is footnoted.

My mother's family never discussed the Western Miners strike; perhaps they would have if asked, but we children did not know to ask. Herman's participation with the United Mine Workers is based on information from a long-time family friend, Harry Georgeson.

This book is dedicated to the miners of Roslyn. In telling this dramatic episode in Roslyn's history, I hope to honor the community and the families who struggled through those tumultuous times.

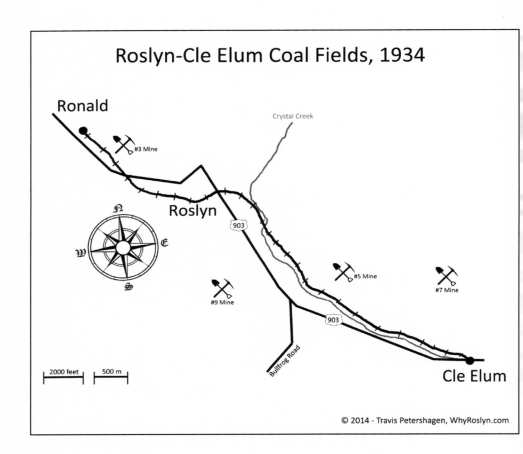

Roslyn-Cle Elum Coal Fields, 1934

Ronald

Crystal Creek

#3 Mine

Roslyn

903

#5 Mine

#7 Mine

#9 Mine

903

Bullfrog Road

2000 feet   500 m

Cle Elum

© 2014 - Travis Petershagen, WhyRoslyn.com

Prologue

The six-month saga of the Western Miners Union in Roslyn, Washington, began in hope and determination, but ended in bitter disappointment and frustration. Communities were torn apart, friends became enemies, and memories of abuses festered for generations.

Why did it happen? What caused the movement to flourish for a time and then to fade into obscurity? What factors pressured miners to take such risks with their friendships and their futures? What prompted the federal government to impose such drastic changes to its economic and labor policies? Why did coal operators refuse to negotiate with a union representing an apparent majority of the miners? What prompted the violence that erupted between mining families in formerly peaceful communities?

Answering those questions requires an investigation of the situation from such diverse perspectives as the miner in Roslyn and the mine owner in St. Paul, Minnesota; the union president in Washington, DC; and the Communist organizer in Seattle. All influenced the events in Roslyn in the spring of 1934 in ways that changed the community forever.

Roslyn was not alone. Similar battles occurred in hundreds of communities across the nation in the early 1930s. Workers in steel mills, auto factories, and garment shops were facing unemployment, wage cuts, long hours, and unsafe and unfair conditions.

With the nation's economy in collapse and banks shuttering their doors, Franklin Delano Roosevelt assumed the presidency in March 1933, with the promise to America's workers of a New Deal—a promise of fair wages and a revitalized economy. His inauguration initiated a 105-day period of frantic bureaucratic innovation seeking work for the nation's one-in-four unemployed workers and cash flow for their employers.[1]

The dreams of Roslyn miners for better wages and hours were ultimately bound to the nation's recovery efforts of those 105 days. Yet a closer look at their struggle reveals dissatisfactions that existed long before the Depression or the promises of recovery from the Roosevelt Administration.

King Coal

The life of a Washington State coal miner in the 1930s was anything but easy. The work was heavy, dirty, confined, dusty, exhausting, and dangerous. Miners earned living wages when the mines were working, but demand for coal was declining, and idle days were becoming more numerous.

Since the early 1890s, coal production had become a major component in the region's economic development. While Washington State's coal production would never challenge the output of the Appalachia fields of the eastern United States, Washington was the second-largest coal-producing state in the West during the first third of the century.[2] And the Roslyn coal field was the largest single coal-producing region in the state, generating 40 to 50 percent of the state's annual coal yield during that era.[3]

Between 1890 and 1900, U.S. coal production had nearly doubled from 118 million to 212 million net tons annually, and then doubled again by 1910 to 417 million net tons. Coal usage, however, began to level off after 1910 in the face of competition from electricity, oil, and natural gas. World War I produced a bubble in demand, and U.S. coal production peaked at 579 million net tons in 1918.[4] Demand tapered downward from the post-war highs to a nationwide production level of 305 million net tons in 1932.[5]

Coal production in Washington State during those years closely followed the national trend. Mines in the state produced two million net tons in 1900, and that number doubled by 1918. After the war bubble, demand declined steadily, pushing production down below two million net tons in 1931.[6]

Coal deposits in Washington State were distributed chiefly along the western slope of the Cascade Mountain range. Important coal fields were located in Whatcom, Skagit, King, Pierce, Thurston,

Coal producing regions of Washington State. *Washington State Department of Natural Resources*

Lewis, and Cowlitz counties on the western side of the Cascades. The Roslyn-Cle Elum coal field in Kittitas County was the single major field east of the Cascades, but it contributed nearly half of the state's annual coal production during the 1920s and 1930s.[7]

Coal is generally classified into four broad categories or ranks reflecting density and carbon content as deposits are, over centuries, subjected to increasing heat and pressure.[8]

- *Anthracite* is the hardest coal with the highest carbon content. It produces the highest levels of heat, up to nearly 15,000 BTU/lb. It burns without a flame and was widely sought for home heating. It was mined prominently in Pennsylvania and used in iron and steel production.

- *Bituminous* coal is a harder black or striped coal. The most plentiful of all coals in the United States, bituminous coal is used in electrical power generation and was in wide use for home heating and rail transportation. Its heat content ranges from 11,500 to 14,000 BTU/lb.

- *Subbituminous* coal is a softer coal and can appear from dull brown to bright black in color. Its heat content ranges from 8,300 to 11,500 BTU/lb.

- *Lignite* is the softest brown coal and is the youngest and least developed of the coal types. With characteristics between peat and coal, it produces the least heat per pound (less than 8,300 BTU/lb.). The Northern Pacific Railroad strip-mined lignite from Rosebud County in eastern Montana beginning in the mid-1920s and called it Rosebud coal. Inexpensive and available in mass quantities, it was referred to by locals as "burnable dirt."[9]

Washington State coal varied from lignite to anthracite with the highest grades of coal coming from the state's mountainous regions. Much of the coal from the Kittitas fields was a high grade bituminous coal, providing some of the highest energy ratings of bituminous coal mined anywhere in the state (12,240 to 13,250 BTU/lb.).[10]

Unfortunately, as the nation's demand for coal dropped in the early 1920s, production capacity increased as speculators drove investments in new mining ventures. The government did little to limit mining investments during the period, so coal mines continued to open. Coal operations, however, were not as responsive to market forces as other industries. Opening a new mine required a major investment of capital. If a mine was not constantly maintained, its shafts could deteriorate rapidly as water filled chambers and beams and ceilings began to crack. So while coal production increased, coal demand and prices dropped, leaving owners to face losing their initial investment or producing at a loss. Many kept producing.[11]

This overproduction of coal pushed prices downward through the 1920s and, along with it, the wages of miners. The number of commercial mines in the country peaked in 1923 at 9,331, but that number moved downward through the 1920s. By 1932, the number of producing mines in the nation had dropped by nearly half that number to just over 5,000. The number of employed miners declined from 700,000 to around 500,000 during that same span.[12] Between 1926 and 1932, the average number of days a coal miner worked per year fell from 215 to 146, and average earnings dropped from seventy-six cents to fifty cents per hour.[13]

Mining Technologies

New technologies in mining were, at that same time, affecting the availability and price of coal. The coal miner of the 1890s performed a number of tasks by hand—chipping slots along the bases of walls of coal with a hand pick, drilling holes for dynamite with a hand auger, preparing charges and blasting the rock surface, and then shoveling the broken coal into a coal car and pushing the loaded car to a passageway to be hauled out of the mine.

One of the major advances in coal production in the early 1900s was the use of coal cutting machines. These chainsaw-like devices cut a path into the base of a coal face with more speed and depth than could be achieved by hand. Their electric motors were intended to prevent sparks from igniting in the gas-filled mines. The machines completed the tedious undercuts much more quickly than hand picks, and the deep undercuts allowed miners to use less dynamite to bring down the coal. With a smaller charge, less coal was blasted into dust and more remained in marketable chunks. The electric cutting machines quickly gained wide industry use; in 1900 machines cut 25 percent of U.S. tonnage, but by 1930 that number had risen to 81 percent.[14]

Cle Elum miner Art Pasa shovels coal onto a jig conveyor in No. 5 mine in 1942. A vertical coal cutting machine at rear left was designed and built by Northwestern Improvement Company engineers and mechanics in Roslyn to accommodate the steep sloped conditions in the mines. *Courtesy of Roslyn Public Library, Roslyn Heritage Collection, by permission of Frank Schuchman*

The introduction of machine mining changed the workplace for coal miners. Mine operators could train unskilled workers in a specialized phase of mining such as cutting, drilling, blasting, or loading. Teams of men operating machines took over the mines, and experienced miners who prided themselves on possessing a wide range of skills saw their value dropping. Miners' pay transitioned in this era from an incentive-based system where they were paid for each ton they produced to a flat-rate system where they were paid by the day.

Another transformation in coal production was the expansion of pit mining. These open-earth operations could employ workers with less skill and experience, many of whom were willing to work without union contracts. Facing declining demands for coal and with a surplus of unskilled workers, mine operators around the country sought in the 1920s to break the backs of the coal unions by

Miners operate a shortwall mining machine in Ronald's No. 3 mine. The use of coal cutting machinery did not come to the Roslyn-Cle Elum coal field until the late 1920s since the machines were designed for use in relatively flat areas. The slope of many of the state's coal fields presented difficult engineering challenges. *Courtesy of Roslyn Public Library, Roslyn Heritage Collection, by permission of Frank Schuchman*

offering work opportunities to miners who would agree to not join a labor union. Membership in the United Mine Workers of America dropped from half a million in 1923 to just over 100,000 by 1931.[15]

Many immigrant workers who came to the United States in the 1910s and early 1920s found good jobs in the mines. They developed specialized skills only to find their incomes and hopes for the future plummeting in the 1930s. Some miners left the fields in search of brighter opportunities, but many in isolated communities like Roslyn were unwilling to pull up stakes and move again to new communities or take up new lines of employment. With a low turnover rate among miners, Washington State had the most stable work force of any coal-producing state in the nation.[16]

Radical Politics

Beyond the numerous work-related and financial concerns vying for a Washington coal miner's attention in the 1930s was a milieu of social and political influences agitating for radical labor reform.

Socialism

The socialist movement in the United States can be traced back to 1877 with the establishment of a Marxist political party in New Jersey that fought for such worker benefits as an eight-hour work day, employer liability, a graduated income tax, government ownership of vital industries and services, and protective laws for female and child workers.[17]

Early socialists hoped that successful utopian communities, where residents worked together for the benefit of the group rather than for wealthy capitalists, might provide the springboard for further growth. Sparsely populated regions of Washington State attracted several such groups. The Puget Sound Cooperative Colony sprang up near Port Angeles in 1887. Although this first colony was short-lived, other colonies were established in the state at Equality, in Skagit County, and Burley, in Kitsap County, in the late 1890s.[18]

A Socialist Labor Party was founded in Washington State in 1890 in Tacoma with nineteen members. But as with the national movement, state socialists suffered fractious internal divisions over such issues as whether they should join with other groups seeking change. Such divisions kept membership low and effectiveness limited.[19]

In the late 1890s, an eloquent socialist leader emerged on the national scene. Eugene V. Debs rallied workers to become involved in politics and to use their votes to effect change. He admired the efforts of utopian communities in the state and found Northwest workers who shared his views on worker oppression:[20] "I am opposing a social order in which it is possible for one man who does absolutely nothing that is useful to amass a fortune of hundreds of millions of dollars, while millions of men and women who work all the days of their lives secure barely enough for a wretched existence."[21]

Some factions of socialist thought believed that Marx had provided scientific proof that a movement toward a socialist society and away from capitalism was inevitable. Others believed more direct means of reform or revolt were required. These divisions undermined efforts at compromise among the several factions of the movement.[22]

One vision did manage to bring together various forces in the socialist movement—a vision to unite workers from all industries, both skilled and unskilled, around a central labor organization in contrast to the conservative American Federation of Labor, which organized skilled workers into hundreds of individualized craft unions. Socialist leaders believed that mass strikes would carry greater impact and eventually bring about systemic reform. A number of prominent socialists met in Chicago in 1905 to form a union for the common worker—the Industrial Workers of the World. Bill Hayward, who headed the Western Federation of Miners, opened the organization's founding convention with these words:

> We are here to confederate the workers of this country into a working class movement that shall have for its purpose the emancipation of the working class from the slave bondage of capitalism…The aims and objectives of this organization shall be to put the working class in possession of the economic power, the means of life, in control of the machinery of production and distribution, without regard to capitalist masters. The American Federation of Labor, which presumes to be the labor movement of this country…does not represent the working class.[23]

Eugene Debs ran for president as a Socialist five times and polled over 900,000 votes nationally in 1912 and 1920. Washington State gave the candidate some 40,000 votes in 1912, and Socialist candidates in the state captured city council offices in Everett, Edmonds, and Pasco as well as one state legislative seat. Party membership peaked in 1913 with some 3,335 members in more than two hundred locals.[24] Nationally, the party elected two U.S. Representatives, a number of state legislators, and more than one hundred mayors.[25]

Socialist voices against American involvement in the World War in 1917–18 provided fodder for those who sought to silence the movement; Debs' last campaign in 1920 was waged from a prison cell. Persecution followed socialists even after the war ended.[26] A *Seattle Post-Intelligencer* advertisement illustrated the sentiments of Northwest business owners in that era: "We must smash every un-American and anti-American organization in the land. We must put to death the leaders of this gigantic conspiracy of murder, pillage and revolution. We must imprison for life all its aiders and abetters of native birth. We must deport all aliens."[27]

In the face of such opposition, socialist activity declined for a time. Yet there were those in mining communities of Washington State who resonated with the 1928 Socialist Party platform statement: "We stand now as always, in America and in all lands, for the collective ownership of natural resources and basic industries and their democratic management for the use and benefit of all instead of the private profit of the privileged few."[28]

The socialist movement can be credited with providing an organizational incubator for those envisioning labor reforms. In fact, many of the original goals of early socialist groups were absorbed into the programs of the New Deal. The movement also spawned more radical perspectives.

Industrial Workers of the World

One of the most radical of labor interests operating in Washington State in the early 1900s was the Industrial Workers of the World (IWW), the "Wobblies." Established in 1905, the IWW set as its goal to enlist working-class wage earners into a single large industrial union that, through a series of strikes, would bring a general strike among workers and force the downfall of capitalism.[29]

The IWW promoted a perspective that saw industry and government coming under the control of labor unions or federations. Some leaders advocated the use of violence and sabotage to achieve their objectives.[30]

Even though IWW members were allowed to hold membership in other unions, the movement received limited support among organized workers, never holding more than 5 percent of all trade union membership nationally.[31] The IWW gained little serious traction among miners in the Roslyn coal fields, but the group did produce a notable following in the early 1900s among nonunionized timber and dock workers.[32] The IWW established a union hall for a short time in Cle Elum, Washington, in 1917.[33]

Wobbly efforts in Spokane in 1909 to recruit lumbermen through street corner speeches prompted mass arrests and led to an organized free-speech demonstration. As soon as police would arrest one speaker, another would step in and continue speaking. Noted Wobbly organizer Elizabeth Gurley Flynn was among more than five hundred jailed during the demonstrations.[34] The free speech action in Spokane preceded numerous similar demonstrations around the country.[35]

Two other events, which came to be known as the Everett and Centralia Massacres, illustrated an intense distrust and hatred of IWW activity in the state. In 1916, more than forty Wobblies in Everett, Washington, were arrested and then handed over by police deputies to a group of vigilantes who beat them savagely. When Seattle IWW members heard of the beatings, they set out by boat for Everett, some two hundred and fifty strong, to rally support for their beaten members. Their boat was met by two hundred deputized Everett businessmen who opened fire on the IWW members, killing at least five and injuring scores more.[36]

Three years later, a group of American Legion members in Centralia, Washington, raided an IWW hall intent on destroying it, but were met by armed IWW members. In the ensuing melee, four Legionnaires were killed and another wounded. One of the alleged IWW shooters was later forcibly removed from jail by vigilantes and lynched.[37]

Between these two events, another devastating blow to IWW effectiveness came during the First World War. Numerous radical leaders voiced opposition to U.S. entry into the war, urging resistance to the draft and recognition of the Bolshevik government in Russia. Many interpreted those ideas as subversive threats. More than one hundred IWW leaders were convicted of sabotage and imprisoned, with sentences up to twenty years. With the loss of leadership, the organization foundered.[38]

In 1919, U.S. Attorney General A. Mitchell Palmer ordered Socialists, Communists, and Wobblies who were not U.S. citizens to be deported to the Soviet Union as subversive aliens. Several additional IWW leaders in the state were captured and deported.[39]

Publicity from the massacres and deportations colored perceptions of the IWW for years to follow. Many saw the Centralia Massacre as part of a planned IWW conspiracy.[40] In the post-war "Red Scare," the state passed a law in 1920 making it illegal to belong to the IWW, and state IWW leaders were forced to work in secret. Some joined forces with Communist labor efforts while others refused, thus splitting the movement further.[41]

Communism

On the heels of the IWW activist period, the work of the Communist Party formed another significant element of Northwest labor history. Communists shared concerns similar to the IWW over worker exploitation and oppression under capitalism. Communists believed that worker dissatisfaction would lead to increasing labor unrest, to numerous strikes, and eventually to cataclysmic nationwide revolt and the overthrow of the government. Following the collapse of the government, Communists envisioned workers establishing a workers' and farmers' government.[42]

Two Communist groups formed in the United States after the Russian revolution in 1917. One group attempted to take over the existing Socialist Party, but their attempts failed and they were expelled. The group then re-formed in September 1919, as the Communist Labor Party, and they attracted a following largely among native-born radicals. Another group formed as the Communist Party of America and attracted a significant following of foreign-born members.[43]

Members of the Communist parties in the early 1920s included former Wobblies. Historian Daeha Ko notes: "Indeed, the Communists hoped to replace the IWW as the militant voice of the Left and worked hard to recruit in the lumber camps and skid-roads where the IWW had been strong."[44]

The Communist Party worked to establish professional revolutionaries in communities, and these individuals dedicated their lives to teaching and promoting the Communist perspective, often at great risk of arrest and persecution, and often without financial support. The party organized into districts, with nuclei groups established among workers. Typical party work included running political campaigns, organizing demonstrations, circulating literature, and raising funds.[45] While the party attracted few members, the work of its professionals carried an impact felt in large and small communities around the state, including Roslyn.

In addition, the party spawned a number of organizations—sometimes labeled "fronts" by their detractors—that provided services such as legal assistance to striking or imprisoned protestors (International Labor Defense), youth education (Young Communist League), and relief of starvation in Russia. Typical of most Communist activity, these organizations were controlled directly by the party.[46]

The two Communist factions united in 1921, but their work began to attract the attention of local and state authorities. Party members were rounded up along with IWW members and other radicals following the Centralia Massacre, and some were arrested and deported. To limit exposure, the party called themselves "The Workers' Party." But much of their work had to move underground, and when they did organize public activities they faced constant scrutiny by state authorities.[47]

Seattle Mayor Frank Edwards voiced a sentiment felt among concerned citizens when he ordered the arrest of Communist leaders in Seattle in anticipation of possible violence during an Armistice Day parade:

> I will tolerate no inciting of riots, no demonstrations against our government, no raising of the red flag of anarchy or any other move to destroy the peace and tranquility of our citizens and to make a mockery of the rights of peaceful assembly and free speeches guaranteed by our constitution. These people do not attempt to avail themselves of the constitutional guarantees; they deride them, mock at them, use a pretense of privileges for wanton license of disorder. That we cannot tolerate—not in Seattle.[48]

Communists in the state continued to work, through the mid-1920s, to assert control over the Seattle Central Labor Council, an affiliate of the American Federation of Labor (AFL). Their attempts were rebuffed by AFL leaders who demanded that the Seattle group expel known Communists. The party fell into decline in the state in the late 1920s.[49]

In 1928, the Communist leadership turned to a different tactic to stir labor unrest. Instead of attempting to gain control of existing labor unions, the party's focus turned to building their own party-controlled unions and establishing unemployed councils.[50] The role of these councils became public demonstration and agitation for government relief.

Police in the state took a hard line on Communist activities, often arresting leaders whenever they held public meetings. Leaders were charged with vagrancy or criminal syndicalism and threatened with deportation.[51]

When it could, the party fanned the flames of unrest wherever it was occurring among workers by publicizing strikes in party newspapers, providing legal defense to strikers, and soliciting funds for striking families.[52]

Radicals in Roslyn

Labor tensions were a fact of life for Roslyn coal miners from the beginning of mining operations in the region, as they were for miners everywhere.

Roslyn's mines began operation in 1886. The Northern Pacific Coal Company operated the mines as a subsidiary of the Northern Pacific Railroad whose transcontinental lines ran through the area. Abraham Lincoln signed the railroad's charter in 1864, granting the company sections of land adjoining the rail line as an incentive to build a northern transcontinental line. The railway sold some sections, logged others, and mined coal to fuel its steam locomotives from mines in Montana and Washington.[53]

In the early 1880s, the railroads used Chinese workers to complete their transcontinental lines. The Northern Pacific alone imported some 15,000 Chinese laborers willing to take on the demanding and dangerous work.[54] As rail lines were completed, the Chinese sought other work in the region. Unemployed whites became angered at seeing Chinese workers taking jobs, and in 1882 the U.S. Congress passed the Chinese Exclusion Act, shutting down Chinese immigration for a decade.[55]

In September of 1885, white miners at the Newcastle mines east of Seattle set fire to the sleeping quarters of Chinese coworkers. A month later some three thousand Tacoma workers drove the Chinese from town. Seattle workers followed, forcing the territorial governor to declare martial law in the city.[56]

A growing industrial labor union, the Knights of Labor, started as a secret society in Philadelphia in 1869, but built a nationwide following among workers after a successful railroad strike in 1877.[57] By the mid-1880s, the Knights represented some 700,000 workers in a number of industries including coal mining, and was described as a "somewhat radical group of industrial unionists," increasingly active in Oregon, Idaho, and Washington.[58]

In the Northwest, the Knights of Labor fanned smoldering fears of a Chinese labor insurgency as a tactic to rally white miners.[59] Roslyn miners organized under the Knights of Labor banner shortly after mines opened there in 1886, but mine operators of the Northern Pacific Coal Company refused to recognize the union and threatened to fire workers who joined.[60]

As tensions simmered in mining camps throughout the region, the Knights of Labor called for a strike in Roslyn in August 1888, demanding an eight-hour day instead of company's required ten or more hours. The coal company refused to recognize the demands of the Knights of Labor and instead imported some three hundred black miners under armed guard to work the mines. The striking miners were forced to yield without a single concession from the coal company, and many strikers were not hired back.[61]

White miners were less than gracious to the black strike breakers. They were known to assign them the toughest mine jobs at the worst locations.[62] But black miners remained an active force in the Roslyn community, constituting 22 percent of the town's population in 1900.[63]

For more than a decade after the unsuccessful strike, the coal company refused to recognize a miners' union in Roslyn. The Northern Pacific Railroad went bankrupt in the economic panic of 1893, but was reorganized and continued operation. The Northwestern Improvement Company (NWI) purchased the Northern Pacific Coal Company in 1899 and managed coal, irrigation, and land investments of the Northern Pacific Railroad for decades after.[64] The NWI, how-ever, was no more inclined to recognize a coal miners' union than its predecessor.

The pathways that brought miners to the Roslyn fields, however, ran for some through the hard rock mines of Colorado and Idaho where a radical industrial union had formed in 1893. The Western Federation of Miners (WFM) took a hardline stand in labor negoti-ations, leading to notable violent clashes with mine operators.[65] At its 1901 convention, the union proclaimed that "complete revolu-tion of social and economic conditions" was "the only salvation of the working classes."[66] Many considered the WFM the most mili-tant labor organization in the country, and by 1903 the WFM had recruited some four hundred miners in the Roslyn fields.[67]

After the demise of the Knights of Labor movement in the early 1890s, a large number of miners gravitated toward another more moderate and growing miners' union, the United Mine Workers of America (UMWA). Recruiters of the UMWA began enlisting Roslyn miners in 1901, and within three years claimed a statewide mem-bership of 3,000, nearly half of them from the Roslyn field. The NWI coal company came to the realization that a failure to recognize the stable and powerful UMWA might encourage miners to move into the ranks of the more radical Western Federation of Miners. So, to avoid further labor unrest, the NWI recognized the UMWA in a for-mal agreement on September 1, 1904.[68]

Under the leadership of John Mitchell, the UMWA remained committed to building a stable working environment that brought better wages and working conditions for miners.[69] Miners accepted a wage freeze and a no-strike clause during the World War.[70] But a postwar wage freeze prompted a period of upheaval for the UMWA and a change in leadership that would affect miners for generations to come.

UMWA and Communism

Communist labor organizers in the United States worked to "drill from within" to establish connections and elect sympathetic lead-ers within the United Mine Workers of America from 1919 to 1928.

The Trade Union Educational League, directed by William Z. Foster, promoted radical change by working from inside existing unions.[71] They attempted to educate workers about the benefits of collective action, and to push for the election of candidates sympathetic to their ideologies. Their attempts to influence the UMWA were met with determined resistance from the organization's leadership.[72]

John L. Lewis

John L. Lewis was perhaps the most dominant force in the labor movement of the 1920s and 1930s, and his leadership shaped the face of the coal industry from the time he assumed the presidency of the United Mine Workers of America in 1920 until his retirement in 1960.

The son of an Iowa coal miner, Lewis had ten years of formal schooling before entering the mines at age fifteen. He became involved in miners' causes in several coal regions before being elected president of the local UMWA in Panama, Illinois, in 1909. His work on behalf of mining safety and fair compensation caught the eye of national labor organizers, and he served as field representative for the American Federation of Labor for six years. After becoming a vice president of the UMWA in 1917, Lewis took control of the largest union in America, with nearly 500,000 members, in 1919 as acting president before being voted as president the following year.[73]

Lewis's work on behalf of coal miners brought many improvements to their lives— shorter working hours, safer

In the 1930s, John L. Lewis led the nation's most powerful labor union. His dynamic and defiant leadership gained the respect of miners across the United States but also earned him many enemies among those who disagreed with his tactics as head of the United Mine Workers of America. *Permission of United Mine Workers of America*

working conditions, better health and survivor benefits, the end of child labor. To millions of mining families, he was a saint. For years after he left the national scene, Roslyn families received their "John L." as they referred to their mining pension checks. A popular story in Roslyn suggested that three pictures hung prominently in many mining homes—Jesus, FDR, and John L. Lewis. By some accounts, Jesus' photo was not always at the top; such was the respect for Lewis.[74]

Lewis was not universally loved, however. He made as many enemies as friends during his tenure with the UMWA. And his enemies viewed him as something of an egomaniac, a pugnacious demagogue, a leader who wielded unchallenged power for his own ends.[75] Photographs of Lewis during his tenure as mining union leader depict a rugged fighter who could command the respect and fear of miners.

Dual Unionism

Confronting Lewis as he took the presidency of the UMWA was a concerted effort among socialist and communist organizers to elect sympathetic miners to key positions within the union. From 1919 to 1922, Lewis sought to cement his hold over the union and to throw out such dissenters. He often referred to those who disagreed with his perspective as "dual unionists," and he was given authority to revoke the charters of any local union chapter that refused to follow his authority. He used the dual unionist label often in reference to any effort to organize a second union to represent mining interests, and often solely as a derogatory epithet against anyone who questioned his authority.[76]

When miners in Illinois walked out to strike against the postwar wage freeze, Lewis revoked their local charters, and a UMWA publication labeled the strikers as dual unionists.[77] Leaders expelled from the UMWA frequently joined forces with Communist organizers attempting to win control of the union.[78]

Lewis's purges made it difficult for those holding radical views to organize a resistance to his leadership. By 1928, Communist organizers abandoned "drill from within" and adopted a dual union strategy. The Trade Union Unity League was established in 1928 as a Communist-controlled labor federation.[79] The mining element of that federation became the National Miners Union.[80] The union found support in the anthracite fields of Pennsylvania between 1928 and 1931,[81] but it failed to attract sufficient support as a national union and was abandoned in 1934.[82]

National Recovery

As the nation's economy worsened in the early 1930s, so did the plight of Roslyn miners. Unemployment brought a downturn in sales, and fewer goods being shipped by coal-powered railroads meant fewer days of work in the mines. The election of 1932 brought a spark of hope to the nation, and the new president's promise of a new deal energized miners with hope of better pay in the nation's economic recovery. Hopes were sparked further with congressional passage of a recovery bill that promised workers greater powers in negotiating fair wages.

The National Recovery Administration (NRA) was established in June 1933 as a major industrial component of the New Deal. The act that created the NRA set broad powers for representatives of business, labor, and government to negotiate fair prices, wages, and working hours in various industries. The goal of the act was to limit the fierce competitive industry practices that economists saw as driving down prices, fueling unemployment, and stimulating overproduction.[83]

The act also established protections for the rights of workers to join unions of their own choosing without discrimination from employers. Labor leaders took this language as a pro-union government endorsement, and they set out to enlist workers around the nation. Membership in the United Mine Workers of America rebounded from 100,000 members to nearly 400,000 during the summer following the bill's signing.[84]

NRA leaders set out to establish codes of fair competition in a number of key industries including coal, but, as in other industries, coal producers were reluctant to accept government interference in their private sector affairs and continued to drag their feet in the negotiations.

NRA chief Hugh S. Johnson, saw that code negotiations could take months or years to coordinate. Seeking swift action, Johnson introduced a blanket code setting basic wages of $12 to $15 per week for a thirty-five to forty-hour work week. The code was mailed to every business owner in the nation. Owners who pledged to abide by the code could post a sign in the window of their business, a blue eagle over the words, "We Do Our Part."[85]

The symbol of business participation in the National Recovery Administration was the NRA Blue Eagle. Business owners who complied with federal wage standards displayed the symbol in their windows, and shoppers were encouraged to shop only at those businesses.
Public domain

In late June 1933, the NRA launched a massive thirty-day propaganda drive to rally public support and to pressure businesses to comply with the blanket code. The effort included mass rallies and parades, speeches, and press publicity, along with a presidential Fireside Chat on July 24.[86] Citizens were urged to shop only at businesses where the blue eagle was displayed.

Talks over a coal code dragged through the summer, forcing President Roosevelt to intercede by demanding that talks continue seven days a week until an agreement could be reached. At the president's urging, the coal for code was established in mid-September at the rate of $5.40 for an eight-hour day and a forty-hour week, despite the union demand for a six-hour day and thirty-six-hour week. Miners did earn the right to union dues check-off (which allowed miners to designate payroll deductions of union dues), an end to child labor, assurance of cash wages, and an end to the company store monopoly.[87]

The NRA was established as an emergency economic measure, set to expire in two years without further legislative action. But before the close of the second year, the U.S. Supreme Court had found the NRA unconstitutional, ruling unanimously that the act infringed on the separation of powers under the constitution.[88]

Historians have concluded that the NRA did little to create jobs or to stimulate economic recovery. The agency, while speaking to the interests of consumers, mostly aided larger corporations in building profits while raising prices for wage earners.[89]

In stimulating support for labor union membership, the legislation prompted an acceleration in the number of work stoppages; 1933 saw an uptick in strike days lost that was higher than any year since 1921.[90] The number of work stoppages doubled in one year, from 841 in 1932 to 1,695 in 1933.[91] The numbers only moved upward in 1934 when some 1,856 strikes involved more than 1,470,000 workers.[92]

The strike of the Western Miners Union in Roslyn was one of those actions.

The Northwestern Improvement Company store in Roslyn was the largest general store in the area, providing food, clothing, equipment, and furniture to families in this remote mining community. Mining families were encouraged to shop for all their necessities at the company store with expenses charged against the next paycheck. *Courtesy of Roslyn Public Library, Roslyn Heritage Collection, by permission of Frank Schuchman*

Chapter 1

Unhappy Days

*H*erman Swanson bounded up the eight stairs to his front porch and swung into his living room in an uncharacteristic hurry that mid-March evening. He'd been chatting with a neighbor down the street about the economy and the Roslyn Bank closing. The neighbor mentioned that the president was about to speak on the radio, and Herman raced back home to catch the broadcast.

He headed across his living room straight to the arched cherry radio cabinet on the oak table. As he clicked on the set to warm the tubes, he called out to his wife, Anna, to get the children and come hear Roosevelt.

Anna was just finishing putting dishes away in the kitchen. Daughters Hannah and Mildred were handling the washing and drying. The meal had been one of Anna's usual Sunday feasts, a four-pound roast with mashed potatoes and gravy. The kitchen cook stove was still warm, and the hot water tank next to it was full and ready for baths in the claw-footed tub.

Anna went to the back door and called out for Clarence, their son, who was up the wood-planked path at the coal shed filling a fresh bucket for the morning fire.

Herman adjusted the radio dial for a clearer signal. As a coal miner, he was more accustomed to brute physical force than to fine tuning a radio knob. His stout arms and legs attested to the physical strains of the work; his blackened knuckles to the persistence of coal tar dust despite abrasive cleansers.

As he settled into his rocker and pulled on his reading spectacles, he read a newspaper headline about the bank closings. Roosevelt had been sworn in as president just seven days ago, and he had ordered an immediate banking "holiday" as he chose to call it—a festive term, Herman thought, for shutting down the nation's financial system in the midst of the worst economic crisis the nation had ever faced.[1]

President Hoover had chosen to call the economic situation that erupted in the fall of 1929 a "depression," in hopes that it would be seen as a minor dip in the economic roadway. He had hoped to avoid the more loaded terms of "panic" or "crisis" used to describe previous economic downturns.[2] Four years later, however, Hoover's word choice had taken on the ominous overtones that would come to define the era—perhaps emotionally as well as economically—as the Great Depression.

Banks in Roslyn and the rest of Washington State had been closed for more than a week by the orders of Governor Clarence D. Martin. Nervous investors had been attempting to redeem gold-backed bank notes for gold. Banks in King County and throughout the country were unable to meet the demand and closed their doors. With banks closed, stores had resorted to accepting checks in payment for merchandise and issuing store checks in change.[3] The Ellensburg newspaper began issuing scrip to pay its employees.[4]

Herman's family trailed into the front room—Anna picked up the crochet needles by her rocker, Clarence sat cross-legged on the floor. The girls started a game of Chinese checkers. The announcer intoned:

"Ladies and Gentlemen, the President of the United States."

Then Roosevelt's cheerful yet penetrating voice filled the room, the first time an American president had spoken so personally and directly into the home of this or any American family:

"My friends: I want to talk for a few minutes with the people of the United States about banking—to talk with the comparatively few who understand the mechanics of banking, but more particularly with the overwhelming majority of you who use banks for the making of deposits and the drawing of checks."[5]

It was March 12, 1933. The nation's economy had been struggling for nearly four years, punctuated by the precipitous stock market crash of 1929. But the economy of Roslyn had been on a downhill slide for more than a decade. Virtually the only work in town was with the Northwestern Improvement Company (NWI). The company owned land and mineral rights in several states, including a large portion of a coal reserve in the Cascade Mountain range of central Washington State called the Roslyn-Cle Elum field.

The town of Roslyn had grown up around the site of the first coal mine to be opened by the railway company in 1886. Of nine major shafts the NWI eventually developed in the coalfield, seven were located in or near Roslyn, and much of the coal was processed there. Worker homes were built close to work sites, mostly wood framed structures from the abundant forests of the surrounding mountains. Most homes were not painted though, adding a sense of rough frontier impermanence to the town.

At the height of coal production, Roslyn's population peaked at nearly 4,000, and the town served as a commercial and cultural center for the other communities of the coal field. But as demand for coal slacked through the 1920s, the population slid as well, to a number that Hannah Swanson would remember long afterward—2,222, matching the town's elevation. In 1933, the NWI was operating the No. 5 mine between Roslyn and Cle Elum and was developing its last active mine, No. 9, about a mile west of town.

While Roslyn's population was declining in the early 1930s, the town of Cle Elum was on the upswing. Situated just three miles southeast of Roslyn, Cle Elum sat directly on the main east-west artery, Highway 10. Ninety miles west was the growing metropolis of Seattle. The highway to Seattle led over Snoqualmie Pass, at 3,022 feet in elevation the lowest mountain pass over the Cascade Range, just thirty miles west of Cle Elum. But the highway was not yet fully paved, and the gravel pass could be treacherous in wintertime.

Cle Elum had another geographic advantage. It sat directly on the lines of two transcontinental rail lines to Tacoma—the Northern Pacific Railway and the electrified Chicago, Milwaukee, St. Paul and Pacific, which hubbed in neighboring South Cle Elum. In addition to its growth as a transportation center, Cle Elum was also the site of the NWI's No. 7 mine. With the 1930 census, Cle Elum's population count of 2,500 had officially surpassed that of Roslyn's.

The third community in the coalfield was Ronald with about three hundred residents. The site of the NWI's No. 3 mine, Ronald was located two miles northwest of Roslyn. Just beyond Ronald was the independent coal mining operation of Archie Patrick, employing another fifty miners. A number of mining families lived in a community just outside Ronald called Jonesville. The communities of the coalfield stretched in a line along a two-lane highway spur that ran northwest from Cle Elum—three miles to Roslyn and another two miles to Ronald and Jonesville.

Heading out of Cle Elum along Highway 10 about twenty-five miles to the east was the center of government for the region, the Kittitas County seat of Ellensburg. Situated in a fertile valley at just over 1,500 feet in elevation, Ellensburg had developed a strong agricultural economy. In addition to its role as a center of government for the region, Ellensburg also housed a growing state college for teacher education.

The distance between citizens of the upper county of the Roslyn-Cle Elum coalfields and those of the lower county around Ellensburg was more than geographic. Educated civic leaders in Ellensburg tended to view the immigrant laborers of the upper county with a fair measure of disdain and distrust. Hard working miners of the upper county, set on protecting jobs and financial security for families, held the slick lawyers, judges, and policymakers of Ellensburg in similar disdain.

The Northern Pacific Railroad was a major consumer of the coal supplied by its mines, and the Roslyn-Cle Elum mines were no exception. Surplus coal was shipped to other parts of the state and to California to supply electric utilities, coke plants, smelters, and manufactured gas plants.[6] But most of the coal mined in the coal field was used to power steam locomotives along the rail lines that ran through Cle Elum.

Production of coal from the Roslyn-Cle Elum fields hit an all-time high of 1.8 million tons the year Herman brought his family to Roslyn in 1920, but the demand for coal began to step downward year by year until it fell to under a million tons in 1930. Over that decade, Roslyn lost six hundred residents, a full 20 percent of its population.[7] The number of coal workers in the state had fallen by one-half to 2,500 over the decade. In 1933, about 950 miners lived and worked in the Roslyn-Cle Elum field.[8]

As the president neared the end of his thirteen-minute address, Roosevelt encouraged his listeners, "I can assure you that it is safer to keep your money in a reopened bank than under the mattress."

Herman looked up at Anna, a wry twinkle in his eye. Just that morning he had discovered a stash of three silver dollars in the top drawer of her dresser. The Swansons had a small savings account at the Roslyn Bank, but they were living month to month for the most part, trying to keep ahead of the dreaded snake—the S-shaped symbol a miner would see on a paycheck when the balance at the company store exceeded wages.

They had moved into their two-story, wood-framed house on Northwest B Street four years earlier. It seemed to fit their family well. Two bedrooms upstairs, a larger room for the two girls, now ages 16 and 13, and a smaller sleeping room for their 15-year-old son. Downstairs a large master bedroom opened off the living room. A dining room housed the coal-burning heating stove. A single bathroom, the family's first indoor facility, had been added to the house, a half-step down from the dining room. A long kitchen had room for a table across from the cook stove. There was a pantry too, that held spices and jars of canned fruit. A washroom behind the kitchen had space for a washer tub with a wringer and lines for drying clothes, boots, and coats during the winter months.

Herman had bought the house for $600 and was keeping up on monthly installments to the bank. During good months there was money to spare. But there hadn't been many good months lately. Most weeks he would work two or three days. A horn at 8:00 p.m. each evening would signal which mines were working the next day. If he missed the horn, he would send one of the children down the block to check the signal lights indicating the coming day's work orders.

Then there were the strikes. Every year or two, it seemed, the union would call a strike until the next new contract could be negotiated. Sometimes the strikes were short, some went on for months. With no income during those strikes, many families harvested gardens as a primary source of food. Herman grew squash and carrots, potatoes and tomatoes every summer. And like many idle miners, he had ventured into the woods with his son to hunt deer and elk for food, and the family had known its share of fish dinners prepared from the day's catch on the Cle Elum River.

The events of 1933 signaled that change was in the wind for the nation's economy. Franklin Roosevelt's New Deal held the promise of jumpstarting a languishing economy by putting people to work.

A Democratic Congress was poised to move quickly to approve new work programs.

Herman reasoned that more people working meant more goods produced in factories and moved by rail, and therefore more coal would be required to power the trains. He subscribed to two newspapers and listened regularly to the radio news programs each evening. He knew that the demand for coal was steadily declining as the region's heating and energy needs were being met more and more by oil, natural gas, and electricity.

New hydroelectric dams along the Columbia River would supply electricity to the area in abundance, and another huge dam project, the Grand Coulee, was proposed 130 miles east of Roslyn on State Road No. 2.[9]

The Northern Pacific was delaying the introduction of diesel locomotives to its line because of its reserves of coal,[10] but the writing was on the wall, and it was not written in coal dust.

Like many people living up and down Northwest B Street in Roslyn in March of 1933, Herman's early hopes and dreams for his life had never included bending over underground to heave shovels full of coal onto coal cars. He was born 57 years earlier in southern Sweden, the second of six children in a farming family. When it became clear that there was not enough land for his brothers to share in farming, he decided to come to America in the 1890s. In America, he found work as a miner near Springfield, Illinois, before moving to Red Lodge, Montana, to work for the NWI.

Anna had come to America from Sweden just after the turn of the century, following her sister who had found work as a maid to a wealthy family in Minneapolis. On a trip to the Twin Cities, Herman met Anna, and after more visits and letters, Anna boarded a train for Billings, Montana, in 1915. Herman met her at the station, her wedding dress in hand, and they headed straight for a justice of the peace.

After four years and two children in Red Lodge, Herman developed a persistent cough. A doctor suggested the cough might be due to the high altitude. Herman had heard that work was available in Renton, Washington. The NWI had operations in both towns, so Herman went to work in Renton loading boxcars. A month later, a third baby joined the family.

But Herman wasn't happy with the work in Renton. He had invested much time and energy in learning the mining trade. Just a few years before, he had purchased half a dozen college-level textbooks from International Correspondence Schools on topics like coal drifts, blasting, surveying, hydraulics, and ventilation. Those texts were part of a mine safety instructional program established in 1890 by the editor of the Mining Herald, *Thomas J. Foster, who was compelled to help miners avoid the tragic accidents he had witnessed as a journalist in Pennsylvania. Herman was proud of his skill as a miner, and mining allowed him to better support his family. So he took the opportunity to get back into the work he loved. Loading his family on a train, he headed over the pass to Roslyn in April of 1920. Back in the mines, he worked with pick and shovel, breaking coal and loading it on cars.*

The days in the mine were grueling. Sometimes Herman would work on hands and knees following a narrow layer of coal, but in most places he could stand to his full six-foot height. Most of the mines were below the level of the groundwater and had to be continuously pumped to remain accessible. Mines left vacant by work

The Swanson family in the early 1920s (left to right): Herman, Mildred, Clarence, Hannah, and Anna. *Swanson family photo*

stoppages might take several weeks to pump out before they could be worked again.[11]

Air fans worked continuously to move fresh air to the miners. But bathrooms were remote corners of the mine, and when the air would become thick with coal dust and water dripped from cracks overhead, humidity mixed with sweat and dust to create a dense, suffocating odor. Men would come out of the mine after a day's work wearing a layer of black silt. Many would shed their mining clothes at the company-provided washhouse, shower off, and don street clothes before heading home. A sign in the washroom reminded miners of the requirement to wash their work clothes at least once per month.[12]

Herman preferred to bathe at home and save the $1 a month washroom fee, much to Anna's frustration. His girls had, a time or two, spotted a blackened figure heading up their front walk and had run screaming from the scary stranger—not recognizing their father after a day in the coal mine.

Some winter days, Herman would go to work before sunrise and come home after sunset, never seeing the light of day. On one such occasion, he had left his miner's lamp lit to illuminate his walk home through the snow. Forgetting to douse the lamp when he arrived at home, he headed straight to the bathroom and leaned over the sink to wash his hands, catching a bathroom curtain on fire.

Before the introduction of machinery, mining had required the miner to master skills such as drilling, blasting, setting support timbers, laying track, and loading coal. As the work progressed, foot by foot down along a wall of coal, the miner would place wooden braces to prevent loosened rock from dropping into the mine.[13]

One family legend held that Herman had once put his shoulder into supporting a ceiling timber in a mine shaft until the proper supporting brace could be driven into place. Those who knew him well could fully imagine the stocky Swede taking on a mountain.

Herman took pride in his mining knowledge. He joined the Masonic Lodge in Roslyn in the mid-1920s, both for the social connection and for the recognition of his skill as a miner. But by then mechanization was beginning to bring significant changes to Herman's workplace.

Herman Swanson coming home after a day of work in the Roslyn coal mines in the 1920s. Herman preferred to wear his mining clothes and gear home each night and bathe at home rather than using the mine washhouse. *Swanson family photograph*

Machine mining came later to Roslyn than to other mines in the country, as the steep grade and narrow turns in Roslyn's mines made it difficult to maneuver machines into place. But by the mid-1920s, mechanical coal cutting and drilling machines were introduced.

The promise of good wages had brought an array of immigrants to the community. As in other parts of the country, early immigrants to the Roslyn-Cle Elum fields were mostly skilled miners from England and northern Europe. But as domestic demand for coal continued to grow, unskilled workers joined the ranks of the mining force, coming in increasing numbers from eastern Europe and Italy. Experienced miners became foremen and held the best jobs, while new and unskilled miners took the worst jobs in the mine.

A 1930 census reveals that about one in five Kittitas County residents were born outside the United States. Three groups of immigrants were nearly equally represented: eastern European (Slavic, Croatian), Italian, and English (and Scottish) with around six hundred in each group. Immigrants from northern Europe numbered around eight hundred (mostly from Sweden, Czechoslovakia, Germany, Denmark, Norway, and Poland). Approximately two hundred black residents were listed.[14]

While the communities around the coalfields of Roslyn represented a wide diversity of background and culture, they did not naturally become a melting pot. Ethnic groups clustered together, joined by common languages, religious beliefs, and cultural practices. Immigrants from eastern and southern Europe were highly concentrated in the communities of Roslyn and Ronald. A number of fraternal organizations arose to provide entertainment, social opportunities, and—when a miner was killed—death benefits to families.[15]

Strikes and the threat of strikes were a constant part of life for miners. Many Roslyn miners believed in the union as their best chance for better wages and conditions. In 1922 they joined with other miners around the nation in a UMWA-led strike for a six-hour workday. Not a single miner worked between April and early August of that year. In return, the miners were handed a wage cut with no concessions on hours.

Coal prices and miners' wages declined through the 1920s and early 1930s. Roslyn miners were paid good wages, but the cost of living in the Northwest was high. Some miners began to wonder aloud just how well their interests were being represented in UMWA wage negotiations.

In 1932 miners were asked to take yet another cut in pay—down 20 percent to $5.40 per day.[16] When the Roslyn miners voted on the contract, 476 voted against, 409 voted for the agreement, and 73½ votes were not cast. Thinking they had defeated the vote on the pay cut, the men were informed that a majority of the working membership must vote against the agreement for it to fail, and since 482½ miners had not voted "against" the contract, it was declared valid.[17]

After the vote, frustration began to churn, but most miners reasoned that some work was better than none at all. The men knew that coal operators in the East were pushing union miners out and hiring nonunion workers.[18]

Miners in Roslyn began to seriously consider sharing the available work by instituting six-hour shifts. The six-hour workday had been on the United Mine Workers agenda through the 1920s and early 1930s. The original impetus for the six-hour day had been postwar mechanization that had taken tasks away from the workers. In order to keep more miners working, the UMWA had proposed to Congress a shorter work week. As the argument developed through the 1920s, the humane treatment of workers also became an issue in the physically demanding and risky environment of the mines.

Miners in the Roslyn field, like those elsewhere, worked an eight-hour day, but the clock started when the men arrived at the rock face. Dressing, preparing lights and equipment, and traveling into the mine shaft were all done on the miners' time. Some mine trips could take nearly an hour. At the end of eight hours at the rock face, the miners would begin the reverse trip out of the mines, stowing equipment, and cleaning up. Miners might easily spend ten or more hours at the workplace. To them, a six-hour day at the rock face seemed a reasonable expectation.

With more workers losing jobs in the early 1930s, the emphasis shifted back to employing more miners by sharing work hours. The 1932 United Mine Workers convention passed a resolution calling on Congress to enact a six-hour day and thirty-hour week to put thousands more miners to work.[19]

Alabama Senator Hugo S. Black—later a Supreme Court justice—proposed an even broader application of the six-hour day nationwide, and his plan was detailed in the *United Mine Workers Journal*.[20] Black's six-hour bill was passed by the U.S. Senate in April 1933 but never came to a vote in the House of Representatives, as the new president's plans for a broader labor bill, what was to become the National Industrial Recovery Act, consumed the attention of Congress in that spring of 1933.[21]

A typical workplace for a coal miner inside Roslyn's No. 5 mine. Miners in 1932 were completing a cross cut between entries in this mine when a coal-cutting machine hit a pocket of gas and sparked a fire. Five miners eventually died from their burns. *Courtesy of Roslyn Public Library, Roslyn Heritage Collection, by permission of Frank Schuchman*

Chapter 2

Spring of Discontent

"Anna!" Herman called out as he burst through the back door. "Anna, you won't believe it." He spoke with a thick Swedish accent, but he almost always spoke English. He wanted his children to have the advantage of speaking the language well.

"The governor has signed it. It's a state law now in Washington. They can't use those electric coal cutting machines in the mines anymore!" It was Monday evening, March 20, 1933, and Herman was just returning from a meeting of the miners at the Roslyn union hall.

"Herman, take it easy," she said, taking his coat. "You'll have another spell."

Anna's admonition frustrated Herman. He hated to be reminded of his need to stay calm, but he knew he should heed the advice. An accident ten years earlier left lasting effects for the burly miner. For all the dangers Herman encountered in the mines, this accident had happened in his own home. It had been just a simple errand to the root cellar to gather some potatoes for the evening dinner. But he had forgotten the low floor joist overhead. He smashed his head on the beam so violently that his glasses shattered. A shard of glass pushed into a nerve center just above his eye. The trauma threw him into an epileptic seizure, the first he had ever experienced.

Ever since that time, when he was jarred by an unexpected noise or became overly excited, he was more apt to suffer a recurrence of the seizures. His children grew up learning to be extra quiet when he was in the house and never to slam a door. The injury seemed not to affect his work, and the seizures were a rare occurrence.

Herman settled quietly into his favorite rocker near the window and pulled on his spectacles, whispering again to himself, "I can't believe it. Andy Hunter and those guys really pulled it off."

Andrew Hunter had moved to Roslyn in 1922 to work as a miner. His house was in a small cluster of homes near the No. 5 mine between Roslyn and Cle Elum. In a day when the measure of a man was his ability to work, Hunter was considered a good man, a good worker.[1] He was fifty years old, slight of build, about five feet seven inches in height, serious, always a smart dresser, and he struck some as possessing the qualities of a lawyer.[2] But any legal training he had was self-taught.

Hunter emigrated from England with his twin brother as a young man. He worked as a miner in Illinois and served in the Army during the Great War.[3] His time working in the mines of Illinois put him in contact with a group of labor activists who were making the Illinois district "a center of radicalism within the trade."[4]

Illinois miners had for several decades advocated government ownership of mines, railroads, and telegraph lines, "in the interest of all the people."[5] Two central elements drove the ideology of Illinois miners, according to labor historian John Laslett. "These were democratic control of the union's system of government, and a form of industrial militancy which pushed not only the coal operators but also their own officers to the limit, and beyond, for as many material concessions as they could get."[6]

It is not certain how much direct contact Hunter may have had with organizers in Illinois during the rise of the movement in Roslyn, but it is clear that he was influenced by events that had occurred there.[7] Most likely he was watching with interest the growth of a militant group of miners in the southern Illinois coal fields.

Four years earlier, in 1929, following a decade of dissention against union leadership, UMWA president John L. Lewis had revoked the UMWA charter for District 12 in Illinois and replaced the elected leaders with his own provisional leadership group. The former leaders, however, refused to surrender their offices, and they prevented Lewis's men from taking charge in the state. The group then claimed that Lewis's failure to hold a convention in 1929 had negated UMWA jurisdiction in the district, and they held their own convention in 1930, labeling themselves the "Reorganized United Mine Workers of America."[8]

Lewis eventually went to court to regain control of the state's union, but he could not quell the dissent that persisted there. By

1932, the situation was no better, and state miners were facing a vote on a contract similar to the one Roslyn miners had attempted to reject that same year. In Illinois, however, ballots on their way to be counted were stolen, and Lewis summarily declared the contract to be ratified. The move pushed a band of outraged miners to create their own union and to negotiate their own contracts with coal operators. The new group dubbed themselves the "Progressive Miners of America."[9]

While in Illinois, Hunter had undoubtedly become aware of the political activity of the Socialist Party in the state; Socialist support there was strong enough to win several local and state elections. In Washington State, Hunter became an active member of the state's Socialist Party. He ran for political office as the Socialist Party candidate for state lieutenant governor in 1928 and for the U.S. Senate in 1932.[10]

Hunter's sharp mind and serious approach to issues drew the notice of his mining peers in Roslyn. Just five years after entering the district, he was selected by the miners as a United Mine Workers district officer, serving as secretary of the miner's hospital, the Roslyn-Cle Elum Beneficial Association.[11] The hospital, built by the NWI in 1908, was the only medical facility in the entire coal industry that was owned and operated entirely by miners.[12]

In this position of leadership, Hunter and other area miners had taken up an issue of increasing concern: the use of the electric-powered coal cutting and drilling machines in gaseous portions of the mines. The graves of Roslyn miners killed in mine explosions—including forty-five in 1892 and ten in 1909—were a constant reminder of the dangers of working in gaseous mines. In a five-year period before 1933, state records verified fifteen injuries as a result of explosions caused by the electric coal cutters in the two mines of the Roslyn coal field that were determined to be gaseous. The gruesome injuries were reported in the *United Mine Workers Journal*: "two of the fifteen died, one man became insane and all others were more or less seriously burned, some with hands and ears burned off."[13]

Sam Nicholls, an amiable and youthful thirty-four-year-old who had worked for the Northwestern Improvement Company for eighteen years, was elected in 1931 to serve as president of the United Mine Workers District 10. At that time, District 10 included the state of Washington, but effectively, the miners in the Roslyn–Cle Elum field were the only miners left in the state organized under the United Mine Workers banner. Many miners west of the mountains had abandoned the UMWA after strikes in the early 1920s.[14]

Nicholls' popularity among the Roslyn miners dropped drastically after the 1932 vote fiasco. Of more than nine hundred votes cast during his reelection in 1932, his margin of victory had been less than ten votes.[15] Nicholls was eager to rebuild his rapport with the miners.

In January of 1933, Hunter and Nicholls pushed for three pieces of legislation to be considered by the state legislature: first was a bill requiring state offices to use Washington coal rather than oil for heating, second was a bill banning electric coal cutting machines in gaseous mines, and third was a bill limiting miner work hours to six per day.

Hunter and Nicholls contemplated their best tactics for pushing the legislation. In early January a thousand unemployed citizens marched on the state capitol demanding money for food, and the legislature had passed a relief bill.[16] So later that month, Hunter and Nicholls used the same tactic, leading some 150 miners to the state capitol.

The miners overwhelmed a statehouse conference room, demanding support for the three mining bills.[17] A photo of the miners on the capitol rotunda steps in front of the state senate chambers shows four banners, one from each of the four UMWA locals in the Roslyn coal fields. One of the signs reads "Gas With Electric Machines is Dangerous to See—Local No. 2589," and another reads "The Miners are asking Your Support on Bill No. 69 and 70. We deserve every bit of your consideration—Local No. 2510."[18]

When the NWI got wind of the proposed legislation, their lawyers went to work lobbying state legislators to bury the bills in committee. In the final frantic days of the legislative session, those NWI lawyers were certain they had accomplished their goal. But when Hunter and the Roslyn miners learned that their bills were being smothered, they swarmed the legislative chambers a second time

More than 150 Roslyn coal miners assemble in front of the senate chamber on the steps of the rotunda of the Washington State Capitol in Olympia in late January 1933 to protest the use of electric coal-cutting machines in the mines. Their protest led to a state ban on the use of the machines in gaseous mines. The legislation was later overturned in Federal District Court. *Roslyn Historical Museum Society*

in early March and demanded that their concerns be heard. Their action prompted the bills to be moved out of the Rules Committee and placed at the head of the legislative calendar.[19]

In the final days of the session, the bill banning electric coal cutting machines in gaseous mines was passed along with the bill requiring the use of state coal. But the bill calling for a six-hour workday for miners failed in the Senate by one vote.

Washington's newly elected governor, Clarence Martin, a conservative Democrat, heard from a number of mining interests prior to signing the bill. He received a three-page letter from Tom Murphy, the NWI superintendent of the Roslyn mines. Murphy stated that the alternative to electric coal cutting involved blasting from solid walls of coal. "In this system of mining enormous quantities of powder were used, and in addition to blowing a large percentage of the coal to dust there were numerous accidents of various kinds caused by the heavy blasting." Murphy noted that the marketability of coal blown to bits was lower than the coarse or lump coal produced with

A coal cutting machine sits outside the Roslyn Museum. The blade of the coal cutter acted like a chainsaw digging a deep undercut into the bottom of a wall of coal. Then holes were drilled and charges of dynamite inserted to blast the coal into chunks for removal. *Author collection*

coal cutting machinery. He further noted that of twenty men killed by explosions in Washington mines in the five previous years, two were caused by explosions from electricity, one from smoking, and seventeen from the use of powder. Murphy's opinion was "Most of the animosity against the machines among the men here is caused by the belief generally held that machines displace men."[20]

Despite the protestations of Murphy and others representing the U.S. Bureau of Mines, Governor Martin signed the bill into law on March 17, 1933.[21]

Hunter returned with his fellow miners a hero. He had led the men multiple times to the state capitol, fought for their safety against the financial interests of the big mine owners, and won. With his leadership, the men had stood together and had seen laws changed to protect them. A local leader was ascending.

As miners in Roslyn celebrated their victory, negotiators in Washington, DC, hovered over early drafts of a policy that would soon have tremendous impact in the upper Kittitas County coal fields of Roslyn, Ronald, and Cle Elum. President Roosevelt and a team of advisers from labor and industry were beginning to craft policies that in June would be woven into the National Industrial Recovery Act—the act that created the National Recovery Administration (NRA).

Coal miners, like auto and steel workers, were fairly well organized and represented by major labor unions. Roosevelt set out to move negotiations in these industries quickly. Looking for leaders among labor as well as industry, the president asked John L. Lewis to suggest the names of individuals to help draft the new policy. Lewis offered the services of his most trusted economic adviser, W. Jett Lauck, to work with a select group of business leaders, administration officials, and lawyers in Washington, DC, to draft the new legislation.[22]

In the Roslyn fields, despite the recent victory, miners were feeling the effects of lower wages, declines in union membership, and cuts in the number of productive working days. Frustrated miners talked openly of taking their union back. Joe Clemente, president of the Cle Elum local and UMWA District 10 auditor, issued a call for help in a letter to John L. Lewis on May 2, 1933:

> The situation in our District is almost desperate. Working conditions are at low ebb, with the mines in operation one or two days a week. Membership is torn by jealousies, gossips, cheap politics, slanders and distrust in the officers; and the coal operators are taking advantage of our dissensions…Now an agitation has been started to remove the District President, who was re-elected by only two votes of majority. All the other officers were defeated, with the exception of myself, being elected for the fourth time. My idea is that the International should take charge of the District; and the sooner, the better.[23]

Negotiators met in Roslyn in mid-May 1933 to discuss terms for a new contract starting July 1. But the miners made a number of what NWI officials termed "radical demands," including a six-hour day and a five-day week with pay increases. Operators countered with the proposal of continuing the current terms for another year. The miners declined, fully expecting that the new coal code would give

them the six-hour day.[24] Both sides agreed to wait until the new coal
regulations were enacted in Congress.[25]

The state law forbidding electric coal cutting machines in gaseous
mines went into effect on June 6. The NWI determined that it was
not profitable to operate using hand labor, so it closed its two gaseous mines, No. 3 and No. 5, idling 450 miners—half its work force.

When the UMWA contract expired on June 30, all of the mines
in the Roslyn-Cle Elum field fell idle. The work stoppage was not
termed a "strike" as it began. Miners were asked to continue working at current wages until federal legislation could be finalized. But
the miners refused unless the NWI would accommodate the 450
workers displaced by the closing of the two gaseous mines. The NWI
held firm, and all work stopped on July 1.[26]

Lawmakers in Washington, DC, continued drafting legislation at
a furious pace. The National Industrial Recovery Act was enacted on
June 16, 1933, one of the last pieces of New Deal legislation to receive
the presidential signature during his first 105 days in office.[27]

A key clause in the legislation, Section 7(a), gave a federal sanc-
tion for workers to join and negotiate wages through labor unions:

> Employes [sic] shall have the right to organize and bargain col-
> lectively through representatives of their own choosing, and shall
> be free from the interference, restraint or coercion of employers of
> labor, or their agents, in the designation of such representatives or
> in self-organization or in other activities for the purpose of collec-
> tive bargaining or other mutual aid or protection.[28]

Idle miners in the Kittitas field read the terms in labor journals
and newspapers. Labor recruiters hit the road in the summer of
1933, showing nonunion miners that the government would protect
their right to organize and bargain as a union. John L. Lewis went
so far as to say, "the President wants you to join a union."[29] UMWA
membership rolls swelled from 100,000 to nearly 400,000 by the end
of the year.[30]

Immediately after signing the NRA legislation, Roosevelt met
separately with mine operators and labor leaders. Then he asked the
two groups to meet together. When operators balked, the president
reminded them of the precarious state of the economy. He reminded

them that they were Americans first and coal operators second. He reminded them that the coal workers were united into a single strong organized group and that they should at least sit down and talk together.[31]

To work effectively, the agreement, or code, for coal would have to be perceived as fair by both labor organizers and coal producers. If wages were seen as too low, then miners would strike. If they were set too high, coal producers would not agree to the terms.

Perceptions of fairness also suggested a nationwide standard for wages and prices rather than the differing regional standards of the past. Wages in the South had typically been lower than in other regions. Where Roslyn miners were making around $5.40 per day in 1933, miners in the South were making less than $4 per day.[32]

Working conditions differed by region as well. Whereas miners in some regions were pit- or strip-mining with bulldozers and dump trucks, Roslyn miners were extracting coal from steep-pitched mine shafts by blasting and loading coal cars. One rumor that persisted in Roslyn was that it was cheaper to purchase coal from Utah and transport it by rail to Ellensburg to heat the Washington State Normal School[33] than to mine and transport coal the twenty-five miles from the upper Kittitas fields.[34]

Negotiations among labor leaders, mine owners, and government officials moved ponderously during the summer. Lewis found himself walking a tightrope. If he held a hard line on wages and hours, he might risk losing the significant gains in worker rights under the NRA—collective bargaining, union membership, minimum age requirements for mineworkers, and the check-off system. If he were seen as caving to industry or government interests, he would lose control of his union. In order to gain the trust of President Roosevelt, he had to show his ability to keep his miners working. "On the other hand, Lewis knew that if the coal miners in fact sat tight and worked diligently, operators would be less likely to bargain seriously with the UMW or to offer the union the terms it desired," Lewis biographer Melvyn Dubofsky noted.[35]

On July 10, a group of idle Cle Elum miners met with representatives of the Washington State Federation of Labor who were meeting there. Cle Elum local president Joe Clemente told the *Ellensburg Evening Record*, "There is no strike. The mines were closed to permit officials of the mines and union representatives to carry on negotiations relative to shortening the work day and boosting wages."[36]

Herman Swanson had savings enough for a couple of months of house payments. His garden was coming in nicely, and a cherry tree in the back held promise of sweet desserts. Neighbors shared extra produce from their gardens, and while some kids may not have gotten a quarter to spend on candy during the summer, few of them went hungry. Daughters Hannah and Mildred worked on sewing simple clothes for the fall school term. Anna had taken to reusing the wax paper that wrapped her favorite crackers.

The July 15 edition of the *United Mine Workers Journal* carried the news that one hundred coal operators meeting with UMWA officials in Washington, DC, had agreed on a minimum wage of $5 per day for inside and $4 per day for outside labor. The journal said that no agreement had been reached on maximum hours per week, and the dispatch said that a code "would likely be submitted with that clause remaining to be settled."[37]

At a gathering of Roslyn miners in mid-July, Herman learned that Andy Hunter was forming a group called the Kittitas County Citizens and Taxpayers League. The group was planning to join with miners in Cle Elum and Ronald to ask the county for relief dollars for the out-of-work miners.

On July 19, the group made its plea for help to the county commissioners in Ellensburg. But, according to the *Ellensburg Evening Record*, commission chair L. J. Richards "informed the miners that N.W.I. Company officials had told the commissioners that if the miners would consent to return to work at the old contract price, the mines would resume work immediately."[38] Since the men could have work if they wanted it, the commission decided that the county should provide no aid. Joe Clemente explained that union negotiations were being handled by the scale committees (who were responsible for negotiating wages for various mine jobs), and district officers, and not by local union leaders. But the commission refused to budge.

Not satisfied with the county's response, Hunter decided to ask the state for relief funds while the negotiations continued. On August 3, Roslyn miners voted a resolution asserting that the county commissioners had acted unfairly. They demanded that miners be put to work on county road projects at a wage of $3 for a five-hour day. The county was providing relief pay of $2.50 for eight hours labor to about thirty needy residents at the time.[39] By the end of August, some Roslyn miners were hired for road work, but most of them quit after six hours rather than working eight hours for their $2.50 grocery voucher.[40]

As the summer months passed, President Roosevelt exerted greater pressure for a coal agreement. He proposed in late July that idle mines reopen under a provisional "blanket code" that would assure miners their existing pay rates until a final decision was reached on the industry code of fair competition.[41]

On July 24, the president made his third fireside chat to the nation, kicking off the Blue Eagle campaign to encourage support for his industrial recovery initiatives.[42] The Blue Eagle, the President explained, was to be displayed proudly in businesses that adhered to the NRA code. Shoppers were encouraged to trade only with merchants displaying the eagle. The Cle Elum newspaper, the *Miner Echo*, ran a black and white version of the emblem each week in its masthead over the names of the editorial staff to show the paper's patriotism in adhering to the code. Roosevelt appealed to workers and employers in his address:

> If all employers in each competitive group agree to pay their workers the same wages—reasonable wages—and require the same hours—reasonable hours—then higher wages and shorter hours will hurt no employer. Moreover, such action is better for the employer than unemployment and low wages, because it makes more buyers for his product. That is the simple idea which is the very heart of the Industrial Recovery Act.
>
> On the basis of this simple principle of everybody doing things together, we are starting out on this nationwide attack on unemployment. It will succeed if our people understand it—in the big industries, in the little shops, in the great cities and in the small villages. There is nothing complicated about it and there is nothing

particularly new in the principle. It goes back to the basic idea of society and of the nation itself that people acting in a group can accomplish things which no individual acting alone could even hope to bring about.[43]

Following the president's directive, John L. Lewis ordered idle miners to return to work under the old contract while negotiations continued in Washington, DC. His attentions were clearly focused more on the 70,000 idle miners in Pennsylvania and Illinois than on the thousand in Roslyn. But, in early August, NWI executives learned of Lewis's orders to the Pennsylvania miners and began to pressure him to issue the same order to the Roslyn miners.[44]

Reports in union journals and newspapers suggested that Lewis was still pushing hard for a six-hour day as well as other initiatives, including the automatic withdrawal of union dues from paychecks, the right of miners to select their own representatives to check their tonnage outputs, the end of child labor in mines, and an equitable grievance procedure.[45] But there was also a strong sense that Lewis and Roosevelt were becoming fast buddies. "They're just like that," miners would say, holding two fingers together.[46] That perception was strengthened when on August 5 the president appointed Lewis to the Labor Advisory Board, the group tasked with resolving disputes under the NRA code.[47]

Coal code negotiations between labor and management resumed in Washington, DC, on August 9 with the lead negotiator for the coal companies restating that the coal producers could not afford higher wages. Lewis responded the next day, demonstrating typical bravado by reading from a fifty-two-page prepared statement: "More and more the framing of codes is a matter of bickering and barter, of surrendering just as little as possible and grasping just as much as possible." He stated that industrialists seem "to be suffering from the delusion that we are on our way back to the conditions which prevailed in the summer of 1929."[48]

Lewis called for a thirty-hour work week, saying: "It will check overproduction and place the industry in a position to produce at least our national coal requirements." He continued, "It will eliminate, so far as practicable, the evils of cut-throat competition. It will stabilize costs and maintain wages at reasonable levels. It will enable the producers to secure fair returns on their investments."[49]

Roosevelt continued to pressure industries to fall in line with the NRA codes. Roslyn miners read threats almost daily in the headlines of the *Ellensburg Evening Record*: "U.S. Will Boycott Firms Refusing to Support NRA Code—First Violating Pledge to Blue Eagle to be Put on Blacklist,"[50] "NRA About Ready to Use More Than Gentle Persuasion,"[51] "FDR Wants Blue Eagle on Coal and Steel by Saturday."[52]

The next week, Sam Nicholls was in Washington, meeting with Lewis and Washington coal operators. At Lewis's direction, Nicholls sent a telegram to union representatives in the Roslyn field ordering them back to work under terms of the old contract:

> At conference arranged by D. R. Swem of NWI Company mines, President Lewis present, our present suspension thoroughly discussed as national code will determine hours work wage and other conditions. Nothing is being gained by continuing suspension. Company's contracts being taken by other companies and railroad being supplied by stipping [sic] operation in Montana and Pacific Coast Coal Company. It is agreed miners should return to work August Sixteenth temporarily under terms and conditions of expired contract until national code is made. Management will re-employ as many men possible now idle as result of closing mines Three and Five. It is our judgment returning to work will prove to government we are cooperating to bring about New Deal as well as proving to nonunion operators who are watching our struggle that UMW of A will do what is right.[53]

Chapter 3

A Battle of Ideologies

*H*erman felt unsettled on that warm Sunday morning in mid-August 1933. He hadn't worked at the mine in more than a month, and the morning breezes brought the scent of pine down the hill and over his Roslyn home just a block from the woods. "Let's take a hike today, kids. Anna, you come too," Herman suggested at breakfast. The girls were ready to go, hoping to beg off of morning chores. Clarence was already up from the table filling his canteen. But Anna opted to stay home. She was expecting a visit from her friend, Ida Gihlstrom.

In the proper Swedish tradition, Herman was not close or demonstrative in his affection for his children. A family activity was rare. But he had a lot on his mind that day, and he didn't mind the company as he pushed himself up the hill behind the house, into the woods, and up to the huge boulders they called "the rocks." Just a couple of years earlier, a miner had chiseled toeholds into several of the big boulders. Even as teenagers Herman's children loved climbing up and over "Dancing Rock," although they had outgrown wearing down the seats of their pants on "Sliding Rock."

Herman pushed on a little farther over the ridge looking for elderberries. He didn't find any on this morning, but he had been known to bring home bulging pockets full. He circled back behind the rocks where he could hear his children plotting a game of King of the Mountain. On a smooth sandstone outcropping, he settled back and looked across the rooftops of the town below.

Despite his efforts, he couldn't turn his mind from his worries about money. The little savings he had was going fast, and there was none coming in to replace it. Why not go back to work, he thought. The union is telling us to go back. They're promising to negotiate better wages and hours. And we could sure use the money right now.

On the other hand, he could hear Andy Hunter and others saying we can get a better deal—fewer hours and better pay—if we hold out a little longer. The twenty-four miners who worked at Jonesville, the independent *mine just past Ronald, had settled with the union and had been operating for a week. They were getting $5.60 for six hours.[1] Not a bad deal, Herman thought.*

In the town below, families headed home from church or over to neighbors for a visit. Like many company towns in the 1930s, Roslyn residents were diverse by background and heritage, yet they shared the bond of life in an isolated community and dependence on the NWI.

Herman could hear the approaching sounds of another family on their way to the rocks. The Zaputil kids from a few doors down the block came into view. Clarence raced to join Stanley and Rudy to boost each other up the toeholds. Herman greeted Stanley Sr. and invited him to sit on a smooth spot next to him.

"Did you hear about the meeting tomorrow afternoon?" Herman asked.

"Sure did. What do you think the guys are gonna do?" Zaputil queried in response.

"I don't know. Sounds pretty official to me. Lewis is ordering us back to work under the old contract. Seems to me like we ought to go back to work." Herman looked up, wondering where Zaputil stood on the issue.

"Yeah, I heard there's a telegram, a direct order. But a lotta guys is wondering why we go back now? What's gonna happen to the guys who's out because of the cutters. They ain't gonna get work."

Days earlier in a Washington, DC, conference room, NWI operations manager D. R. Swem met with Lewis, Nicholls, and UMW International board member Walter Smethurst. Swem demanded that Lewis order the miners in the Roslyn-Cle Elum district back to work under existing contract terms until a code for coal was established.[2] Roslyn miners met on the following Monday to consider the order.

Just after lunch, Herman set out to walk down the hill to the union hall. It was another warm mid-August afternoon, but a light breeze kept the temperature bearable. The meeting was set for 2:30, but he wanted to arrive early to catch up on the latest news from his coworkers.

As he crossed First Street, he noticed a small group of men on an opposite corner. Approaching the group he heard the speaker declaring in no

uncertain terms that Roosevelt and Lewis were working for fat-cat corpo-
rations and not for the working men. "They've entered into a pact to break
the strike in Pennsylvania, and they're trying to do the same thing here,"
the man said as he passed around a copy of "Mining Notes," a typewritten
newsletter published by a group calling itself the Labor Research Institute
in New York. As the paper came around, Herman noted the title of one of the
articles, "NMU Organizes in New Mexico."[3] *National Miners Union, he*
thought to himself. That's the communist union that the UMWA is always
warning about.

Just three months earlier, the May 15, 1933, cartoon cover of the
United Mine Workers Journal had shown what it termed a "dual"
union member walking by a UMWA worker. In the drawing, the
dualist's sinister shadow was holding a bomb with a lit fuse. The
shadow was labeled "Communism."[4]

A miner's letter in that same issue highlighted the passionate Bib-
lical and patriotic fervor of the UMWA position on Communism:

> We men in the United Mine Workers all believe in the tenets of the
> Christian religion and the Commandments as handed down by
> the Holy Bible; we believe in the institutions of our government.
> On the other hand, the communists do not believe in the church or
> state, and it is their purpose to destroy completely every form of
> government we have here. So, brother miner, read your *Journal* and
> study it and live up to its teachings. Let's put a United Mine Work-
> ers charter on every coal tipple in our land, and if the communists
> want to spread their lying propaganda, let them go to Russia and
> spread it, for we have no place for them in our organization. [5]

Communist labor organizers in Washington State had found some
success organizing in Seattle among workers who were frustrated
about being paid war-time wages after war had ended. Organizers
had visited the Kittitas fields at intervals since the party organized in
the state in 1919.[6] But these efforts never gained much of a foothold
among miners in the Roslyn-Cle Elum field.

Still, the values embraced in Communist labor publications did
hold an attraction for oppressed and struggling workers and especially for workers who had moved just a few years before from eastern and southern Europe where communist values were either being

practiced or seriously considered. In the United States, the Communist Party had gained more members among the foreign born, and a good number of those were of Slavic descent.[7] The party's most successful efforts with organized labor would be in locating and encouraging existing labor unrest.[8]

Workers in the Roslyn area and elsewhere gave serious attention to messages about the rights of workers to benefit from their labors rather than to add to the fortunes of East Coast labor barons. A popular communist interpretation of the banking moves made by Roosevelt in his first few days in office held that he was placing vast amounts of wealth into the hands of rich bankers at the expense of workers.[9]

At the speaker's feet Herman noticed a stack of newspapers bearing the name Voice of Action.

The Seattle-based newspaper began publishing in March 1933 and praised the triumphs of the state's Communist Party labor organizers. It had been Communist organizers who had led the one-thousand-person hunger march on the state capitol just weeks before the Roslyn miners arrived there in January 1933.[10]

Another labor group active in the decades leading up to the summer of 1933 was the Industrial Workers of the World (IWW), or the Wobblies. Devoted to the principal of "one big union," the Wobblies had attempted to organize unskilled workers in the Roslyn area, making inroads from time to time, especially among the state's timber workers.[11]

In 1919, the NWI had taken note of attempts by IWW organizers to gather supporters among Roslyn miners. A company memorandum stated that the company hired speakers who: "lectured all over the State for Americanism and against radicalism and advised employes [sic] to be loyal to the Companies furnishing them employment."[12]

The company went so far as to hire special agents to talk in support of the IWW in an attempt to lure vulnerable miners into exposing their hidden radical interests. One agent apparently did his job too well, prompting the NWI Seattle manager to "dispense with his services as he was stirring up trouble and doing us more injury than good," the memorandum noted.[13]

Efforts of the IWW were hampered by the flaring of violent and highly publicized labor disputes such as the Everett Massacre of 1916 and the Centralia Massacre of 1919.[14] The group was, however, active in the Roslyn area in 1933. As work progressed on improving the dam at Lake Cle Elum in mid-May, IWW agitators rolled logs onto the roadway near the head of the lake in an attempt to stop trucks from hauling supplies. The state patrol sent in twenty-one officers to maintain order, and the situation was quickly calmed.[15]

Herman was concerned about the rights of workers, but he had never become politically active. His political views were based largely on prag-matic decisions about which candidate could bring stable, well-paying jobs. Several of his cousins who had remained in Sweden had become members of the Social Democratic Party, supporting a program of socialized govern-ment-provided services paid for by a progressive tax—a variation on the socialist views of Karl Marx.

Herman had voted for Hoover in 1928 based on the Republican's experi-ence as a former mining engineer and on his stand favoring prohibition. But he switched in 1932 to Roosevelt because he thought the Democrat promised more hopeful and innovative leadership to rebuild the economy than Hoover had provided.

Indeed, many immigrants in the Roslyn area had spent a good deal of time considering the several contrasting forms of govern-ment that had been emerging around the world between 1917 and 1933. They still believed strongly in the ideals of freedom and liberty that had drawn them here. But they had to wonder whether Amer-ican capitalism was going to survive the economic depression the nation was facing.

A decade and a half before, newspapers had carried accounts of a Communist revolution in Russia and Lenin's promises of remov-ing class differences and working together for a common good.[16] On another extreme, Italy's Mussolini had been demonstrating since the late 1920s the efficiency of a strong centralized authority in bring-ing order to government and the economy. And within the last few months the name of Adolph Hitler had been emerging in news reports about Germany's attempts to rebuild its economy under National Socialism.

Heated political discussions were common on street corners and across neighborhood fences. As Herman turned to leave the crowded street corner, the speaker thrust a Voice of Action *paper into his hands. He folded it tightly and stuffed it into his hip pocket as he headed toward the union hall.*

The hall was packed as Herman arrived. He found a spot near the front by Gus Jaderlund, one of his Swedish friends. John P. Pasquan, the president of UMWA local No. 2510, gaveled the meeting to order, but it took several tries to quiet the hundreds of men in the hall.

Thirty-nine-year-old Pasquan had emigrated with his parents from Croatia as a child and had been working in the Roslyn mines for more than twenty years. Like many people in the community, he was better known by a nickname; the men called him "Pots." Pasquan had been at the center of a controversy at the No. 3 mine the previous winter. A popular miner, he had lost his job over infractions of safety rules. But he and his fellow miners had raised such a squabble that the mining company finally relented and put him back to work.[17]

The frustration of the miners was evident. The Communist newspaper, *Voice of Action,* reported the miners' response to the order to return to work:

> The new minimum scale for which local miners are fighting is practically the same as that demanded by the miners of Pennsylvania, who have just gone on strike again, says Basquan [sic], in spite of efforts of the entire national administration to form a "truce."
>
> The more than 600 miners who met here at 2:30 last Monday, August 14, for the strike vote went on record unanimously to reject the wired instructions of Lewis to return under the old scale. Instead the local voted a fine of $25 on any man who went to work.[18]

It didn't take these miners long to do the calculations. A fine equal to a week's wages for going back to work. That was enough to make anyone stop and think. But local leaders were not willing to let their actions stop at the point of issuing fines on their fellow workers. They wanted control of the state district. The *Voice of Action* report continued:

> "A recall of the district president of our union has been started and will gain the support of every local this week," says Basquan

[sic]. "'Local number 2269 has already voted for a recall." When asked why this move was being made, Basquan said, "He promised to stand by the miners. Then we sent him back to Washington and he wired us to accept the old scale." Miners here report that Nichols [sic], District 10 president, last year forced the men to accept a 20 percent wage cut through a crooked referendum vote in which he counted "dead men"and miners out on farms waiting for work. Although there have been no definitive moves made as yet, it is rumored that Lewis and the gang in control of the mine union nationally may try to expel the locals in the state involved in the strike and take away their charters.[19]

Herman had come to the meeting harboring doubts, and he left with even more. Snubbing the direct order of a union president was a bold and dangerous act. Ousting a union district president was serious business, too. The UMWA had the clout of hundreds of thousands of workers, not to mention millions of dollars in the pension fund. Was he ready to risk his pension for this, he asked himself? But the crowd at the union hall was insistent—close to becoming a raucous mob—and it was hard to stand up against them when they got going.

Several days later, Cle Elum's local union members met to consider Lewis's call to work, but they were overwhelmed by Roslyn miners led by Hunter. Walter Steele Sr. described the meeting in a letter to John L. Lewis:

Friday evening Aug 18th, Mr. Hunter and this gang, came down from Roslyn, and Hunter asked me, how about the Eagles Temple, and why we had not rented it for this meeting called, I said that there was no mass meeting called, that the Local Union would take care of all the business we had. So when the meeting was called, our President let them know that this was not a mass meeting and only the business of the Local 2512 would be taken care of, but this gang would not let us get anywhere, It was 'gang' Rule. They hist [sic] every member of our Local that tried to have anything to say, if it was not in acord [sic] with what they wanted to put over. They wanted to know what we intended to do with one of our members. After receiving the telegram signed by you and Mr. Nicholls to go work, this bunch wanted us to fine this Brother $25.00. We tried to tell them that this man was an Elictrician [sic], and as you know that it is the custom for these men to get the mine in shape before opening, we didn't see why this Brother should be fined only working one day, but this Gang forced a vote by the "I and No." So we don't know if 2512 had much to say about it. Can we legally fine this Brother?

I tried to get the floor several times and did ask if the Gang that had come down from Roslyn, thought they were doing the right thing by telling us how to run our business. [B]ut all we could get out of them was that they wanted 2512 to go on record in asking for the recall of Mr. Sam Nicholls. We told them it was not necessary, all that they had to do, was to get 35 percent of the members to sign. This set them wild. When they were told that the International may take a hand in this recall, they said that it was not any of the International business. Now instead of Mr. Hunter telling his men that this was not an open meeting, and to let us run our business, he told them, that the International was not running them, or District #10. And that they did not intend to listen to what they had to say, that the recall was going through, and that when the U.S. Code for the coal was set, that they, Hunter and his men was goin' to make a Code for the State of Washington, that the Miners in this State would work under. He said to Hell with the Code at Washington.[20]

The stage was being set for a labor war unlike any that the Roslyn coal fields had ever seen. In previous labor battles, the men had united behind a single union banner, standing in solidarity as a unified body, fighting against a common taskmaster, in the same community, for the same purpose. But the letters from UMWA loyalists to John L. Lewis in the spring and summer of 1933 reveal a different kind of battle, one that pitted miners loyal to Lewis and the United Mine Workers union against those who were totally disillusioned with the UMWA, its leaders, and its ability to represent their interests.

Adding to the fray of this emerging battle were those individuals promoting a radical agenda. Whether Roslyn's leaders sought it or not, a week after their refusal of John L. Lewis's order to return to work, a letter arrived at the Roslyn union hall addressed from W. K. Dobbins, president of the Unemployed Citizen's League of Seattle. The letter promised the full support of the Communist Party in the state, including the help of unemployed workers, unions, and fraternal groups affiliated with the state committee. Dobbins asked the miners to regard the *Voice of Action* as their own paper, ready to publish their views as the need arose.[21]

Chapter 4

Fevered Pitch

*H*erman *pulled on his best trousers. Hat in hand, he poked his head up the stairwell and called to his children that he was going to start walking to the ballpark. This late-August Sunday was a big day for the Roslyn All-Stars baseball team. They were playing Renton in one of the last games of the season.*

As Herman and Clarence strolled to the ball field, Herman could hear nervous conversations among clusters of men. The talk was not of strikes and balls that day, but of strikes and recalls—staying off the job, or going back to work.

The stands were crowded. Husbands and wives, dressed in their Sunday finest, were sharing sandwiches from home—no extra money for ballpark hotdogs. And, at least officially, there was no beer at the park that day. The state's vote to repeal prohibition was set for the following Tuesday.[1]

The ball team was in fine form as well. The second-hand uniforms from a Seattle-area team had been restitched, the old team name removed.

As Anna and the girls joined Herman in the stands, Clarence remained at field level, his face pressing the screen, watching the Renton catcher strap on his chest protector, don his facemask, and grab the catcher's mitt.

Herman was struggling to grasp the enormity of the situation that he and his mining buddies faced. The *Ellensburg Evening Record* a few days earlier had reported FDR was putting pressure on coal and steel negotiators for a deal on new codes by that Saturday.[2] Now that date had come and gone with no deal.

Sam Nicholls had met with Roslyn miners the previous week to urge them to return to work, but he found nothing but hostile resistance.[3] Instead, he wrote to John L. Lewis, he was "compelled to take much abuse from a group who run rampant over the east side disrupting meetings and causing disturbances in general."[4]

Nicholls then set a meeting of the District Executive Board for August 25 seeking an official order. He got nothing. He sent a plaintive telegram to John L. Lewis: "I have not had proper support from International representative of this field and through my effort to place back to work membership are demanding my recall. Unless help is sent at once I am at a loss to control this situation."[5]

Lewis responded by sending in a trusted aid, Walter Smethurst of Montana, to manage the situation.[6] The forty-one-year-old Smethurst had, for the past four years, served as a member of the international executive board of the United Mine Workers of America, representing the western United States, and had successfully quelled uprisings in other districts. He had earned his miner's stripes working in the Republic Coal Mine in Roundup, Montana, for nearly sixteen years. His military stripes were just as impressive. He had served with the U.S. Allied Expeditionary Force in the battles of the Meuse-Argonne and St. Mihiel in France in 1918 during the Great War.[7]

The day after the Sunday ballgame, Smethurst met with members of the District Executive Board. In a two-day session, he pled with the board to accept the union's position and return to work, but the board would not be moved.[8]

On Tuesday, Washington became the twenty-fourth state to repeal prohibition. Andrew Hunter received 2,330 votes in Kittitas County to become a delegate to the state's constitutional convention. The second-place delegate was Ellensburg attorney Austin Mires, a signer of the state's original constitution in 1889.[9]

Meanwhile, NWI coal manager D. R. Swem kept the pressure on Lewis to get the men back to work. "Roslyn miners still on strike," Swem wrote in a telegram to Lewis. "Nicholls and Smethurst apparently having difficult time with radical leaders who disregard all contract obligations and international orders. Unless these men are disciplined will make conditions intolerable when we attempt to make new contract with men."[10]

While Lewis followed the state situation carefully, his attention was mostly consumed with negotiations on the federal coal code in Washington, DC, that had begun in late June and were running seven days a week from 9:00 a.m. until at least midnight. The only break came on September 4 for a Labor Day holiday celebration.[11]

As negotiations toiled on into September, the pace of Roosevelt's pressure for a deal between coal operators and the union mounted daily. Newspaper headlines trumpeted the virtues of the NRA and the president's demands for haste.[12] Miners in Pennsylvania called a strike to protest delays in drafting a coal code.[13]

In Washington State, the District 10 Executive Board went back into session on Tuesday, September 5. Their first action was to exclude outsiders from future meetings to avoid vociferous guests.

The board took up the recall of President Nicholls. With 442 signatures tallied, they had more than the 35 percent required to trigger a recall. An election was set for mid-October. The question was raised whether the vote should include only those who were members in August 1932, when Nicholls was reelected, or include new members, who were mostly from the west side of the state where Nicholls enjoyed stronger support. The meeting ended without a decision on the vote or a resolution to call the miners back to work.[14]

It appeared that Roslyn miners were playing a high-stakes waiting game, betting that their solidarity would bring better wages, a six-hour day, and full employment for all the miners.[15]

John L. Lewis continued to pursue the six-hour day, but he also recognized the need to reach an accord. Roosevelt had opposed the six-hour day from the beginning, believing it was not realistic to force struggling businesses to hire more workers.[16] Using powers granted him under the NRA, the president dictated the final decision on the coal code: eight-hour days, $5.40 per day, five days per week.[17] On the evening of September 18, Roosevelt signed the code for soft coal.[18]

Herman heard the news from a neighbor. The grapevine was buzzing from house to house in Upper Kittitas County. A mass meeting was scheduled for the next evening at Roslyn's Rialto Hall. Walter Smethurst was to speak.

Herman listened as a group of his neighbors chatted angrily over a fence the night before the meeting: "Who the hell does he think he is, thinking he can just come in here and tell us what to do? Who runs this union anyway? Is it John L. and his boys or is it us, the guys who do the real work?"

"Whatever the wage is, we're locked in. It's the government that sets the wage isn't it? What can we do?"

"What good has this crazy layoff done for us? We got nothing. Three months of no work and we got nothing."

"I can tell you for damn sure, there's a lotta guys who aren't going back to work until all of us can work. I'm not going back if the company's only taking half a crew."[19]

Unbeknown to the miners, the NWI was planning legal action to nullify the state's ban on coal cutting machines. Ever since the legislative ban was voted in the previous March, lawyers for the NWI had been working on a plan to have it declared invalid. The NWI had developed safer machines and had them tested by the U.S. Bureau of Mines.[20] They also prepared affidavits from engineers as well as Roslyn miners swearing to the safety of the machines.

In mid-September, NWI lawyers brought an action against the State of Washington in federal district court to overturn the coal-cutting ban. Company executives were hoping the action might remove the last objection the men had to returning to work by promising employment for all the miners.[21]

As Herman and a neighbor approached the meeting hall, he could hear strong accents mixed with broken English in spirited conversations.

"Why should we go in? We didn't call this meeting. He did."

"The union has just sent their lackey out to tell us to go back into the mines for starvation wages."

Herman noticed that no one was entering the hall, so he joined a small cluster near the door. One of the men piped up, "He'd have to pay me to go in and hear him." And another chimed in, "Why don't he just rent the hall if he wants to hold his meeting?" Others agreed, and an informal group formed around "Pots" Pasquan, insisting that he charge Smethurst the $10 rental fee to use the hall.

The men refused to enter until Smethurst paid.[22] Being pressured to pay a fee to use a union meeting hall was the ultimate insult to the special envoy of union president John L. Lewis. But Smethurst saw no other way to share his views with the men, so he agreed.

With the miners finally inside the hall, Smethurst began the meeting by lauding the NRA and the powers it gave workers to organize and bargain collectively, with rights now protected by the government. The main purpose of the NRA, he said, was to "assimilate the unemployed by shorter hours and increase purchasing power by an increase in wages."[23]

"What we seen didn't get us no shorter hours or increased pay," one of the miners shouted.

Smethurst agreed, but he noted that the new contract gave significant raises to three-fourths of U.S. miners. When he cited Alabama pay rates, several miners pointed out, "We're not in Alabama, we're in Washington."

Smethurst reminded the miners that the price of coal had been dropping because of inroads into the home heating market by gas, oil, and electricity. He noted that since 64 percent of the cost of producing coal went to labor, raising wages would only increase costs, making coal less competitive.

The miners asked whether they might push for a six-hour day in negotiations with coal producers at the state level where their contracts were finalized. Smethurst responded, "I would say no if the code calls for eight."

As the meeting closed, many miners felt even more distant from their UMWA leaders. Many still felt abandoned, frustrated, and seething from the lack of understanding. Smethurst set out for his drive that evening back to Renton just as frustrated. In a letter to John L. Lewis the next day, he gave a dismal assessment of the situation.

> I was again in Roslyn in connection with the trouble at the N.W.I. Co. mines, but with no results. I had a conference with Mr. Swem [NWI manager of coal operations] today at which I placed the whole matter before him, stating that it was my opinion that the time for appealing reasonably to his employees was passed and that it looked that we would have to apply some other method, and suggested that he notify the Dist. that he was going to blow the whistle for work and those who failed to report would no longer be considered employees of the company, and that I would notify the men that all of those that returned to work would be given the full protection of our Union, while I was rather reluctant

to resort to this method it was the only thing I could see to do, and still retain our relationship with the company. However Swem suggested that it might be the best plan to let my suggestion wait until the code is effective believing that a new set of circumstances will be brought about that [may] be the means of avoiding much trouble that is now anticipated. With this suggestion coming from the company involved I agreed that it should be tried that way. The mess here has all the earmarks of an attempt to start a dual movement, I am watching it closely, but have been unable to place my finger on any one to make an example out of.[24]

The "new set of circumstances" that Swem referred to became clearer to Roslyn-area miners when they opened their Tuesday evening newspapers on September 26 to learn of the legal action nullifying the state ban on electric coal-cutting machines. Under the headline, "Mine Firm Wins Law Injunction," ran the following story:

The Northwest [sic] Improvement company yesterday won a temporary injunction in Spokane Federal court restraining officers from enforcing an amendment to the state mining laws prohibiting use of electrically operated cutting and drilling machines in coal mines alleged to be gaseous, pending trial before a special master on the merits of the case.[25]

The Northern Pacific Railway western counsel, L. B. daPonte, stated in the article, "Seventy-nine percent of the bituminous coal mined in the United States is produced by electrically operated equipment similar to that our company has installed." He continued, "These machines have been made safe under regulations of the U.S. bureau of mines. Machines permissible under the bureau's code have never caused an accident and are considered incapable of causing an accident."[26]

With two solid blows in one week, the world of this remote mining community was reeling. First the coal code had blasted at their dream of a six-hour work day, and now the Spokane federal court ruling had allowed the coal cutting machines back into the mines, undercutting their show of unity before the state legislature months earlier.

With few men working, idle miners had time to chew on the rumors about who had testified the new machines were safe. The Communist newspaper, *Voice of Action*, identified the "rats," a term it said miners were using to signify the men who had signed affidavits declaring the machines safe. Among the men identified as signing affidavits were Sam Farrimond and Bernard G. "Bun" Henry.[27]

Herman did a double take when he heard the name Sam Farrimond. Farrimond had been selected by the union men of Roslyn to lobby against the machines in Olympia last January. Now he was signing an affidavit that the machines were safe?[28]

And "Bun" Henry? The saga of Bun Henry was a long and lurid one in Roslyn's recent past. Eight years earlier, Henry had been arrested on a rape charge, along with Jack Boose and Joe Morris. More accurately, a warrant had been issued for Henry's arrest, but he got wind of the pending warrant and headed for the hills. Sheriff's deputies spent several days looking for him around Fish Lake without success. Henry had blackened his reddish hair to avoid detection. But he eventually surrendered to police.[29]

Arthur McGuire was the Kittitas County prosecutor, and the venerable defense attorney E. K. Brown was retained to defend Henry. The trial had drawn such interest that the old court building in Ellensburg was reported to have swayed under the weight of spectators, so a judge had ordered some one hundred watchers out of the courtroom.[30] The litigants went through two trials, which ended with an acquittal for Morris and convictions for Boose as an accomplice and for Henry on the rape charge.

E. K. Brown appealed the admissibility of some of the testimony in the case to the State Supreme Court. But the court, in 1927, affirmed the lower court decision, and Henry served time at the state's penitentiary in Walla Walla.[31]

After returning to the community, Henry worked for the NWI by day and built something of a boxing career by night, appearing in a number of boxing matches in the state, some promoted by his brother Bud. The brothers boxed as part of the same card in Rialto Hall on January 20, 1933, at about the time that some of his fellow miners were trekking to Olympia to fight for the ban on machines. That evening, the young lightweight Bun defeated Tommy Santos to the cheers of a large audience from both the upper and lower county.[32]

When word came in September 1933 that Henry testified for the safety of the machines, public denunciations and threats followed. At a special mass meeting of the union's local members, the miners set up a trial committee to investigate the charges against the men.

One of the committee members assigned to investigate the charges was Bob Ruff. A thirty-nine-year-old machinist at the No. 5 mine, Ruff was a Mason and a respected member of the volunteer fire department. He was well-liked among his peers.[33] He also supported the notion of starting a new local union and abandoning UMWA affiliation, a position that put him on the opposite side of the issue from union loyalists like Farrimond and Henry.

Henry supposedly met Ruff on the street just the day before the charges were brought to the union local in Roslyn against the signers. According to Henry, Ruff handed him the newspaper in which Henry was identified as a "rat," and said "Here Bun, read that. This ain't nothing to what I'm going to do to Farrimond. We paid that [expletive deleted] money and the [expletive deleted] went over there and brought the machines back to the mines."

Henry claimed that Ruff threatened him, saying the men were going to hang him at the next meeting. "I've heard that. I'll bring the rope," Henry replied.[34] Displaying perhaps more bravado than wisdom, Henry showed up the next day with rope in hand, stood up in the meeting amid shouts and accusations and challenged the men, "You fellows said you were going to hang me. Here's the rope."[35]

The group managed to finish the meeting without using Henry's rope, but immediately after the meeting, Henry became involved in a brawl with none other than his former friend and co-defendant, Jack Boose. Farrimond and Ruff reportedly scuffled during that brawl as well. As Henry and Boose fought, Boose's cheek was bloodied, and Boose claimed the injury was the result of a bite from Henry.

The trial committee, with Ruff as one of its members, met several times but were unable to reach a decision on whether testifying about the safety of machines should merit expulsion from the union. The rest of the miners were not satisfied with that outcome, however, so they directed the committee to come to a decision. The committee finally voted to expel Farrimond, Henry, and three others for 99 years.[36]

Herman was losing patience with the lengthening stalemate. He needed the work, not a bunch of infighting at his local. If the president said to work eight hours a day, and if John L. said $5.40 was the rate, then let's get the state contract signed and get back to work, he reasoned.

But many of the men who worked with him in the No. 3 mine disagreed. They weren't ready to give up on their dream. The language of Section 7(a) of the NRA kept ringing in their ears—"employees shall have the right to organize and bargain collectively through representatives *of their own choosing*" [emphasis added]. They had sensed the power of a group of gritty, ragged miners, standing together, and they were prepared to fight on.

Chapter 5

Tapping the Ceiling

Experienced miners seemed to possess an uncanny ability to determine when a mine ceiling was safe. By listening to the sounds of a pick handle tapping on the rock surface overhead, their keen ears could determine if it was solid or likely to cave in. Young miners learned to heed their advice, or they didn't live to be old miners.[1]

But tests that worked well in the mine were not easily transferred outside. The difficult political situation emerging in the Roslyn coalfields in late September 1933 left experienced miners with no safe place to stand.

The scale committee, selected by local miners to negotiate the union contract with state coal producers, had become bogged down during planning sessions. Members of the scale committee were determined to push for the six-hour day and substantial increases in pay, but their union leaders were under orders from John L. Lewis to negotiate rates and hours based on the nationwide coal code just signed by President Roosevelt.[2]

Walter Smethurst, the international union representative sent by Lewis to settle the problems in Washington State, had pushed the committee for a statement ordering the miners back to work under the existing contract terms, but the committee refused to act. Smethurst took matters into his own hands and issued a letter to the miners.[3]

The notice, dated September 30, 1933, was signed by Smethurst, Sam Nicholls, and a local miner selected by the miners as their representative to the international union board, Sam Mikulich.

Greetings:

> For the past five days a scale committee representing all of the miners of Dist. 10 has been in conference at headquarters in Renton, familiarizing itself with the provisions of the Bituminous

Coal Code as approved by the President of the United States, and by the United Mineworkers of America, and which becomes effective Oct. 2nd. Inasmuch as the code was approved by our Union it is necessary that our membership be governed by its provisions. The maximum hours of labor are eight with $5.40 as the basic minimum wage for inside skilled labor, and $4.00 for outside unskilled. A conference committee was selected from the main committee to work out in joint conference with the operators the labor provisions as provided in the code and to set wage scales in accordance with the rates scheduled therein. They will also negotiate for a contract consistent with provisions of the code embracing the newly organized sections which have been unorganized for so many years. If this is accomplished it will greatly improve the conditions of all the membership of Dist. 10. It is needless to say that they will secure the best possible contract consistent with the provisions of the code.

The code as approved by the President of the United States and the United Mine Workers becomes effective Oct. 2nd, and will then become the law of the land. This being the case the scale committee agreed that they have no authority to submit any agreement reached between the operators and committee to a referendum vote of the membership. The effective date of any agreement reached in joint conference will be Oct. 2nd.

You are hereby advised to return to work. By so doing you will greatly assist your scale committee in making an agreement. Your failure to return to work will jeopardize the committee's chances of making the best possible contract. Act quickly upon this advice. Your scale committee meets the operators Oct. 2nd and there is no doubt it will be confronted with the question of your idleness and the Union's position regarding the same.

We, therefore, urge that upon receipt of this communication you immediately comply with the suggestion and advice contained herein.[4]

Another mass meeting was called at Roslyn's Rialto Hall. Even though hunting season had opened, nearly every miner was in the hall. Union local president "Pots" Pasquan put the options on the table for the group to consider—to follow the clear directive of the union and go back to work under the eight-hour, $5.40 pay scale, or to continue their holdout. He explained that the state committee had selected six delegates to represent the union in meetings with mine operators the following Monday, and he noted that he was one of those six.

He explained that the new coal code had specified a minimum rate of $5.40 per day for skilled labor but did not specify which positions were skilled. So he argued that rope riders (who coupled coal cars together, checked coupling ropes and chains, and rode cars into and out of the mines), drivers, motormen, and pumpmen should be considered skilled labor. They had been making $5 per day under the old contract. He argued that they should be raised to $5.40 per day and miners should receive forty cents per day more than that, or $5.80 per day.[5]

The group also initiated a recall on Sam Mikulich because his name appeared on the Smethurst letter. In the end, the group voted overwhelmingly to reject Smethurst's call to return to work, although some miners did not vote.

Herman was one of the miners sitting on his hands that evening, and as he slipped away into the night, he was more than a little concerned that he might be the only man who was growing disillusioned with the direction of his local leaders. It seemed to him that some pretty good guys were getting carried away, headed in a direction that was going to get them and everybody with them in a whole lot of trouble.

Outside the meeting hall, pressure was mounting on the miners to close a deal. An October 6 editorial in the Cle Elum *Miner Echo* estimated the economic loss to the community because of the miners' refusal to work in the month of August alone at $127,039.50, an amount that was "lost for good as the coal was supplied from other sources."[6]

Seattle Times articles reflected President Roosevelt's growing concern as miners and operators, especially those in the Pennsylvania fields, balked at negotiating union contracts under the terms of the new coal code. The newspaper's October 8 front page carried the headline, "Roosevelt Demands Coal Peace." Another headline in that same paper stated, "Roosevelt Warns Capital, Labor to Cease Quarreling." The next day's headline read, "Roosevelt Scans Coal Field; Asks Work Resumed." Two days later, Roosevelt told reporters he would ask Congress for the power to step in and end labor disputes unless organized workers settled differences quickly. And three days after that, miners learned they could lose federal relief if they went on an unjustified strike.[7]

Intense negotiations on the state coal contract opened between the union committee and state coal operators on October 2. Some days the meetings extended to sixteen hours.[8] By October 14, D. R. Swem, the NWI manager of coal operations who was negotiating on behalf of NWI, reported to company executives in St. Paul that the wage scale had been clarified at $5.40 for miners with a lower wage for drivers, motormen, rope riders, and pumpmen.[9] John L. Lewis had been consulted as negotiations progressed and had clarified the dispute, but not in the direction Roslyn miners were hoping.[10] An agreement was finalized two days later that set the state contract in line with the national coal code—$5.40 per day for an eight-hour day.

As the final touches were being added to the state coal contract, another whirlwind enveloped the negotiations. Votes on the recall of District 10 union president Sam Nicholls were tallied, and the results left little doubt as to the sentiments of the miners. Sam Nicholls was ousted. The miners had voted Andrew Hunter as their new District 10 president. As Roslyn-area miners heard the news, some were jubilant, certain that Hunter's leadership would bring them the shorter working days, better pay, and attention to local concerns that they felt Nicholls had failed to deliver.

On the other hand, UMWA loyalists, those who had worked under union contract for years, those who would become eligible for pensions in a few years, were shocked and afraid of what might lie ahead. Even before Walter Smethurst saw the final vote tally, he advised Lewis:

> While the votes have not been counted in the recall election but the various reports coming in indicate that Nicholls is defeated, and Andrew Hunter is elected, while Hunter keeps his tracts [sic] well covered there is no question that he is the leader of the insurgents in the Roslyn-Cle Elum field, and is not a fit man to hold office in our union, and while I write this I am seariously [sic] considering asking you to revoke the charter of the Dist. on the grounds that on numerous occasions the Dist. Board and Scale

committee has been asked to take a stand regarding the idleness of the miners of the east side of the mountains and they have constantly refused to do so, further, the east side of the mountains has complete control of the district, in that the newly organized miners are barred from participating in the affairs, at least in running for office, and upon the restoration of the District charter they would have equal rights to run for the offices of the district.[11]

Lewis was prepared to take action against the upstarts in Washington State who refused his orders. Andrew Hunter did not have the chance to enjoy a single day as UMWA district president. On Wednesday, October 18, the day the vote was announced, Lewis revoked the charter for District 10 and established a provisional charter. Adding insult to injury, Lewis named the man who the miners had just ousted to return as president of the provisional district—Sam Nicholls.[12]

The miners were in a state of shock and denial. Many couldn't believe that they had worked for months within the system, recalled their district president through a valid recall vote, elected their own representative per union rules, and then had their choice so deliberately rebuffed by Lewis. For some the action was seen as ultimate proof that union leadership had lost touch with local interests, more evidence that the UMWA was nothing more than a "company" union. "Pots" Pasquan withdrew from the union negotiations in Renton and returned to Roslyn.[13]

Talk of leaving the United Mine Workers and starting a new local union was rife in parts of the upper county. Andrew Hunter sent a telegram of protest to John L. Lewis, but Lewis did not respond, asking Smethurst to handle the issue.[14]

Another mass meeting was called for 2:00 p.m. Saturday, October 21, at Roslyn's Rialto Hall.[15] The *Voice of Action* reported the meeting with breathless passion:

> The miners of Kittitas County thunder their defiance of efforts by John L. Lewis and corrupt leaders of the United Mine Workers of America to force them back into the pits at a starvation scale.
> "How many of you men are ready to roll up the charter and send it back to Lewis?" challenged [Sam] Mikulich, militant International Board member of the union, deposed by the Washington,

D. C. burocrats [sic]. And six hundred miners assembled in a mass meeting here last night rose to their feet in an almost unanimous vote.[16]

The miners instructed their local officers to meet with the scale committee and to draw up a plan of action that the men could agree on. Pasquan returned to the negotiations the following morning and participated in marathon sessions for the next three days.[17]

Meanwhile, NWI officials continued to pressure Lewis to push harder to get the men back to work in Roslyn. D. R. Swem told Lewis that unless operations were resumed immediately, the railway would be forced to look elsewhere for coal.[18]

Still squabbling over the length of the work day, members of the union scale committee finally struck upon a plan that would put men back to work under terms that both the miners and the mining companies might accept, even if it delayed an inevitable clash. The proposal called for the men to accept a six-month contract under protest with the understanding that their concerns over the six-hour day would be resolved within that six-month period.[19]

"What are the prospects that men will accept agreement and follow orders of scale committee?" came the query of the mining company vice president to the company's lead negotiator.[20] Swem responded quickly: "Scale Committee are confident men will accept agreement and follow orders and [Mine Superintendent Tom] Murphy reports general opinion in Roslyn men are expecting to return to work this week and anxious to start."[21]

Another mass meeting in Roslyn on October 24 brought 550 miners to Rialto Hall, now badly divided and questioning the steps to be taken next. A contingent of loyal UMWA members was ready to follow the union back into the mines, trusting that the contract was the best deal to be made and wanting to do their patriotic duty under the Blue Eagle.

With bills mounting and winter coming, another contingent badly needed the work, but they were bitter that union leaders had ordered them back to work without regard to the men displaced by the coal-cutting ban. They were frustrated at the union's failure to stand and fight for the six-hour day, and ultimately they were

disenfranchised when their recall and election votes were so bla-
tantly disregarded by the UMWA leadership.

Still another, more radical group was considering bolting from
the UMWA in favor of a new local independent union to better represent the men of the Roslyn coal fields. But clear leadership and
direction among members of this group was not yet focused. The
Voice of Action chided the timidity of its leaders:

> Certain leaders were very vacillating and hesitant in their action,
> which had much to do with preventing the workers from break-
> ing away from the reactionary leadership and the United Mine
> Workers of America, and carrying on a broadening struggle long
> ago. These leaders created doubts in the minds of the strikers as
> to whether the west side would back them and follow their exam-
> ple. They injected fear that the government would interfere with
> their troops and there would be bloodshed; that the company
> would not recognize the new independent union.[22]

Divisions long unspoken began to surface at the meeting hall.
Speeches came from every sector of the mining community. They all
needed the work. And nearly all could agree that they were not willing to pay union dues while their charter was revoked. Most were
willing to consider working under protest as long as their concerns
about the length of the work day were being addressed. The final
vote was nearly unanimous—to return to work, under protest.

The next evening four hundred more "aye" votes from Cle
Elum sealed the decision. Under protest, the men would work for
six months. On October 26 the mine whistles blew and the mines
opened at near full production. All the mines began operating five
days a week except No. 7, where two groups of miners split a six-day
work week. Superintendent Murphy said the men could expect full
work for some time as back orders for coal had piled up during the
four months of idleness.[23]

While the NWI had made a few wage concessions, the terms of
the interim contract were much the same as the terms of the previous
contract. Summing up the situation, NWI executive J. M. Hughes
told the railway president: "Taking it all together our company
seems to have fared very well in this negotiation."[24]

Chapter 6

Go West

After four months of inactivity, Herman could feel the strain on his muscles from a full day of work in the mine. With his empty lunch bucket tucked under his arm, he wearily pushed himself out of the back seat and thanked his neighbor for the lift. The evening sky was dark with clouds, but Herman's eyes were used to darkness and the snow on the ground reflected what light there was.

At lunch that day, miners had been discussing the prospects of another mass meeting that evening, the first day of November, at the Roslyn miner's hall. Another mass meeting. What could be brewing now, he wondered? We've got a contract, we're working, what else could anybody want?

As Herman turned up Arizona Street toward his house he could see his son coming down the hill to meet him. After school that afternoon several of Clarence's friends had traded magazines. Clarence had picked up an April issue of Popular Mechanics *and had been drawn to a diagram for a Morse code practice set. He wanted to know if his father might be willing to advance him twenty-five cents to go with the forty-five cents he had saved so he could buy two No. 6 dry cell batteries for the project. Herman said he would see when he got his pay at the end of the week.*

The meeting that evening featured many of the same players that Herman had heard at other mass meetings. Still smarting from the revocation of their district charter, a few vocal leaders had taken control of the group and were calling for a meeting of the rank-and-file members, what union leaders would label a "rump" meeting.[1]

Reviewing the list of abuses, leaders suggested that John L. Lewis should not be allowed to break the spirit of unity in Roslyn that had taken years to build. They quoted the Industrial Recovery Act—workers had the right to choose *their own* union. The spokesmen set a meeting date to take formal action on forming their own new labor union.[2] Seattle was chosen as the site for the organizational meeting;

attracting miners from west of the mountains might add legitimacy to the effort.

Some of the impetus for the formation of a new union was coming from the state Communist Party. A twenty-year-old labor organizer by the name of Mark Haller was assigned to work among the miners of Roslyn and generate interest in the communist-based National Miners Union. Haller had grown up in a West Virginia coal-mining camp and could speak a little Serbo-Croatian. He later recalled the building coalition of dissent: "It wasn't long before I realized that while the huge majority was anti John L. Lewis, the opposition was split. I proposed that since the programs of the Progressive Miners [favored by Hunter], IWW, and the National Miners were basically the same, we could combine and form an independent union with connection among all three."[3]

The chief of the Washington State Patrol, William Cole, was keeping a wary eye on the activities of all known communist organizers in the state, and he noted the strengthening coalition in a letter to the governor in late September 1933: "I find the Communists agitators and Industrial Workers of the World are trying to form some alliance so as to be more effective."[4]

Sam Nicholls, president of what was now the UMWA provisional district, sent a letter to each union member warning that anyone attending the Seattle meeting would be expelled from the UMWA.[5] Nicholls's letter contained a check-off slip for payroll deduction of union dues. He suggested paying dues was the best way for members to protect their UMWA membership. But Walter Smethurst admitted, "The slips are coming in slow."[6]

As men arrived at the Labor Temple in Seattle on Saturday morning, November 11, a number of residents elsewhere in Seattle were preparing festivities for a five-day Recovery Act carnival, including a bazaar with afternoon teas, dinners, and programs at Trinity Church Parish.[7] Others around the country were observing the first of the great black blizzards sweeping through the nation's heartland in what became known as the Dust Bowl.[8]

Ten delegates entered the hall, resolute on setting a new course for coal miners in the state, perhaps even the nation. The *Voice of Action* reported: "Every delegate spoke with bitter tones of J. L. Lewis and his machine. Innumerable cases were brought up for which the UMWA did not do a thing; the Roslyn blacklisted miners, the 20% wage cut put over last year by the UMWA; Lewis' henchmen, Smethurst being sent here and openly working with the coal operators, and to top it all, the installment of the provisional government."[9]

The eight Roslyn delegates voted to break away from the UMWA. The two western delegates did not vote because they had no instructions to vote at the meeting. The next vote was to form a new labor organization for miners, and to name it the Western Miners Union of America. The delegates selected Andrew Hunter as president, Mike Petrovich (the former vice president of the district) as vice president, and John P. "Pots" Pasquan as secretary.[10]

A representative of the Industrial Workers of the World, Arthur Boose (no relation to Jack Boose) of Portland,[11] spoke to the group, promising the support of his organization. Haller was next to address the new union leaders, cautioning that the action to form a new union might be hasty and suggesting greater efforts to involve locals in the western part of the district.[12]

The leaders of the new Western Miners Union were anxious to find support wherever they could. Communist organizers in Seattle could offer free publicity through their newspaper, the *Voice of Action*, provide legal counsel through the International Labor Defense, and produce a crowd of demonstrators on demand. But tight communist affiliation could also impede the new union's push for acceptance. Perceptions of communism in the state were far from positive—a Congressional hearing in the state in 1930 had brought to the forefront government concerns over communist activity and its surveillance of activists.[13]

The new union organizers continued to meet in Seattle through Monday, November 13. One of Hunter's first acts as president of the new union was to attempt to secure an endorsement from the American Federation of Labor. The AFL was the oldest labor union in the nation, and had been led by labor giant Samuel Gompers from 1886 to 1924.[14] An endorsement from such a venerable labor organization would have given the new union instant credibility. But the AFL refused such an endorsement.[15]

News of the new union traveled quickly to John L. Lewis. Walter Smethurst telegrammed for help the next day:

> Rump convention held November eleventh and twelfth at Seattle. Start dual union name Western Miners. Andrew Hunter President, Mike Petrovich Vice President, John Pasquan Secretary. Attempts being made to secure membership. Much confusion ensues. As a result have warned members how to protect their membership. Our union still have some local conditions to work out under our contract setup. Would like two or three men immediately. Impossible to give proper attention to all interests since the last move. Letter follows.[16]

That same evening a telephone message, transcribed for Lewis from Eugene McAuliffe of the Union Pacific's mining company, signaled the threat felt among mine owners in other parts of the country over the formation of a dual union in Washington State:

> Mr. N. D. Moore [a representative of the Dale Coal Company of Ravensdale, Wash.] telephoned from Seattle at 10:45 p.m. November 13th that about one thousand men employed in the Roslyn District, led by Andrew Hunter, are definitely communistic. Hunter is the man who ran for President against Sam Nicholls.
>
> Hunter, with these men, called a convention to meet in Seattle Saturday November 11th, meeting continuing through Monday the 13th. Hunter has secured the support of local leaders in the western part of the state and they are now trying to get the one thousand to twelve hundred men west of Roslyn to join in organizing a new union, alleging that President Lewis has failed to secure the shorter day and increased wages promised in numerous public utterances. They also promise relief from exorbitant national dues. The proposed state organ[ization] is pledged not to collect in excess of from twenty-five to fifty cents per man per month, with self-government.
>
> Mr. Moore states that provisional president Sam Nicholls and Walter Smethurst, National Board Member from Montana, on the ground are trying to combat the situation but he is fearful that it is too serious for them to control without help.
>
> He asked me to get in touch with Mr. Lewis urging him to send out one of his strongest men, first offering Nicholls and Smethurst the help suggested, but not mentioning in any way that Mr. Moore doubts their ability to combat the situation, or

has made request, in which he states that Mr. D. R. Swem of the Northwestern Improvement Company joins him.[17]

Lewis responded, immediately assigning three more UMWA international representatives to Washington State to fight the dual union.[18]

By stepping away from the UMWA, the leaders of the new union were taking an immense risk. They knew that their actions could not be undone. They were now marked men. They could never again reclaim standing as UMWA members. If their gambit failed and their new union should fold, they would never again work in the Roslyn mines. The course of their lives would be changed, their families upended, their careers stymied. Without work in the mines, they would have no option other than to move away and start over.

The new movement had a strong following, especially among workers in Ronald and much of Roslyn. If the men could stay united, stay the course in protesting for the six-hour day with full pay, attract new members west of the mountains, and achieve recognition as the majority mining union in the state, there was hope of reaching their goals and establishing a lasting organization.

Reasons for joining the new union were as varied as the diverse backgrounds of the workers. Many immigrant miners who could not read or write English were undoubtedly swayed by the convincing speeches of the movement's leaders—the promises for a better life, better pay, better working conditions. Many others felt the pull of family and friends and responded with loyalty to those vital relationships.[19]

Some joined because they felt that their safety in the mines could be better protected by a local union than a national or international group that had little contact with their daily lives. Still others believed that it was wrong for capitalists in the East to profit from their spilled blood in the mines, and they saw the local union as a means of taking care of themselves and others in their community.[20]

Western Miners set out with a passion to recruit every miner in the state. West of the mountains the work went slowly. Few men could afford to travel, and the Western Miners were competing with UMWA organizers who were also working to maintain and build their numbers west of the Cascades.

In Roslyn, Ronald, and Cle Elum, Western Miners organizers pushed especially hard for support. Tensions between the miners grew as men loyal to the UMWA responded to the efforts of the Western Miners by putting pressure on their coworkers to stay loyal to the larger union. UMWA organizers at times went into the mines and threatened miners with expulsion unless they signed check-off slips for union dues.

A number of miners signed on with both groups; some didn't care which union won out, while others thought they could play both sides of the fence to assure being on the winning side.

On a late November Friday evening, Herman answered a knock at the door. His daughters were upstairs and crouched in the stairwell to hear the unexpected visitors. "Anna, can you make us some coffee?" Herman gestured to his wife as two men entered the dining room and took chairs at the round oak table.

"Listen, Swede," one of the men started. "I'm gonna get right to the point. I ain't seen you at the Western Miners meetings. You know we're startin' this new union for you and every working man in the district. We're pushing hard for six dollars for a six-hour day, and we're gonna get a union that listens to us here in Roslyn and not to Washington, DC."

"You've been in the mines a long time," the other picked up. "A lot of people respect you and the work you do there at No. 3. We got a lot of signatures already from the guys up there. We know that just about everybody is ready to sign on. We really want you to join with us. What do you think?"

Herman paused for a moment. The English words didn't come so easily when he was stressed. "I've been with NWI and John L. a long time. They always been fair to me. I just got a few more years to my pension," Herman's voice became more resolute and steady. "Why should I change now?"

"Well, what have you gotten from John L.?" the first man asked. "A 20 percent punch in the gut last year and a bunch of promises. Then this new contract, and it's for the same pay as last year. How are we ever gonna get ahead if we just keep followin' John L. backwards?"

"But what good has all this ruckus done?" Herman replied, his voice rising in intensity. "What's it got us but four months poorer? I think it's time we got to workin' and stoppa den här skiten." The girls gave a silent gasp as they recognized their father swearing in his native tongue.

"Look, Swede, we're in this thing now. We're gonna win it. You don't want to be left out. It's gonna be big, and it could get rough, but we're gonna win. You know, it would sure be too bad if something happened to you in the mine, you bein' this close to the pension and all."

Herman was taken aback by the thinly veiled threat. He knew that some of the "accidents" that had occurred in the mines, some of them fatal, had not really been accidents at all. He felt a cold chill come over the back of his neck as he rose from the chair. "Yah, you just better watch out for your-selves, that's all I can say. I know lotsa fellas whose stayin' with John L. and if you give us any trouble, there'll be hell to pay. Now get outta my house!"

"Whoa, Swede, take it easy. We're not here to fight you, but we're gonna win, with or without you. So you'd just better get on the right side of this thing. You take care of yourself, old man," the second man sneered as he stood to leave.

Herman's hands were shaking as he watched the men head for the front door. As it slammed shut, he exploded at Anna for not having the coffee ready sooner. Then he noticed his head beginning to throb. He went straight to bed. Anna followed and clenched his hand as his back began to arch in an epileptic fit.

Charles Rushton experienced similar pressure to join the new union:[21]

> I worked in No. 3 mine at the time. The majority of the fellows wanted to go for this new union, but these guys that were going to be the head guys would come and tell me, "C'mon Charlie, you better sign up. We won't have to work hard after this." I says, "No, I can't see that." I said, "How in the hell are you going to run these mines if you don't work?" I says, "You are not going to have any work." I said, "No, I don't think I want to sign with you." And I didn't. I don't think there was more than about ninety or a hundred men that stayed with the United Mine Workers out of probably six hundred miners. And it was hell for awhile.

Two international representatives of the United Mine Workers arrived in Roslyn in late November and met with local branch members to begin to repair damage caused by the exodus of key leaders, including John "Pots" Pasquan. One of their first acts was to expel the leaders who had defected to the new union. They also exonerated the men who had been thrown out earlier for signing affidavits supporting the electric coal-cutting machinery.[22]

In early December, UMWA representative James Ferns and district president Sam Nicholls showed up for a UMWA meeting at Roslyn's union hall only to find it filled with Western Miners. A confrontation ensued over the use of the hall for mass meetings. Pasquan and the Western Miners claimed that the union hall belonged to the miners of Roslyn as trustees and not to the United Mine Workers.[23]

The UMWA filed papers in Ellensburg suing the Western Miners over ownership of the hall. Andrew Hunter decided that his new union would not contest the case.[24] Arthur McGuire, now a superior court judge, ruled that the UMWA local had right and title to the property.[25] So the Western Miners were forced to find other meeting spaces.

As the dual union began to take hold in the upper Kittitas coal fields, the local newspaper, the *Miner Echo*, remained silent about the movement, apparently sensing the strong feelings and unsure what editorial position to take. Rather than take sides, the paper provided a December 22 open forum with side-by-side statements from opposing leaders.

Writing for the Western Miners Union, Andrew Hunter recounted the abuses inflicted on the men by the UMWA and stated that the Western Miners represented more than 90 percent of the miners in the Roslyn-Cle Elum coal field. He reported four new local branches in Roslyn, Ronald, Cle Elum, and Issaquah. He concluded with a ringing denunciation of UMWA pressure tactics:

> Repeatedly representatives from the outside of the United Mine Workers of America, with the consent and cooperation of the operators, in violation of Federal Law, have gone into the mines and have intimidated miners into signing up with the United Mine Workers of America under threats of expulsion and discharge. On the contrary, the Western Miners Union of America has scrupulously obeyed every law and regulation of the United States and of the State of Washington and every principle of fair dealing.[26]

Nicholas Fontecchio, one of the three UMWA international board representatives sent to the district by John L. Lewis, provided the union's perspective. His appeal called for national unity to overcome the difficult economic crisis. The country, he said, needed a strong, responsible union to promote the interests of industrial recovery. "Elements who are creating discord in the miners' union and bringing about industrial conflicts are a menace to the country and cannot be tolerated. Miners and mining communities have suffered much in recent years because of misunderstanding. The confusion that now exists in this region must be eliminated."[27]

The Christmas season was anything but peaceful in Roslyn that year. With saloons and bars now open across the state, miners collected to let off steam among friends and argue their side with enemies in the labor dispute. Local police attempted to keep a lid on the situation, but they sensed a growing pressure. A few days before Christmas, one policeman delivered an intoxicated reveler to his family with the warning, "Keep him home tonight. There's gonna be trouble."[28]

The policeman's warning was all too prescient. In the early hours of Christmas Eve, one disagreement erupted into violence. Shots rang out, and a man fell to the ground, dying.[29]

The corner of Pennsylvania Avenue and Second Street in modern day Roslyn. On the far corner, near the pickup truck, an altercation led to a shooting that took the life of one Western Miner and further divided sentiment in the community between miners loyal to the United Mine Workers and those supporting the new local union. *Author collection*

Chapter 7

Murder at Christmas

*M*ildred skipped ahead of Hannah as they rounded the corner of First and Washington by the NWI company store. The girls had coaxed their mother into a holiday outing on this snowy Christmas Eve. Mildred's fourteenth birthday was six days earlier, and she wanted to make sure her mother didn't plan on celebrating the two occasions with a single present.

The company store always had the biggest window display of the season, and the girls were anxious to gaze at every ornament, light, and Christmas outfit one more time. A few rays of sunshine had dried the well-shoveled walks in front of the store.

As the girls pored over a mechanical squirrel picking up a nut, Anna noticed an unusual gathering at the end of the next block. She recognized one of her neighbors, Esther Whitaker, at the edge of the circle, so she ventured down the block a few minutes later with her girls in tow.

"What happened?" Anna asked Esther as she joined the circle.

"Didn't you hear? It's Bob Ruff. He was shot here last night, just after midnight," Esther reported.

"Is he hurt bad?"

"He's dead. He was shot on the sidewalk here, in front of Pete's Place." A group had formed by the hardware store near the front door of the tavern, directly across Pennsylvania Avenue from the Masonic Lodge.

A murder in a small town is no small news. A murder at Christmas, even more newsworthy. "He was a Western Miner," another added. "Sam Farrimond shot him. They'd been arguing for months, you know. Farrimond is the one who testified for the coal cutters, remember? Ruff hated him for that."

"Well, you know Sam. He could never back down from a fight," a third chimed in. "Cops got him red-handed. No way he'll get outta this one."

Bob Ruff had lived in Roslyn most of his life. He would have been forty in another month. He had been married with two children but divorced twelve years earlier.[1]

Ruff's shooter, Sam Farrimond (who also used the name Krahen-buhl[2]), reportedly fired four shots at close range with a 32-20 revolver, hitting Ruff once. Ruff died en route to the hospital. Farrimond was immediately taken into custody.[3]

Because he was a Mason and a volunteer fireman, Ruff's funeral was held the following Thursday at the Masonic Lodge across the street from where he was shot, his casket carried by fireman's sled to the Masonic Cemetery.[4] Herman, a fellow Mason and miner, joined more than five hundred miners who marched in the funeral procession. A number of business owners closed their doors and joined the procession.[5]

Rumors of the shooting ran wild in the isolated community. One version had Ruff peacefully talking with friends on the street when Farrimond ran up behind him and kicked him. As Ruff turned, Farrimond shot him in the side.[6]

Another version suggested that Farrimond had really intended to shoot Andrew Hunter and had mistaken Ruff for Hunter since both men dressed well and were of similar build.[7] Yet another story had Farrimond consuming several shots of liquor and then saying, "I'm just going to kill somebody," whereupon he headed out of the bar and shot Ruff in the back.[8]

But numerous witnesses had heard Ruff and Farrimond arguing at Pete's Place, and several had witnessed the shooting. There was little doubt that the source of the disagreement was the battle between the Western Miners and the United Mine Workers.

J. C. McGovern, the mayor of Roslyn, was working as a special officer that evening and had helped Special Officer Graham arrest a drunk just before the shooting. As the men were headed to the jail they heard shots, and Graham went back to investigate.[9]

With the help of several men, Farrimond had been disarmed and arrested. McGovern returned to the scene and stayed with Farrimond until he was turned over to Sheriff Art Byars in Cle Elum. Byars took Farrimond to the county seat in Ellensburg where he was arraigned. Concerned over the widespread animosity in the community toward Farrimond, the sheriff moved the shooter out of the county as a precaution before his trial.[10]

County prosecutor Spencer Short, a thirty-three-year-old gradu-
ate of the University of Washington Law School, had grown up in
Ellensburg.[11] Short practiced law with his father at G. P. Short and
Sons before his election as prosecutor in 1930.[12] Seeking assistance
in trying his first murder case, Short invited a special prosecutor,
F. A. Kern, to serve as the lead prosecutor. Kern, aged fifty-one, was
an experienced Ellensburg attorney who had been practicing in the
area since 1909.[13]

E. K. Brown, the savvy, fifty-four-year-old veteran of many court
battles, including the Bernard "Bun" Henry rape trial of 1925, was
retained to defend Farrimond. A wealthy property owner, Brown held
the mortgages for a substantial number of residents of the county.
Speculation circled that perhaps that fact may have accounted for his
unusual record of success in defending murder cases.[14] Those who
kept records said that Brown had seventeen acquittals in eighteen
murder trials. One local later said of Brown, "He was a good lawyer,
crookeder than hell. If you had the money he would get you free. If
you didn't have the money he would probably help you get free too,
because he was that kind of guy."[15]

Farrimond did not have the money to hire Brown, but the United
Mine Workers put up $500 to assist in his defense. The Northwest-
ern Improvement Company added another five hundred to retain
Brown for the trial. NWI president J. M. Hughes explained his rea-
soning to Northern Pacific Railway President Charles Donnelly:

> Farrimond is one of our machine runners and at the Company's
> request signed an affidavit as to the use of the machines...Ever
> since these affidavits were obtained the radical element in the
> field have persecuted the men who made them on the ground
> that they were disloyal to union labor. These men have had to
> endure threats of physical violence and social ostracism. Farri-
> mond has had to stand his share of this abuse and apparently the
> altercation which resulted in the killing was the culmination of
> months of quarreling.
>
> Farrimond has no resources. The United Mine Workers are
> going to finance his defense and the representative of the Union
> has approached Mr. Swem [NWI Manager of Coal Operations]
> with the suggestion that, under the circumstances, the Company

might be willing to contribute. Mr. daPonte [NWI Western Counsel] and I discussed the matter at some length last night...and we are all of the opinion that the trouble having developed as the result of Farrimond's action in our behalf, there is some obligation on our part to assist in his defense.[16]

Among Western Miners supporters in Roslyn, there was little doubt that the murder had been ordered by the company. "They killed him to scare the others," recalled Camilla Saivetto, "to see that they stayed in, bowed to their orders."[17] The Communist newspaper reported that mine superintendent Tom Murphy was seen bringing a turkey and groceries to the Farrimond house on Christmas Eve after the shooting.[18]

Prosecutor Short attempted to gather evidence that would tie the union, the company, or both to the shooting, and he collected some fifty affidavits before the trial.[19] But he never got the chance to develop that strategy fully. Brown acted quickly to limit the scope of the trial solely to the actions of the defendant and the deceased and to avoid questions of union or company complicity. Brown was, however, quite willing to expand the scope of questions as they related to possible Communist influence among Western Miners supporters. Judge Arthur McGuire struggled to maintain a close focus during court testimony, allowing from both sides only exhibits and testimony that were shown to have direct relevance to the shooting.

Seven and a half weeks after the shooting, jury selection began in the Kittitas County Superior Court in Ellensburg, in the first trial of the February term of the court, with the honorable Judge Arthur McGuire presiding.

Interested court watchers from the upper county as well as from Ellensburg packed the gallery in anticipation of a fiery trial. Jury selection began on Valentine's Day, but there were few thoughts of love in the courtroom that blustery Wednesday morning. Questioning centered again on the hatred and division that had consumed the Roslyn coal fields for months. E. K. Brown questioned prospective jurors on their knowledge of the local labor conditions, their attitude toward labor unions, Communism, radicalism, the NWI, and

The Kittitas County Courthouse, as it appeared in the 1930s, was the scene of several legal battles that brought to the fore the differing views of upper and lower county residents about the legitimacy of a new miners' union in the Roslyn-Cle Elum coal fields. *Courtesy of Ellensburg Public Library, WSU Digital Collections*

various union officials.[20] Jurors from the upper county were systematically excluded from sitting on the case because of their presumed prejudice.[21]

Judge McGuire ordered the seating of one alternate juror. The witness list contained some eighty-seven names representing those on both sides of the mining issue. To limit the length of the trial, both lawyers stipulated that no character witnesses would be called.

The prosecution opened with testimony establishing the death of Bob Ruff and the circumstances surrounding the shooting. From prosecution witnesses, the story emerged of a dispute in the tavern that was taken outside, where an intoxicated Farrimond drew a weapon in anger and shot Ruff.

Joe Cusworth testified that he had heard shots while he was inside Pete's Place and came out to the street to investigate. He tried to take the gun away from Farrimond when the shooter said, "Get away Joe, or I'll shoot."

Joe Morris testified that he had been headed to Swede's Hall when he heard shots and came running. He approached Farrimond and said, "What's the matter, are you crazy?" Farrimond replied, "Get away from me. I don't want to shoot you but I will."[22]

Cusworth moved to grab Farrimond, and in the struggle for the revolver, two more shots were fired. The shots hit the pavement, and no one was injured. Cusworth said Farrimond was easily disarmed in the confusion when he was distracted by the efforts of the others. He said that Farrimond had previously shot twice, one shot hitting Ruff and the other scattering three of his companions.

Joe Raffle testified that he had brushed against Farrimond in the bar and felt something hard inside his shirt. When Raffle said he thought it must have been a bottle, E. K. Brown cast an aside that brought a titter from the packed courtroom. Judge McGuire halted testimony and told the gallery that he would clear the courtroom if he heard further outbursts.[23]

Mayor McGovern of Roslyn testified about the arrest and Farrimond's behavior after the shooting. Prosecutor Kern asked the mayor whether, in his opinion, Farrimond was drunk. McGovern testified, "I would say he was intoxicated."[24] A number of other witnesses, including friends and acquaintances of the defendant and members of both labor organizations, testified that Farrimond had shown signs of being under the influence of liquor.

The last of the prosecution witnesses was Lawrence Barrick, a Roslyn miner of Croatian birth who was with Ruff when he was shot. Barrick gave much the same story as the earlier witnesses about the facts of the shooting. But during an hour-long cross-examination, E. K. Brown tore into Barrick, accusing him of being a Communist and a bitter foe of Farrimond's.

Barrick responded in what the newspaper described as "a noticeable accent," that he was not a Communist. He quickly admitted that he was a member of the Industrial Workers of the World and that he opposed "capitalism and all capitalistic tools." He said he had been critical of Farrimond since he learned of the signing of the affidavits supporting the machines. But he denied that he or other members of the Western Miners Union of America were Communists.[25]

Brown took Barrick back over his testimony about what had happened during the shooting. Barrick said that after the first two shots, Farrimond stood with the gun in his hand, and somebody said, "Look out, he's going to shoot again." At that, Barrick said, "I turned and ran."[26]

Some in the courtroom could not contain their laughter at Barrick's statement. Having issued several warnings, Judge McGuire sent out the jury and made good on his promise to clear the courtroom. The prosecution rested its case later that day before an empty chamber.[27]

While testimony continued in Ellensburg, another act of violence was reported in Roslyn on the evening of February 15. Communist labor organizer Mark Haller had been in Ellensburg attending the trial during the day, and in the evening he was headed toward his place of residence after a Western Miners meeting in Roslyn when he reported being attacked:

> I was walking on Second street towards Hoffmanville [a section of Roslyn]. I saw a car parked ahead and a man standing outside. I was about to pass the car when the man came up to me and demanded, "Who are you?" Before I had a chance to answer I was slugged. I recognized my assailant as Bernard Henry. The attack was so unexpected and I was taken by surprise that I couldn't defend myself. I hollered for help. He was choking me and hit me again on the head with the weapon, ran to the waiting car and driver, and went. I picked myself up and felt the blood pouring down my face. I managed somehow to stagger in a neighbor's yard and he took me in. I have several holes in my head. My coat, shirt and a copy of the *Voice of Action* I had in my pocket were soaked with blood.
>
> The authorities were very hesitant in swearing out a warrant. When they finally made one out on a charge of third degree assault I was still dazed by the attack and signed it.
>
> I was attacked in an effort to either kill me or to scare me into leaving town. The superintendent's son also threatened me. But I'm staying in Roslyn.[28]

A month later, assault charges against Henry were dismissed at the request of Henry's defense attorney, E. K. Brown.[29]

Back in Ellensburg, the trial entered its fourth day on Saturday morning, February 17, and spectators again filled the courtroom. The pervasive Ellensburg breezes were milder and a bit warmer than they had been over the past week, and court watchers were eager to see Brown begin his defense.

Brown did not disappoint. He opened by declaring his intention to prove that the hostile actions of one group of miners, and particularly the attitude of Bob Ruff, were responsible for the tragedy. The story Brown told the jury was that the labor troubles in Roslyn over the past six months had kept two factions of miners in a continuous state of turmoil, that Ruff had threatened Farrimond on several occasions, and that on the night of the shooting, Farrimond had reason to believe that his life was in danger. The shooting, Brown suggested, was an act of self-defense.

For his first witnesses, Brown called brothers Harold and Richard Duff, who had gone on a deer hunting trip the previous fall with Sam Farrimond and Bernard Henry. Harold was a brother-in-law to Henry. He testified first, and both men gave similar accounts, stating that they had heard shooting in the woods and encountered Ruff with two companions.

They said that Henry asked Ruff, "What's the idea of shooting across a deer run?" Ruff, they said, replied that he was "practicing up for you [Henry] and Sam [Farrimond]."[30]

In cross-examination, special prosecutor Kern asked both witnesses whether they thought Ruff had been joking when he made the statements, but the men were noncommittal.

Brown then called Bernard Henry to the stand. Known by many in the area for his skill as a boxer,[31] Henry was described as "a willing pugnacious witness."[32] Apparently none the worse from the alleged altercation with Haller a few nights before, Henry testified that he and Farrimond had been "pally" ever since they both signed the affidavits on the safety of the coal cutters the previous summer. Signing that affidavit, Henry testified, resulted in a great deal of hostility from their fellow miners, including Ruff.

Brown moved to place the affidavit in evidence, but the prosecution objected about the relevance of the document to the issue of the murder. Judge McGuire ruled that "only that portion of this evidence which actually showed the animus of the deceased to the defendant, or the animus of an organization tied up with the deceased and expressed through him might be admitted." McGuire admitted the affidavit.[33]

Henry then testified about the incident where he said Ruff had handed him a copy of the *Voice of Action* newspaper and threatened him. Brown offered the newspaper into evidence and again the prosecution objected. The judge later allowed only the article naming Henry.

Henry told about his fight with Jack Boose after the mass meeting, refuting with "much heat a prosecution inference that he had bitten Boose on the cheek." He explained that he had merely grabbed Boose, and he offered to demonstrate his hold on Prosecutor Kern. "Try it on Brown," Kern suggested. So defense attorney Brown became an unwilling participant in a wrestling demonstration before the court. Henry's grip "left a red mark on the attorney's cheek for some time after."[34]

The defense next introduced several "surprise" eyewitnesses to the stand who produced their accounts of the events surrounding the shooting. Russell Miller, an eighteen-year-old Yakima Civilian Conservation Corps worker, was the first witness to take the stand as a disinterested spectator.

Miller testified that he was standing beside the Masonic dance hall when he heard loud talking across the street. He said Ruff had come out of the bar with his arm around Farrimond. "They was standing in the doorway. They came out in the street. One fellow called this fellow (indicating the defendant) a _____. This fellow (the defendant) backed away. The other fellow turned as if he was going to fight him. Then he was shot."[35]

The next eyewitness turned out to be a surprise for both camps in the legal battle. Norman Thompson, an eighteen-year-old Roslyn newsboy, was on the street at the time of the shooting. He testified that he was attracted by what sounded like an argument. He started across Pennsylvania Avenue from the dance at the Masonic Temple to Pete's Place. "As I got to the middle of the street, the quarrel ended and some people came out of the door." Thompson said he saw Far-rimond come out of the tavern. "Then I seen Bob Ruff walking away from the doorway. Sam took a few steps out of the doorway. When he and Bob Ruff was six or eight feet away, for some reason Bob Ruff turned around. As he did, Sam shot him. Then he stood on the side-walk threatening everybody. Then he fired again."[36]

Thompson said he couldn't recall whether Ruff had taken steps forward before or after he was shot. "After he was shot, I think. Then he turned around and ran to the street and fell over."[37]

Special Prosecutor Kern came back to this testimony on cross-ex-amination, trying to emphasize for the jury the witness's testimony that Ruff had taken no steps toward Farrimond before he was shot. But E. K. Brown intervened. "I'm plainly surprised at this matter. Didn't you tell me when I questioned you before that they came out of the doorway together," he asked Thompson.

"I didn't," Thompson said.

"Who's been talking to you since I saw you?" Brown bellowed. "Didn't you tell me you saw Ruff take a step or two toward him before he was shot? Why did you tell me that?"

"Because you asked me too quickly up there. I don't know whether he took the steps before or after he was shot," Thompson responded.

"Who's been talking to you?" Brown repeated.

"A lot of people."

"Get you confused?"

"Yes," the witness admitted.

Brown was then forced to challenge the credibility of his own wit-ness, and it was Special Prosecutor Kern attempting to rehabilitate Thompson's testimony. "Forgetting all that, tell the jury what is your honest opinion of whether Bob Ruff took any steps toward Sam Far-rimond before he was shot."

"It seemed to me that he did," said Thompson. "How many?" "Two."[38]

So Kern's attempt to salvage testimony supporting his case had failed, and the jury was left with conflicting accounts of Ruff's actions at the time of the shooting.

Mike Padavich of Cle Elum was the next to take the stand. Padavich testified that he had driven by Pete's Place moments before the shooting and seen Farrimond standing in the doorway with Fred "Happy" Dullahant. Padavich then saw two men coming at a run from the diagonal corner of the intersection. One of the men resembled Ruff, Padavich said.

Padavich had parked his car and was sitting in front of the Masonic Temple. When he heard a shot, he turned his head and saw two men running away from Pete's Place. Farrimond had a gun stuck in Dullahant's stomach and was backing him toward the door and warning him to stay away. Padavich said he did not see the shooting.[39]

Farrimond's next door neighbor, John Bator, testified that he had witnessed much of the abuse that the miners had heaped on Farrimond and Henry after they had signed the coal cutting affidavits. Bator testified that on one occasion, he had met Ruff on the street, and Ruff had said, "They ought to hang the dirty _____ for signing the affidavits to bring the machines back to the mines."

On the night of the shooting, Bator stated that he had passed Pete's Place at about 11:15. He said he had heard loud voices coming from the tavern, so he glanced inside to see what the commotion was about. Bator said that Farrimond was talking in loud tones with Dullahant, Bob Pasquan, and John Kauzlarich. He said he heard Farrimond say "That's all of it. That's enough," and then Farrimond turned away.

A few moments later, Pasquan and Kauzlarich came outside. Bator reported that Kauzlarich said, "I should have slapped the _____. Shall I go back and do it?" Pasquan replied, "No, it's too late now. Come on," and the two left.[40]

As the trial moved through the afternoon, one juror became ill and had to be excused. The foresight of Judge McGuire in impaneling an alternate juror allowed the trial to continue.

Farrimond's wife testified that he had consumed two "shots of mule" and a glass of home brew before leaving the house on the night of the shooting. The defense also put local NWI officials Jack Lewis and Tom Murphy on the stand to testify to rumors they had heard about a "certain element" in the town that was out "to get Sam."[41]

Defense attorney Brown was trusting that his last witness would be his most convincing. He called the defendant, Sam Farrimond, to the stand. Facing a day of difficult testimony, his life on the line, Farrimond had spent most of the previous night chasing a bedbug in his cell. "I struck a dozen matches looking for him," he said. "If there's one in the place I can't sleep."[42]

But Farrimond appeared controlled and calm as he took the stand. His attorney led him through the events surrounding the shooting and to the scene itself. Farrimond described the shooting with no change of demeanor. "There was some men standing on the sidewalk, but I didn't pay any attention to them because Ruff came up to me as I opened the door. He was standing at the corner of the doorway. He had just got through knocking his pipe out, I think. He started an argument about the union.

"I was kinda surprised. He pulled me out on the sidewalk. He didn't pull me roughly. (Here he demonstrated how Ruff put an arm around his neck and pulled him.) He pulled me out about three feet. We talked there. He cursed me. He called me a _____ rat.

"I started backing away from him. About six or eight feet. He started coming for me. His right hand was clenched and his left hand was near his pocket. Then I shot."[43]

Prosecutor Kern took up the cross-examination of Farrimond by taking him carefully back over every step of his testimony. Then Kern "loaded and fired his big gun."[44] He asked Farrimond if he recalled an informal hearing three days after the shooting with Spencer Short, Sheriff Byars, and a court reporter. Farrimond said that he did recall the hearing. His testimony in court matched much of his earlier statement, but differed dramatically in his accounts of the shooting itself.

In the earlier testimony, Farrimond had said he had not been outside Pete's Place, but in court he testified he had been out "several times." He said in early testimony that he had been sober, but on the stand he said he was "intoxicated to a degree." In his earlier statement he described a lengthy quarrel with a number of men, but on the stand he spoke only of a disagreement with Ruff. And of the shooting itself, his earlier statement had been that he was lying on the ground when he fired and that he got up and walked into Pete's Place and put the revolver on the bar. On the stand, his testimony aligned more closely with that of other witnesses who said the gun was wrestled away from him after the shooting.

As Kern confronted Farrimond with the inconsistencies, Farrimond responded repeatedly, "I don't remember you asking those questions." He also countered that his memory was hazy because the officer had struck him with a "sap" [billy club] at the time of the arrest. Kern took the opportunity to read Farrimond's earlier statements into the record nearly in their entirety.[45]

As the defense rested its case and the testimony concluded, the trial turned to the closing statements. Before a still packed but now more serious and silent audience, E. K. Brown characterized the troubles in the coal fields as a battle against the "radicals, the wobblies, the reds, the hotheads," which he said had, "all gone into the new organization, the Western Miners." He held them responsible for the tragedy.[46]

Brown noted that a majority of those in the Western Miners movement were good citizens. But he believed the prosecution of Farrimond was an attempt to "save the face of the Western Miners," and Brown warned the jury that convicting Farrimond would send the message that the "red flag of communism should replace the star-spangled banner over the upper county."[47]

Kern responded with an equally passionate prediction of the dire consequences of an acquittal. "You have before you one of the most serious situations this county has ever faced. If you want to prevent further bloodshed, the best way is to deal out justice in this case."[48]

Judge McGuire then read to the jury a number of instructions relating to the law of self-defense and the element of intoxication. Among his instructions, McGuire stated:

> The court instructs you that to justify killing in self-defense there need be no actual or real danger to the life or person of the party killing, but there must be or reasonably appear to be at or immediately before the killing some overt act of the person killed, which either by itself, or coupled with words, facts or circumstances then or theretofore occurring reasonably indicate to the party killing

that the person slain is at the time endeavoring or immediately to endeavor to kill him or inflict upon him great bodily harm.[49]

After a Christmas Eve altercation left a Western Miner dead, vaunted Ellensburg attorney E.K. Brown defended the shooter on grounds of self-defense. *Courtesy of Ellensburg Public Library, Washington Rural Heritage Collection*

Court records indicate that Judge McGuire read some two dozen instructions to the jury before their deliberations.

After a full day of testimony, closing arguments, and jury instructions, the jury was handed the case at 8:30 p.m. Tuesday evening, February 20. They continued their deliberations through the night, breaking only for a breakfast the next morning. Wednesday morning at 9:30 the jury indicated that they had reached a decision, exactly one week after the trial had begun.

The courtroom filled again. Defendant and attorneys held their breath in anticipation as the jury foreman read the decision. "We, the jury, in the case of the State of Washington versus Sam Farrimond, find the defendant—not guilty."[50]

The courtroom erupted once again in gasps of disbelief and cheers of surprise. Bob Ruff's former wife, Mrs. L. B. Davis, fainted at hearing the verdict and collapsed in the back of the courtroom. She was carried into the corridor outside the courtroom where a doctor attended her.

E. K. Brown now stood at eighteen of nineteen in murder acquittals. For a portion of his fee, he added to his gun collection the 32-20 Smith & Wesson revolver that had been the murder weapon.[51]

Chapter 8

Prelude to the Storm

*C*larence had finished his chores for the morning. The bucket of coal was full and sitting by the heating stove, his bed was made, and the front porch was swept. Now a robust sixteen-year-old and an avid baseball fan, he finished oiling his catcher's mitt while listening to the sports news on the radio that Sunday morning, February 25. The newscaster had brought word of the death of legendary baseball manager John McGraw of the New York Giants.[1]

Clarence was itching to play some catch, and although the ground was still damp and soft, the air was not as cold as it had been the past week. So when he saw the neighbors across the street returning from Sunday mass, he decided to see if one of the Hawkins boys was willing to join him.

Half an hour later down at the ball field, the boys were just warming up, throwing fly balls to each other, when a car stopped beside the grandstand and three women began sizing up the space and barking out tasks for their children. "I think the speaker stand should be right here near home plate. We can put some of the signs there on the grandstand where everyone can see them," said one of the women. "Say, would you boys mind giving us a hand here? We're going to have a mass meeting here in an hour or so and we need some help getting these banners in place."

Clarence wasn't sure what all the commotion was about, but he agreed to help the women tie some signs to the screen and set up tables near the parking lot. As the women's attentions turned to other tasks, he skipped back home to tell his mom about the meeting and to ask if he could return and see what it was about.

Anna didn't answer right away. She had heard frustrated friends claiming that the Western Miners had a majority of the men in Roslyn and that the United Mine Workers and the NWI were running scared. They shot one of the Western Miners as an example, then finagled the legal system to get the killer freed.

The verdict in the Farrimond trial four days earlier had sent shock-waves through much of the town, and now Western Miners leaders were preparing a response, a show of strength and unity in the face of what they saw as a direct challenge from their UMWA and NWI foes.

Anna was more than a little curious about what would be said at this mass meeting, but she knew that Herman would not stand for her being seen at such an event. So she told Clarence that he could go back to the field and "play some more catch" and see what was going on.

Crowds were gathering when Clarence slipped onto a bench near the top of the grandstand. He had been there no more than a few minutes, trying to blend in with the group, when a slight young man with a red mark on his left cheek moved to the top row and began handing out leaflets. Clarence had seen the man around the school a few times. His name was Mark Haller and he was organizing a chapter of the Young Communist League in Roslyn. Haller's face still displayed the bruises and a split lip he had suffered from the beating ten days earlier. His voice, however, carried a softer tone.

"Say there young fella', how about you joining us after school tomorrow?" Haller called out as he approached Clarence. "We'll be planning a march to help miners like your pop get better pay and working conditions. There's a lot of guys joining in from all over town, and a lot of young fellas getting involved. Gals too. They're tired of their folks taking it on the chin for John L. It's time those who work get what they deserve around here so we all can live better, and we're ready to fight for it. Here, this explains a lot more." The man thrust a mimeographed page into Clarence's hand.

Clarence averted his eyes from the man's steady gaze and thanked him for the invitation, knowing he had no intention of showing up the next day. As the man moved on down the row, Clarence scanned the flyer:

FIGHT THE TERROR IN ROSLYN

For the second time, gun thugs, agents of the Coal Operators and the UMWA, have assaulted leading members of the militant Independent Western Union. Why is this terror being carried on against the Western Miners Union?

A new Coal Code is being drawn up. The provisions of this code depend upon the militancy of the miners. A solidly organized militant miners Union will force better conditions for the miners; A defeated Mine Union under the control of the Lewis

Controlled UMWA will mean worse conditions and wage cuts for the miners.[2]

FIGHT THE TERROR IN ROSLYN

Gov. E.g. A.
Hearing held on may 25

For the second time, gun thugs, agents of the Coal Operators and the UMWA, have assaulted leading members of the militant Independent Western Miners Union. Why is this terror being carried on against the Western Miners Union?

A new Coal Code is being drawn up. The provisions of this code depend upon the militency of the miners. A solidly organized militant miners Union will force better conditions for the miners; A defeated Mine Union under the control of the Lewis Controlled UMWA will mean worse conditions and wage cuts for the miners.

The miners of Roslyn and Cle Elum learned that the UMWA was a union controlled by the Coal Operators, working against the interests of the miners. They broke away from the UMWA and built their own Union, the WMU.

The UMWA, in cooperation with the Coal Operators, have tried to terrorize the miners and herd them back into the UMWA. First Bob Ruff was killed. This failed to terrorize the miners. Then Mark Haller was slugged, and finally the Coal Operators fired two leaders of the WMU. The terror in Roslyn is just beginning:

The miners had faith in the Prosecuting Attorney and the County Courts. They thought Farrimond would be found guilty of killing Ruff, but the Prosecutor and the courts acted in the interests of the Coal Operators and the UMWA- -Farrimond was freed: Now the miners can see that the Coal Operators, the Courts, and the UMWA are all lined up against the miners.

The miners must, more than ever now, preserve their Union and defeat the terror in Roslyn, Mark Haller was slugged, and told that if he will not leave town he will be killed, because Haller represents the interests of the miners against the Coal Operators. Haller is organizer of the Communist Party and the Young Communist League. Organizations of the workers that are in the foreground in the struggle for better conditions for the workers. The Communist Party and the Young Communist League are YOUR best guarantee for the preservation of the WMU as a militant fighting rank and file Union of the miners. A large Communist Party and Young Communist League will defeat the terror in Roslyn.

Every honest worker should join the Communist Party. Every honest young worker should join the Young Communist League. In this way will the miners be able to build and preserve their own Union. In this way will they smash the terror.

The Communist Party and Young Communist League call upon all the miners to carry thru the following in order to preserve the Union and smash terror.

1. Demand that the Prosecutor change the charge from third degree to first degree assault with intent to kill, against B. Henry.
2. Demand that the miners be allowed to choose their own special Prosecutor, so that the County Prosecutor will not be able to do what he did in the Farrimond case.
3. Organize defence groups in each local of the WMU to protect the Leaders of the miners.
4 Organize a mass march to the trial of Haller, demanding the full prosecution of Henry.
5. Force the Coal Operators to reinstate the two militant members of the WMU
6. Join the Communist Party and the Young Communist League:

Handouts trumpeted the travesty of justice in Roslyn in early 1934 and encouraged individuals to join the Communist Party to help protect their rights. *Author collection*

Before Clarence could read on, the first speaker of the day approached the lectern and the crowd of several hundred erupted in loud applause. It was Dick Prescott, one of the local leaders of the Western Miners movement, clambering onto the wooden speaker's stand.

Although his exact words were not recorded, the substance of Prescott's speech might have gone something like this:

"Thanks everybody. I bring you greetings from Andy Hunter who is just now returning from Washington, DC, where he has been meeting with federal labor leaders the past two weeks."[3] *A small chorus of cheers filled the space between sentences.*

"As many of you know, Andy has been working to make sure the Western Miners get recognized as the majority union here. On January 3, we met with Mr. Swem of the NWI, and he assured us that he would negotiate with us if we had a majority of the men when the current code expires the first of April.[4]

"Now the John L. Lewis machine is doing everything it can to keep us down, and the real, ugly face of the UMW is being exposed. They shot Bob Ruff in cold blood just a couple blocks from here, and then last Wednesday they got their man acquitted." A chorus of hoots and boos followed, but Prescott pressed on. "Alright now. We're gonna hear from the lawyers on that in just a bit. But let's not forget the other times we been pushed around and slapped in the face on this.

"The end of December, the Western Miners in Cle Elum voted for a new checkweighman, giving our man there almost two hundred votes. The United Mine Worker man couldn't muster even twenty votes. But what does old Tom Murphy do? He goes and puts their man in charge anyway.

"Then, just a couple weeks ago, two members of the Western Miners get laid off at No. 5 and told there's no work for 'em. There was plenty of work for those guys. All the other guys working in that area got other places to work, but not those two. So the men at No. 5, most of 'em, signed a petition saying they would share the work with the two that got laid off. But then Murphy says the men can't share the work.[5]

"And most of you know that Mark Haller got beat up pretty bad here in Roslyn a while back. So it's been a tough fight, and it's gonna be a tough fight before we're through. We just gotta stick together and we can make it. The worst thing we can do right now is to accept another John L. deal."

*The grandstand broke into a strident chorus of cheering as Clarence spot-
ted a buddy a few rows away and slipped down to the seat by him during
the break.*

The crowd heard a succession of speakers, five in all, expressing
for the first time in such a public setting in this community their support for the work of the Communist Party in upholding the rights of
workers. One of the speakers likened the outcome of the Farrimond
trial to two widely known cases considered to be travesties of justice—the 1916 sentencing of Socialist Tom Mooney on false charges
related to a San Francisco bombing, and the ongoing case of nine
blacks in Scottsboro, Alabama, falsely accused of a 1931 rape.[6]

Next, the lawyers in the Farrimond trial were invited to speak.
County Prosecutor Spencer Short said simply that he had done his
best and had no apologies to make regarding the prosecution of the
Ruff murder.

F. A. Kern, the special prosecutor in the trial, was growing increasingly concerned at the strong Communist tone taken at the gathering.
He attempted to distance himself from the earlier speakers, saying
he had understood that the Western Miners movement was based on
American values and stood by the American flag. If the movement
now was adopting Communistic values, its leaders could, he said,
"count me out." Kern went on to say that the rumblings from the
community that he had heard since the trial bore out the prediction
he had made before the jury a week before that "unless justice was
administered, there would be further violence."[7]

E. K. Brown was the next to approach the speaker's stand, fresh
from his victory in the Farrimond case a week earlier and now
defending "Bun" Henry on an assault charge. Brown turned his rhe-
torical venom against the mimeographed paper that Clarence was
holding. "The fact that an organization would put out a paper like
that proves the correctness of my contention made during the Farrimond trial that unless Farrimond was acquitted the jury would
in effect be replacing the Star-Spangled Banner with the red flag of
Communism over the Roslyn coal fields.

"I reiterate my statement that the rank and file of the Western
Miners union, in my estimation, are not Communists, but there

won't be any rank and file left when they learn the color of the agitators and ring leaders—they will return to the United Mine Workers organization."[8]

Clarence slipped away from the meeting before the final speaker took the stand. As he headed up the hill back home, he finished reading the mimeographed paper:

The miners must, more than ever now, preserve their Union and defeat the terror in Roslyn. Mark Haller was slugged, and told that if he will not leave town he will be killed, because Haller represents the interests of the miners against the Coal Operators. Haller is organizer of the Communist Party and the Young Communist League. Organizations of the workers that are in the foreground in the struggle for better conditions for the workers. The Communist Party and the Young Communist League are YOUR best guarantee for the preservation of the WMU as a militant fighting rank and file Union of the miners. A large Communist Party and Young Communist League will defeat the terror in Roslyn.[9]

Herman read the flyer over several times that evening before throwing it in the fire. "Anna," he commented, "You know, we're going to be in for a whole lotta trouble here. These people are not gonna back down, they just keep pushing, but there's no way they can stand up to John L. and the NWI and win. I just don't understand why so many people are ready to give up on the United Mine Workers."

"Well, I don't know, Herman," Anna responded quietly. She rarely challenged Herman directly on a major decision, but she couldn't ignore the anti-UMWA sentiment pervading her community. "A lotta people are talking, saying the Union hasn't been doing that much for us. What if these Western Miner fellas are right? What if they have the votes? Where are you gonna be then? You know the mine is gonna hire good workers no matter what side wins out."

"That's not what they're telling us at the mine. They're saying if we get involved with the Western Miners, we may lose our jobs, even our pensions. I even heard 'em talking about closing the mines instead of working with Hunter and that group."

"Oh-yoy-yoy," Anna sighed. "What a mess. Nobody's gonna win in this fight, are they? Everybody's just gonna get hurt. Oh, for stupid."

Since the formation of the Western Miners Union in November, its president, Andrew Hunter, had been pursuing every available avenue to gain recognition for his new union. He wanted to make sure that when the new coal contract was negotiated, his Western Miners Union would be representing Roslyn miners. The first NRA coal code covered just six months, giving negotiators more time to resolve differences in wages and hours. It was set to expire April 1, 1934.

Hunter had sent numerous letters to representatives of the National Recovery Administration in Washington, DC, and to the regional bituminous coal labor board in Denver stating that he represented a majority of miners in the Roslyn district. He had called for a secret ballot vote of the district to determine which union the men wanted to represent them, but to no avail.[10]

The United Mine Workers, meanwhile, wasted no time in acting to remove the mutinous Western Miners leaders from their ranks. One week after the formation of the new union, the heads of five UMWA locals in the Roslyn coal fields brought charges against thirteen members for violating the UMWA constitution. In addition to Hunter, the charges named the new union's vice president, Mike Petrovich, its secretary-treasurer John P. Pasquan, Lawrence Barrick, William Senuty, George Gasparich, Joe Lennox (Lenac), Frank Klopcie, Richard Prescott, Robert Ruff, Jack Boose, George Mitchell, and John Andriosevich.[11]

After Ruff's death, the charge was amended with a hand-written note beside his name reading: "died 12/24/33 before Comm. [Commission] heard charges."

The remaining twelve received a letter from John L. Lewis dated December 28, 1933, notifying them of the charges filed against them. The men were given the opportunity to respond at a hearing before a three-man UMWA board headed by district president Sam Nicholls. The hearing was set for the evening of January 6, 1934, at the Travellers Hotel in Cle Elum.

Just a few minutes before the hearing was set to begin, Hunter entered the hotel lobby and left a letter with the clerk. It was signed by eight of the men charged. The committee waited some time, but the other four men made no appearance.[12]

The letter was on Western Miners letterhead. Clearly the leaders of the new movement were not concerned about being ousted from the UMWA. "We are members of the Western Miner's Union of America and we left the United Mine Workers of America knowing well that we have the right to belong to an organization of our own choosing."

The letter was factual in tone, reciting the injustices that drove the men to found a new union—the 1932 vote count, the recall fiasco— but Hunter did allow one paragraph to lecture his nemesis and to vent frustrations:

> Now, Mr. John L. Lewis, let me tell you something about your attitude and that of the officers representing you. You and your officers have not treated the members of District 10 in the proper manner for many years and you have forced the Mine Workers of District 10 to break with your organization by forcing them to submit to reductions of wages and the breaking down of working conditions.[13]

On February 1, 1934, the UMWA International Executive Board expelled the men and notified them that they would need the permission of the International Executive Board to regain admission to the union.[14] The letter announcing the expulsion arrived at Hunter's home during the opening rounds of the Farrimond murder trial in mid-February.

Hunter was not around to read the mail, however. He was in Washington, DC, calling on an NRA Code Administrator, Wayne P. Ellis, and a representative of the NRA legal counsel. Hunter argued that he represented 80 percent of the miners in the Roslyn-Cle Elum district, and asked again for the opportunity to vote on union recognition. Hunter then met with U.S. Senator Homer Bone of Washington State to plead his case. He also met with the regional director of the bituminous coal labor board, T. S. Hogan, to push for an election confined to the Roslyn field. Hogan said he was reluctant to consider a limited election since the current coal contract covered the entire state district.[15]

Hunter's efforts to organize and gain recognition for his Western Miners movement were not going unnoticed. Among those carefully monitoring the situation in Roslyn was Eugene McAuliffe, president of the Union Pacific Coal Company. McAuliffe was keenly concerned that a successful Western Miners union movement in Washington State would bring more intense radical union organizing activity to the Rocky Mountain coalfields of the Union Pacific.

McAuliffe urged John L. Lewis to intensify recruiting efforts in the Roslyn field, stating in early January that no union officials had been there since December 14.[16] Just a week later, he wrote again to Lewis stating: "I am inclined to think that the Washington situation is the most critical one that you have at the present time in the West."[17]

By the end of January, McAuliffe reported that sources who had visited Roslyn described the situation as "much worse than known by the outside and will develop into serious trouble unless early adjusted." McAuliffe suggested that UMWA state district president Sam Nicholls was "following line of least resistance," while Western Miners president Andy Hunter was "cocksure of himself, is politically shrewd," and "gathers weight by aggression."[18]

Leaders of the Northwestern Improvement Company were well aware of the trouble brewing in Roslyn. Memos between NWI president J. M. Hughes and the Seattle manager of operations, D. R. Swem, in early January show the company's concern over the lax recruiting efforts of UMWA officials. "They [UMWA state leaders] must certainly know that unless they can have convincing proof that they represent the majority of our employees we will not be in a position to deal with the United Mine Workers when the present working agreement runs out. If they do not realize that it should be brought to their attention quietly."[19]

The NWI president had a strong interest in maintaining ties with the UMWA since the union represented a vast majority of their mining employees in the West, and John L. Lewis had proven a tough but reasonable rival in past negotiations. The Western Miners presented an unknown entity that threatened the balance of profitability and stability for the mining company. In January, Hughes offered a plan to extend the UMWA contract in the district without putting the matter to a vote of the miners:

> We think the Washington [coal producers] Association is entirely justified in negotiating an extension of the present agreement at

the time specified in the contract on the ground that it is dealing with a party that, according to the last information, was truly representative of the employees and if John L. Lewis and the district officers would be willing to extend the agreement as now constituted for another year without a referendum we see no reason why the Association should not have such an understanding. Of course, the representatives of the Western Miners will be present to protest. If they cannot show by proper evidence that they represent the majority they need not be considered and they can appeal to the Labor Board of Division V. Proper evidence can only be produced in the shape of signed authorization by each man for the check-off of dues. No list of names which the Western Miners might produce will be acceptable evidence.[20]

So the plan for a contract extension without a rank-and-file vote was floated for consideration to UMWA leaders and NRA representatives. Union Pacific's Eugene McAuliffe suggested that the NWI immediately fire ten to fifty Western Miners agitators, but the company was reluctant to aggravate the situation.[21]

To prepare for the labor unrest that the NWI might be facing, Hughes ordered the installation of a four-foot security fence topped with fifteen inches of barbed wire around the Roslyn and Ronald mine sites and properties.[22] He also ordered a buildup of coal reserves in bunkers and rail cars over the next several months.[23]

Apparently some of Hunter's visits and letters to NRA leaders in Washington, DC, did bear fruit. In late February, the regional labor board of Seattle notified UMWA leaders in the state of its intention to conduct a vote among miners of the state over union affiliation. When UMWA state district president Sam Nicholls got wind of the order, he immediately notified John L. Lewis, who squashed the plan, stating that the NLB had no power to disturb existing labor contracts.[24]

In early March, the Roslyn-Cle Elum Beneficial Association removed Hunter as its secretary. Nicholls communicated the news to John L. Lewis: "it sure has given the gent a blow that he feels very much. He has threatened to enter suit stating that he has just commenced to fight, but as we get it much of the fight has been taken out of him when his salary was cut off, usually $190.00 per month not picked up every day and the dues are slow coming into the dummy union."[25]

Hunter's supporters rallied around him and started a petition to recall the entire association board. They collected signatures from what they said were more than half of the members of the hospital association and then instituted an unauthorized election with Western Miners representatives on one ticket and the old UMWA board on another. Hunter's group claimed that the results showed an overwhelming majority for their ticket. "The vote for each of their six candidates, they said, varied from 562 to 573; that for the old board from three votes to eight."[26] But the UMWA ignored the vote and retained the existing board.

At the insistence of Union Pacific Coal president Eugene McAuliffe, a March 5 meeting was called in St. Paul with Northern Pacific Railway and NWI top administrators. McAuliffe said he had received word that Lewis was agreeable to an extension of the current coal contract, provided that any changes in wages or working conditions offered in pending NRA coal code negotiations would become effective immediately. McAuliffe suggested that Washington's coal producers enter such an agreement with union leaders without referring the matter to a vote of the members. NWI president J. M. Hughes restated his concern that such plan might add fuel to the fire of the radical movement. He preferred to seek the endorsement of a representative group of miners for the contract extension. He recommended taking the matter to a vote of the district officers who represented each of the union locals.[27]

Later that day, Hughes and Swem were called back to NPR president Charles Donnelly's office where they laid final plans. Swem would meet with John L. Lewis in Washington, DC, to confirm the agreement for a contract extension. Lewis would be asked to send additional UMWA board members to the district to persuade reluctant miners to agree to the contract extension.[28]

Just over a week later, again at McAuliffe's prompting, T. S. Hogan, head of the NRA's labor board for the western United States (Division V), called for a face-to-face meeting in Salt Lake City with representatives of the NWI. D. R. Swem took an overnight train out of Butte to attend.[29] Meeting together with several representatives of the coal operators of Washington State, NWI president J. M. Hughes outlined the plan calling for an extension of the current contract to be ratified only by the UMWA district officers. Reports from Roslyn measured UMWA membership and dues check-off at around 450 men in mid-March. Hogan noted that of some 2,300 total miners in the state, about 1,800 belonged to the UMWA. Hogan stated his opinion that no vote would be necessary and none would be ordered.

Hogan noted that Andrew Hunter had made contacts with attorneys of the Progressive Miners Union in Illinois, and Hogan was "sure that the Washington State situation was being fostered with a view to creating a radical center which would affect not only the state but Montana, Wyoming, Colorado and Utah as well. Hunter had told him as much and he expected every effort would be put forth to get a hold at Roslyn."[30]

Hogan expressed full agreement with the plan calling for the contract extension as voted by district officials and urged that the meeting be held soon in the state in hopes of influencing undecided miners to stay with the UMWA.

Hogan wrote to Andy Hunter of the Western Miners Union and Walter Smethurst of the UMWA asking each to draft a statement of their understanding of the situation in the Roslyn field, and both complied.[31]

The meeting with the state district officers was set for mid-March. Western Miners leaders were not included; only the leaders selected by the men who had remained loyal to the UMWA participated. But the district officers were anticipating new terms coming from the next round of NRA coal negotiations, perhaps even a seven-hour day. So they were reluctant to agree to a one-year contract extension. In what was termed a "spirited" meeting, the officers voted to extend current contract terms only until the federal coal code terms were announced, giving themselves a ten-day window to then negotiate a new agreement based on the modified code.[32] The local newspaper carried the full agreement and statement of UMWA loyalty in both the March 23 and 30 editions.[33]

As soon as Hunter got word of the contract extension agreement, he called Swem to demand that his union be recognized, but Swem sidestepped, saying that an agreement had been signed and then extended with the UMWA, and the NWI could not recognize their union. Hunter responded that he would refer a decision to the men, and he suggested that the Western Miners were considering a strike on the first work day in April.[34]

Did Hunter and his Western Miners supporters have enough support to pull off a full-scale strike at four mine sites scattered in the hills around the three communities of Roslyn, Ronald, and Cle Elum? Would the United Mine Workers loyalists attempt to cross the picket lines in large numbers? No one seemed to know for sure as the last days of March passed.

NWI president Hughes considered the possibility of firing any miners who refused to show up to work. Brainstorming with his representative in Seattle, Hughes suggested that perhaps the company could close the No. 3 mine for a month and work a smaller consolidated crew at No. 5 and No. 7, cutting some two hundred positions.[35]

Hughes also reassured his railway bosses that he had taken steps to prepare for a strike, building up a reserve of 70,000 tons of coal in Cle Elum storage and filling another sixty rail cars to capacity to meet commercial contracts during the anticipated work interruption.[36]

April 1, 1934, was a Sunday and marked the first day of the new contract. Monday had been declared a mining holiday in the previous contract. So the real showdown over the new contract would come on Tuesday morning, April 3.

Word began to spread through the streets and alleys that a new coal code agreement had been reached—that it called for a shorter, seven-hour work day for miners, and promised a slight increase in hourly pay. The miners would get $5 per day for seven hours rather than $5.40 for eight.[37] But the Western Miners supporters had come too far to settle—they were still hoping for $6 for six hours, and the only way to that goal was a strike to gain union recognition.

At a large meeting on April 1, Hunter asked his Western Miners for a vote. The result was an overwhelming order to strike.[38]

Chapter 9

The Gauntlet

*A*nna had a pot of oatmeal and a tea kettle bubbling on the kitchen stove as Herman slid into his usual chair at the table. Even on a workday, 5:05 a.m. was an early breakfast hour, but Herman was determined to get a jump on the picketers. He usually caught a car ride with one of his co-workers, but he figured the main road might be blocked today, so he and two other miners had plotted the night before to head through the woods by foot and arrive before 6:00 a.m. in hopes of avoiding some of the commotion they anticipated at No. 3 mine in Ronald.

The Ellensburg newspaper Herman read the evening before had trumpeted the story with a banner headline: "Miners Nervous As Strike Nears; Western Union Issues Call for Action Tomorrow; United Workers Ordered Back to Work; Aid is Sought."[1]

Anna was more than a little jumpy that morning, fretting over what might happen to her husband between their back door and the mines. "Did you hear those women this morning, must have been 3:00 a.m." She said in a hushed voice, not wanting to awaken the children.

"I think I did," Herman responded. "Was there one with a cowbell?[2] I thought she would never stop."

"Then just when I was about asleep again, I heard, it sounded like a truckload of women. What were they saying? 'Join our cause?' Something like that."[3] Anna paused a moment, then wondered aloud, "How many of them will be out at the mines today, I wonder?"

"There'll be plenty, but I think we should be able to get through okay," Herman said, more confidently than he felt. "And don't worry. If it looks too bad, me and the guys won't do anything dumb."

"Well, don't take any chances, and don't forget your lunch pail. And, Herman," she caught his arm at the back door, "please be careful."

"I will, Anna. I'll see you when I see you, I guess." The kiss goodbye was just a bit more meaningful that morning.

Herman met his two working companions in the alleyway behind his house. The course they had plotted seemed clear. Creeping along in the *darkness, they traveled side roads and alleys near the edge of town while carefully surveying movements in the streets below. Just about every house had a light on by now, and the smell of coal smoke was thick in the cold morning air.*

As they came to the last house at the edge of town, the trio of miners headed up a miners' road that went straight over the hill that separated Roslyn and Ronald, rather than following the main highway that circled the hillside. Herman knew the route was steeper but shorter. It was the route he had used often, and he was hoping he was early enough to avoid trouble.

The miners listened intently as they came to the crest of the ridge. They could hear voices and chanting on the main highway a quarter mile away. Through the trees they could make out fires glowing in two or three barrels and picketers gathered around warming their hands. Herman's eyes studied the route ahead, and he could see picketers blocking the path to the washhouse.

A sound behind him made him whirl in his tracks. A miner about a hundred yards behind him was heading up the same path, but a large woman from the Western Miners picket lines detected the movement and confronted the man. Herman could hear the woman lecturing the miner, urging him to go back home rather than work as a scab. As other hecklers gathered, the man turned around instead of challenging the crowd.[4]

Herman and his pals scattered into the woods and circled the hill above the washhouse. From there he could see men and women massed on the main road, but he had a clear path to the washhouse, and the three men started to jog the last two hundred yards. As they came into the lights of the mine yard, their movement caught the attention of picketers guarding the main road.

"Hey, you sneaky scoundrels!" one of the picketers shouted. "Didn't you read the announcement? Mines are all closed today. On strike."

The men kept their heads low as they trotted the last few yards to the washhouse.

"Swanson, you lousy bastard. You can go to hell in that mine if you want to, but you'll have to come out sometime!"

Inside the men met a handful of others who had come early enough to make it through the picket line. One said a woman had made a grab for his dinner pail, but he had managed to fight her off. Another was tending to a cut over his left eye. A rock had smashed the windshield of his car, sending shards of glass flying in every direction.

The men waited in the washhouse, listening as the tumult outside intensified. As miners from Ronald came from their homes to the main entry road leading to the mine, they met the hostile mob of picketers. Men, women, teenagers, and children lined the entry, chanting "swine," "rats," "finks," "traitors," and vile insults of the four-letter variety.

But the epithet that burned as much as any was "scab." In the eyes of a loyal union miner, a scab was the lowest of the low, a traitor who cared so little about his fellow workers that he would work while they starved. And now to be termed a "scab" because of their act of loyalty to the UMWA was more than some men could take. A few threw punches at picketers. Others thought better of their odds in fighting an angry mob.

In some places, the women picketers locked arms across the mine road. The men stayed back of the front lines a bit, providing support from an arsenal of pine cones, cow pies, branches, and rocks. In addition to the verbal and physical assaults, some women readied prized stashes of rotten eggs, specially aged and putrefied for this moment.

As individuals or small clusters of miners attempted to break through the picketers, the women would start pushing at them, grabbing their lapels and imploring them to stop. If the miners persisted, the pleas took on a more abusive tone. Some women spit as they pulled at the miners' clothing, hurling verbal insults.[5] Dinner pails were knocked out of hands and kicked about, the contents trampled in the dirt. Jackets were torn off and tossed about the crowd as the women celebrated their triumph in humiliating opposing miners.[6]

A large woman at Archie Patrick's mine near Ronald caught more than a little attention as she stood on a tree stump and flipped up her dress, exposing her bare bottom to approaching miners.[7]

As Ernest Cusworth picked up his dinner pail at 5:45 that morning, prepared to head to No. 5 mine, his two children began to protest. "Don't go, daddy," said his ten-year-old, Claire. "You haven't any right to go."

"I must go as a matter of principle," Cusworth replied.

"What's that?" Claire asked.

"That means if I believe a thing's right, I must go and do it or acknowledge myself yellow. You wouldn't want me to be yellow, would you?"

"No-o-o," said Claire.

"But daddy, I'd rather have you yellow than dead," his eight-year-old, Jean, added.[8]

Cusworth faced the gauntlet of epithets and abuses the entire two miles he walked to the mine. Near the mine yard entrance he met a solid wall of female picketers. He considered fighting his way through the line. "I've always believed that when a woman takes on a man's job, she should take on his responsibilities. But I couldn't bring myself to apply it," Cusworth told an Ellensburg reporter. He turned back rather than striking out at the sea of women who blocked his path.[9]

A riot nearly erupted at No. 9 mine when a miner's dinner pail was taken. Miners who had assembled to start their shift decided to march en masse on the group of picketers to retrieve the pail, but before the groups met, cooler heads prevailed and the confrontation was averted.[10]

Miners who dared to confront the groups of women experienced the most severe and humiliating consequences. In several instances, the women succeeded in knocking miners to the ground. As soon as they could get a man down, several of the women would hold down arms and legs while one of the bolder women would straddle the man's face and attempt to urinate on him.[11] In one instance, women were said to have rubbed a miner's face with a used menstrual pad.[12] Law enforcement officers received some of the worst abuse. One woman was reported to have rubbed her bare behind on the face of a county sheriff.[13]

One miner, heading to the No. 5 mine, met a line of protesters and attempted to run through the line. He was grabbed and jostled, cursed at and held up by the women. Unable to free himself and unused to such close physical female contact, he tried to kiss one of the women. The Ellensburg newspaper reported: "Another woman landed a well-aimed blow between the miner's eyes, knocking him to the ground. With the aid of other women picketers, the miner's pants were removed and tied around his neck and he was chased down the road."[14]

Law enforcement officers were positioned at each of the mine entrances and did what they could to maintain order. In some instances, strike leaders helped the police maintain or restore order. But at times law enforcement officers were at a loss to keep the peace. Roslyn police chief Robert Ronald was at the No. 3 entrance road attempting to direct traffic when a car carrying two miners approached. He tried to clear the roadway, but he found himself physically moved from the center of the road by a mass of women while another group pelted the car with rotten eggs. The driver attempted to flee down a side street and eventually arrived at No. 3 mine, but his car was thoroughly covered in eggs.[15]

In other areas, local police, many of whom were close friends and neighbors with the picketers, chose not to become involved in the developing situation. A deputy sheriff at the time, Bob Bell later explained his thinking. "I told the captain of the state patrol, hell, it's up to you fellas. I'm not going to get mixed up in here…I've got to live here with these people after you boys are gone. I want to try to stay out of everything I can."[16]

County Sheriff Art Byars was quick to admit that he lacked the manpower needed to handle the disturbances. He summoned help, and a dozen state patrolmen responded from all parts of the state,[17] but a large number were in the western part of the state in connection with the governor's "safety week" observances.[18]

Camilla Saivetto was on the picket lines at 5:00 a.m. the first morning of the strike. But when she saw men throwing rocks at a car, she recognized the passenger as a man she had hired to install a bathroom at her house. "I would no more throw a rock at him than I would to a dog," Saivetto said. She decided pretty quickly that she didn't have the stomach for picketing. "If they go at it to have a strike and to be as ornery as that, I don't think I'm going to be in the strike no more. I don't want it," she recalled.[19]

Gus Jaderlund had decided to get through the lines in his '28 Chevrolet sedan. He met a large crowd near the mine entrance and "a bunch of guys took hold of that dang car and they just about turned it over. But it happened to be one of the fellas that was in the picket line, they noticed, and they was good friends with us and all, and they said, 'Hell, don't do that.' But we was up on two wheels you know, ready to tip us over."[20]

Clyde Fisher encountered a huge crowd in Ronald, and the group began rocking his car. Several windows were smashed, and Fisher was cut on the chin by a piece of glass. He managed to back his car away from the group and found another route to the mine. But he was stopped again by a large gang near a railroad crossing. He was carrying a German Luger handgun, and he fired a warning shot. The group ran into the woods for cover.[21]

A similar confrontation occurred at No. 5 mine when "Spud" Murphy, the son of mine superintendent Tom Murphy, was reported to have fired a warning shot at a crowd of protestors.[22] UMWA member George Turner reported firing a single shot into the ground in warning as he approached No. 9 mine.[23] Tom Murphy himself may have provided arms to some workers for protection as they entered the mines.[24] A number of guns were reportedly taken from miners during the first several days of the confrontation.[25]

A report that one woman had been hit by a stray bullet was later denied. Another report that a black washroom attendant had been seriously wounded at No. 3 mine and was near death was also later denied. One woman was injured when she attempted to stop a car from crossing the picket lines; mine sub-foreman Jack Richards was struck by a rock on the head; and physicians reported treating a number of injuries from flying rocks and other objects during the day.[26]

In the face of the violence that erupted in the early hours of April 3, the strike leaders maintained that they were calling for a peaceful picketing effort. Andrew Hunter held a meeting of the picket committees shortly before noon and told the group of sixty men attending, "We want no violation of the law, no violence."[27]

Tom Murphy began receiving counts on the number of miners who had made it to work at each mine. Murphy had expected crews of around two hundred at each of the three large mines, Nos. 3, 5, and 7, that day. But his crews tallied 26, 45, and 75 respectively. The just-opened No. 9 Mine reported 40 of its crew of 61. The independent Cascade Coal Company at Ronald was closed tight with not a single miner able to report.[28] In all, Western Miners picketing had succeeded in reducing an expected work crew of around 650 to less than 200.

Company officials, caught off-guard at the ferocity of the picketers, attempted to assess the damage and determine what course
of action to follow. A Northern Pacific special agent in Roslyn suggested that the state patrol might need a force of forty to fifty men to
maintain the peace.[29]

Calls were placed to the governor to step in with additional force
from the state patrol or the National Guard. Governor Martin faced
the difficult balance of protecting public safety without playing
favorites in the labor dispute. To respond with massive force might
be seen as favoring the United Mine Workers position, while a lack
of response might favor the protesting Western Miners. The governor met with coal operators and United Mine Workers representatives and pledged state protection. "[R]egardless of their union affiliations, miners who return to work can count on protection from
state law enforcement agencies," the governor announced later in
the week.[30] Martin immediately dispatched Washington State Police
Chief William Cole with eleven troopers to the area.[31]

Back on the streets of Roslyn, Ronald, and Cle Elum, picketers
had taken note of the miners who had successfully crossed their
picket lines. While a contingent of picketers remained at each mine
site, other bands went into the towns and paid unexpected visits at
the homes of strike breakers.

*As Anna was in the midst of measuring cornmeal for supper, she heard
voices outside and looked out to see a group of thirty women assembling
along her sidewalk and up the side of the house along Arizona Street. She
had no idea what they were doing there, and she wasn't about to step outside and ask. She retreated to the kitchen to give her lentil soup a stir. Then
she heard the chanting: "Swanson is a scab. A dirty rotten scab," "Your
husband is a _____ strike breaker," and "We got your husband good today,
Mrs. Swanson!"*

*Anna wasn't sure what to make of that last statement. She was quite
sure she would have heard something if Herman had been hurt, but still she
had no idea what might have happened at the mine during the day, and her
worst imaginings sent a chill up her spine.*

*After about ten minutes, the group moved on to its next home. Anna
was glad that her children were in school and didn't have to hear the insults.
But she was deeply unsettled that a group of that size would assemble at her*

house and threaten her and her family. Where were the police? Could you just threaten somebody like that without taking any responsibility for your actions?

William Bednar was a tracklayer who had managed to get through the lines at No. 5. As the band of women arrived at his home, his daughter Aggie, age eight, was upstairs. When she heard the vicious screams and shouts coming from her yard, she crawled under the bed to hide.[32]

Some UMWA miners who had been unable to get to work that morning banded together and drove around the town looking for Western Miners picketers to harass.[33] The newspaper reported that both sides "resorted to minor acts of violence."[34] In one instance a group of UMWA loyalists began mimicking the chants and hoots of a group of Western Miners supporters. The verbal jousting became so obnoxious that a neighbor came out on his front porch carrying a shotgun and ran the whole crowd off.[35]

In Ronald, a group of picketers from No. 3 Mine met a group from the nearby Patrick's mine in the late afternoon near the company store. Together they determined to teach John Madzuma a lesson. Madzuma had worked that day as a mine guard. His job was not a union position, so he was not technically involved in the dispute, but the group of Western Miners supporters was not paying attention to such subtleties. Madzuma had crossed their picket line, and he must be taught a lesson.

The group spotted Madzuma and his wife shopping in the company store and waited for them to emerge. Tillie Madzuma later testified that she heard shouts and threats to her children, ages two and six, if she failed to come out. She emerged to see a crowd of between 150 and 200 men and women, shouting and calling her and her husband names. Mrs. Madzuma came down the steps of the store and said two women reached out to grab her. She threw her grocery bag at them, spilling the milk, cabbage, bread, and meat on the ground.

At that moment, her husband emerged from the store and spotted his wife confronting the crowd. He grabbed a pick handle from a store display and headed into the crowd in an effort to protect her. Several of the men grabbed the handle away from him. Without any defense, Madzuma made a dash for his front gate, but he was jumped from behind. The couple fought their way into the safety of their house, Madzuma claiming to have been struck with a pipe in the back of the legs in the melee.

Stories differed on the exact turn of events, but several witnesses said that after the Madzumas made it inside their home, they threatened to get a gun to disperse the crowd. At any rate, the crowd scattered when the police arrived.[36]

Herman took a long shower at the washhouse after work. In no hurry to face the crowd outside, he lingered nearly an hour before putting his coat on to leave. Along with three or four men, he made a break for it during a lull in the chanting. As the men turned the corner of the washhouse, they could see a larger crowd waiting along the route they hoped to take. But the group had fewer women this time, and Herman could see a few openings in the line. He and the others, still wearing their mining hats, put their heads down and made a break into a cluster of trees. The picketers hurled every insult in the book at them, along with numerous missiles. Herman deflected a stick with his arm and kept moving. It wasn't until he had cleared the group that he noticed the moisture of a raw egg on his pants.

He headed into Roslyn along the same route he had taken in the morning, keeping to back roads and alleys. About a block from home, he turned up an alley when suddenly a group of teenagers and children popped up from behind a fence and started pelting him with eggs and pine cones. He took three or four more direct hits before hopping the back fence onto his own property.

Sometime late in the day, coal operations manager D. R. Swem and mine superintendent Tom Murphy assessed the violence they had seen on the picket lines. Very few men had made it through the lines, and there was a lack of police support. They determined that the mines should be closed until the safety of their workers could be assured.[37]

As the evening wore on in Roslyn, the violence did not stop. Swem sent a quick telegram to his company president summing up the situation: "Night of disorder in Roslyn with Western Miners harassing men who worked yesterday. Several men called from their homes and beaten up and others threatened if they attempt further work. Many automobiles had broken glass and several badly cut."[38]

Heads New Union

Andrew Hunter fought to convince company authorities that
the WMU should be recognized as the majority union in the
mining district. A photo caption in the April 14, 1934, *Ellensburg Evening Record* reads: "Andrew Hunter is president
of the Western Miners Union of America, a group which is
battling for recognition in the Roslyn-Cle Elum coal fields."
Permission of Ellensburg Daily Record, *courtesy of Ellensburg
Public Library*

Chapter 10

Tense Waiting

*H*annah pushed her locker door closed and double-checked the latch. Her eyes were still moist, but she quickly dabbed at the tears with her finger. She didn't want anyone to notice her distress.

Just minutes before she had been confronted in the restroom of Cle Elum High School. A group of four girls entered just behind her and started bantering. "Hey Hannah Banana, so your dad's one of those stinking scabs, huh?" She tried to ignore them by heading into an empty stall and locking the door. Then she heard them banging on the walls from the next stall. "You'd just better watch yourself, blondie. You never know who might be waiting for you. You know what happens to scab kids, don't you?"

At that moment, the restroom door popped open and Miss Berlin stuck her head in. "Is everything all right in here, girls?" She queried. "Oh yes, Miss Berlin, everything is fine," one of the girls responded a bit too sweetly. Hannah breathed easier knowing the long-time Roslyn English teacher was listening just outside.

Hannah waited a few extra minutes after the girls left before grabbing her history book and heading to class late. More and more, her life was being disrupted by the strike. The morning before, as she had waited for the Roslyn school bus, an argument erupted, and the bickering continued the entire two-mile ride into Cle Elum. School officials considered providing separate buses for children who refused to ride with children of "scabs."[1] Clarence, who most mornings was off on his own with his pal, Harry Georgeson, was under strict orders from Herman to keep an eye on his sister at the bus stop.

Hannah had felt relatively safe at school—until the restroom incident. Now she was shaken to the core, jumping at every dropped pencil and checking around every corner. At lunch she made sure she was sitting with a group of United Mine Workers kids.

In Roslyn, the threats were real enough to those in the Bednar household that for several weeks an uncle came by to escort Aggie to the elementary school each morning.[2]

Children and teens took up the causes of their parents. Jimmy Hunter, the son of Western Miners leader Andrew Hunter, would go block to block, standing on a corner fence post and delivering impassioned speeches to a growing group of young followers.[3]

While most households found themselves on one side or the other in the conflict, the Zager family faced an unusual dilemma. Pete Zager remained loyal to the UMWA while his wife joined the Western Miners picket lines. The *Ellensburg Evening Record* reported that the couple's son, Pete, opted to stay with family friends in Cle Elum.[4]

Divided loyalties caused rifts not only among neighbors but within families as well. When the son of Dick Prescott, a Western Miners leader, said he was going to work that day despite the strike, he was ordered out of his family's home.[5]

Western Miners youths from Roslyn's south side reportedly paid visits to nearly every UMWA miner who had crossed the Western Miners picket lines and "made them kneel down on the floor, clasp their hands and swear that they won't scab any more."[6] The *Voice of Action* reported some were scared into joining the picket lines the next day.

Emotions ran especially deep in Ronald. A school principal who had been assigned to the Ronald School in the fall of 1933 chose to take his family on frequent weekend trips to visit their grandparents in Ellensburg rather than face the open hostilities of his new community.[7]

The threats were clear and vocal. A young Ronald girl recalled a group of picketers shouting to her mother as she watched from a porch, "You know, your husband wouldn't be the first boss that got killed."[8]

Stories were told of family members pulled from their homes, of women and children physically slapped and assaulted for their loyalty to the United Mine Workers. UMWA member George Turner Sr. reported for work at No. 9, and afterward was threatened. His son recalled, "They told my dad they were going to come and kick the crap out of him, and he had his shotgun sitting right by the door. If someone had come, he would have killed them, you know. It was a bad deal."[9]

Families of Western Miners felt little safer as the strife persisted. Fathers insisted on keeping tabs on family members whenever anyone ventured outside, even to fetch wood.[10]

Word spread quickly through the community that the mining company, the NWI, had decided to close the mines because of the strike. But the picketers kept up their vigil, arriving at the mines again the second morning at 5:00 a.m. in numbers estimated at four to seven hundred.[11] Miners had no reason to cross the lines because the mines were closed, but several company officials were halted as they tried to report for work.[12]

Police responded to complaints sworn out by individuals on one side of the issue against individuals on the other. When arrests were made, however, large groups of protesters would gather at city hall, their shouts and protests making it difficult to administer justice. Local magistrates in Roslyn postponed trials and moved others to Ellensburg.[13]

Some twenty-five cars were damaged on the first day of the strike.[14] One of those cars, at the No. 3 mine in Ronald, was rolled by picketers.[15] William Hall of Cle Elum and three passengers approached No. 5 mine "to visit," he later said. When picketers stopped his car, two of his windows were smashed by rocks.[16] A state patrolman and a deputy sheriff came to the scene and warned picketers to keep the roads clear. Andy Hunter addressed the picketers, saying he was doing everything in his power to prevent the use of force by police. He assured the officers of his cooperation and appealed to the picketers to refrain from violence. He said that the women, who had been leading the pickets, were to stay behind the front lines.

"We are keeping only skeleton pickets at the mines now," Hunter said. "But if and when an attempt is made to reopen the mines, we will put our entire membership back on the job. We will line the roads for a mile on both sides if necessary. We do not want violence and will do our best to see that there is none."[17]

Hall swore out a complaint against Helen Pasquan, claiming she had thrown the rock that broke his windshield. Pasquan was arrested and taken to Ellensburg the next morning and, at first, refused to give her name to the court. So the initial court documents were prepared under the name, "State of Washington v. Jane Doe Pasquan, whose true Christian name is unknown."[18]

Pasquan's testimony and her feisty demeanor made quite an impression in court, as an Ellensburg reporter described the scene. "Far different was the version given by the spirited young woman who is named in his [Hall's] complaint. Her vigorous explanation and flashing eyes leave no doubt as to her sentiments, she branded the car's occupants 'trouble-seekers.'"

Pasquan's version of the incident suggested that picketers had asked the men in the car to go back rather than to try to enter the work site. The driver then started backing up and pulling forward, very nearly hitting an older woman and Pasquan's husband. Helen Pasquan stated: "I was standing beside the car, trying to get them to go back, when the eggs started. Several hit me. I stepped back into the crowd and the window went crash."[19] A $500 bond for Pasquan's release was posted by Richard and Flora Prescott and Andrew and Clara Hunter.[20]

With the mines closed, the state patrol withdrew its extra men with a promise to the mining company to provide sufficient support when the company reopened.[21]

"We've won!" declared Andrew Hunter as he exhorted his followers.[22] The Western Miners leader sought to capitalize on the strong support of women in the community by organizing a women's auxiliary. When Hunter and Dick Prescott appeared at an April 5 meeting to help the group take its first organizational steps, they were told "the women can take care of themselves."[23] Hunter's daughter, Clara, was named president of the women's order. Helen Pasquan, just released on bail, was vice president, and Camilla Saivetto was secretary-treasurer.[24]

Word from the UMWA was that the union was readying for a long siege; they were prepared, "like General Grant, to dig in for all summer, if necessary."[25] But calls for help were being made from within the community to find some resolution to the standoff. On the evening of April 5, the mayors of Roslyn and Cle Elum sent a telegram to President Roosevelt requesting federal mediation:

> The coal miners of the Roslyn-Cle Elum field employing 1,000 men, are idle following a strike called by the Western Miners

Union on April 3. We believe that there are no present prospects for a resumption of work and that the friendly mediation of our national government is needed and that it will bring about a speedy settlement. We, on behalf of our citizens, earnestly and respectfully request your friendly mediation.[26]

The NWI was also working to assure adequate police protection at the state level and a favorable resolution of the contract dispute at the national level. Governor Martin was traveling at the time of the strike, but on his return he met with mining officials and gave them assurances of complete state backing. D. R. Swem, Seattle manager of coal operations for the NWI, reported to his company president, J. M. Hughes, on April 10: "In Olympia all day yesterday. Governor gave us good interview and assured us would furnish all protection required with full force of state patrol and call for federal troops if necessary. Chief Cole of patrol requests 48 hours notice before attempting reopening."[27]

The request of the mayors of Roslyn and Cle Elum went to the desk of President Roosevelt and then on to the Conciliation Service of the Department of Labor. The labor department placed the responsibility in the hands of the western Divisional Labor Board chair, T. S. Hogan.

Seeking an official federal decision on the legitimacy of the UMWA contract, NWI coal manager Swem cabled Hogan to come to the district and render a decision at once.[28] Hogan was in Washington, DC, and harbored doubts about how a decision of his board would be received by the hostile Roslyn miners. "Am prepared to go [as] soon as I can reach other members of Board but would not like to take any action which would be harmful. Am doubtful if any order issued by our Board would end strike, but it might pave the way for enforcement of Code,"[29] Hogan wrote in a telegram to Swem.

Swem replied, "If such an order is issued, we will have support of local and state authorities and public generally in endeavoring to reopen mine. Evidently the radical group do not intend to present matter in orderly manner to Board and the initiative is apparently with the Board and us."[30]

Shortly thereafter, Hogan embarked on his trip west. Despite the fact that Hogan had close ties to NWI mining company officials, and to UMWA president John L. Lewis, he was described in press reports as a "mediator," and depicted as something of a disinterested third party to the conflict, a federal official responding to local requests for federal mediation.[31]

Hogan's trip by rail took several days to complete, and the miners in Roslyn, Ronald, and Cle Elum waited in nervous anticipation for a decision in the dispute.

On Sunday, April 8, more than twelve hundred men, women, and children gathered on the streets of Cle Elum to march in a mass demonstration of Western Miners Union solidarity. Western Miners leaders rode in cars at the front of the parade, followed by officers of the new ladies auxiliary and two flag bearers.[32]

Stretching for more than a mile, the parade proceeded along Second Avenue then through the downtown area before converging on Pennsylvania Avenue for several speeches. Marchers carried placards emblazoned with slogans: "We are Not Reds," "No Gunmen in Our Ranks," and "W.M.U. 100 percent Americans." Using a truck-mounted microphone and loudspeaker furnished by the Roslyn radio shop, Cle Elum City Attorney Stanley Seddon greeted the assembly on behalf of the mayor, who was at home ill.[33]

Col. J. L. Mitchell, a Yakima lawyer and disabled war veteran, addressed the gathering, urging the miners to have a vote and then to stand by the results of that vote. "If the matter is properly presented to the U.S. Mediator who is now on his way to this district, the outcome will be an election," Mitchell stated. "You have a right to select your own representatives, and the president has declared you have that right. I don't know what is wrong here, and I don't want to know. I am satisfied that neither side is perfect, and the question for you to answer is which side is nearest perfect? Then by a majority vote you should guide your actions."[34]

Next Andrew Hunter took the microphone, reminding the assembled crowd of the abuses that the miners had suffered over the past several years at the hands of John L. Lewis and the United Mine Workers. "All we are asking is that we be given our rights under section 7 of the NRA, interpreted in the same manner as given by President Roosevelt," Hunter stated over mounting applause. "Until we get that, there has been no justice," he shouted to the approving crowd.[35]

STRIKING MINERS HEAR TALKS IN CLE ELUM
SUNDAY FOLLWING SPECTACULAR PARADE

A part of the crowd of 1200 persons at a mass meeting in Cle Elum, Sunday, in connection with a strike which has tied up the coal mines of the area. They were called out by the newly organized Western Miners Union of America which is seeking recognition. The nationally affiliated United Mine Workers of America has the existing contracts in the field. (Record Photo.)

The April 13, 1934, *Ellensburg Evening Record* covered the parade and rally of the Western Miners Union. The caption reads: "A part of the crowd of 1200 persons at a mass meeting in Cle Elum, Sunday, in connection with a strike which has tied up the coal mines of the area. They were called out by the newly organized Western Miners Union of America which is seeking recognition. The nationally affiliated United Mine Workers of America has the existing contracts in the field." *Permission of* Ellensburg Daily Record, *courtesy of Ellensburg Public Library*

Hunter struck back at reports of Communism in the ranks of the Western Miners, stating his union was 100 percent American. He also welcomed the arrival of the divisional labor board chairman to resolve the dispute. "The sooner he gets here the better," Hunter said.

The newly elected leaders of the women's auxiliary were the final speakers of the day. Milling among the crowd as they spoke were mine company employees, taking careful note of the men who were participating in the parade and reporting those names to mine superintendent Tom Murphy. His count listed fifty-seven NWI men from No. 7 mine and about four hundred men in total at the parade.[36]

As miners in the Roslyn-Cle Elum coal fields awaited the arrival of the Divisional Labor Board chair, something of a siege mentality set in. Western Miners supporters diligently kept up the vigil morning after morning on the roads leading to the mines, wary of what might happen if they were to let down their guard. UMWA loyalists awaited word from mine foreman Tom Murphy on the next steps they should take.

Andrew Hunter surmised that much of the support for the strike rested on the ability of his fellow miners to continue their holdout. To sustain the families of the striking miners, Hunter appealed to the federal government, the state and the county for relief aid for the striking miners. But no federal relief was forthcoming without a decision on the legitimacy of the striking union from the Divisional Labor Board. And the state deferred to the county in granting aid requests from the miners.

On Monday, April 9, a decision of the Kittitas County Welfare Board found no merit in Hunter's request for aid. The report stated:

> Upon investigation by the County Welfare Board we find that giving relief to this striking or rioting group of miners is unalterably opposed by the taxpayers of this county.
>
> They consider the strike unjustifiable. The county commissioners, as a body, have absolutely refused to spend the taxpayers' money to support these strikes and the Kittitas County Welfare Board concurs in that stand.
>
> The new union, or organization, has merely been set up as a result of the fact that there is a dissatisfied individual in that community who is a strong leader and organizer.[37]

When notified of the report, Andrew Hunter, president of the striking Western Miners' Union, declared the welfare board report "all wet." "We are entitled to relief and we'll get it anyway, as we have a lot of support in this strike," he declared.[38]

Hunter then turned back to the state seeking relief. On Tuesday, April 10, he led a delegation of 10 miners in an appeal before the state welfare board. But state relief administrator MacEnnis Moore told the delegation that he could not override the decision of the Kittitas County Welfare Board.[39]

Ellensburg attorney Austin Mires summarized the perceptions of many in the lower county in a diary entry: "The strike is still on at Roslyn and the miners want the county commissioners to grant them relief. I'd see them perish first. When men have a chance to work and won't, they are entitled to no consideration."[40]

On that same Tuesday, April 10, Ellensburg Judge Arthur McGuire dealt another blow to the Western Miners cause. In a citizenship hearing, the judge held up the applications of fourteen upper-county men because of their association with the Western Miners Union.

As the judge questioned the men at the hearing, they gave a variety of reasons for their involvement with the new union. Some men said they felt John L. Lewis had lost touch with the miners, while others said the new union provided greater opportunity for better jobs and wages. All the men denied involvement in or allegiance to Communistic or IWW principles. Several said they had been to the picket lines and seen missiles thrown at miners, but others said they had chosen to stay away from the fracas. None seemed to have knowledge of how the women picketers had been organized and none were aware of efforts to organize children. Holding their future citizenship status in his hands, the judge took the opportunity to lecture the men regarding their involvement with the striking miners:

> A man has a right to organize under the law, to preach his doctrine and seek recruits by peaceful means, but he has no right to obstruct another's attempt to go to work by even so much as the weight of his finger or the throwing of missiles of any kind.
>
> If you, yourself, aid or instigate another or even approve of his unlawful actions then you have made yourself responsible for that action. That means that under the law you could not be held for an utterance of a fellow member unless that utterance is brought home to you and then gets your endorsement at which time it becomes your act or statement.
>
> There appears from the evidence that you knew the women were doing those acts of picketing in violation of the law. I am not taking rumors for that opinion, but rather the testimony of you applicants...The men are charged with knowledge and are responsible for the women picketing and doing the unlawful things shown in the testimony.
>
> If your claims are based legitimately for recognition, then more secure would have been your case had you stayed at home quietly until a mediator arrived. Then your cause would have been just as legal and your record far more clear. Now should the N. W. I. company be so disposed, actions in violation to the law

can be placed before the federal mediator, which may have some bearing in his attitude.[41]

On reports of a children's organization being formed, the judge said "such a group could serve no useful purpose in the strike and could be termed as pursuant to methods that newspapers report the communists are adopting to gain ascendency in the minds of children."[42]

So the pathway to citizenship, sought by many immigrants living and working in the Roslyn-Cle Elum coal fields in 1934, was suddenly becoming clouded amid concerns of Western Miner-Communist Party affiliations.

T. S. Hogan arrived in Tacoma on Sunday, April 15, in the early afternoon, accompanied by fellow regional labor board member James Morgan. The pair was met at the train station in Tacoma by NWI coal manager Swem, who had lunch with them before driving them to Seattle. On Monday, the members of the Regional Labor Board met with three representatives of the coal industry and five United Mine Workers representatives to gain "an insight of the United Mine Workers position in the controversy."[43]

Following a thorough discussion of the issues leading to the strike, Swem told Hogan he believed that the mine operators and the UMWA had entered a valid contract on March 23 continuing the current contract pending a decision of the Bituminous Coal Code Authority on a federal coal code. Hogan responded that he thought Swem's position was "absolutely correct" and that he believed the board would follow along the course that Swem had indicated.[44]

Hogan had wired the mayors of Roslyn and Cle Elum saying that he would meet with them on Monday, and so later in the day, Swem arranged for the labor board members to travel to Cle Elum by auto to meet with the mayors. Swem understood that Hogan did not plan to give Hunter an interview at that time, but planned to meet with the mayors only.[45]

Hogan apparently had other plans. The *Ellensburg Evening Record* reported that Hogan met not only with the mayors that evening in Cle Elum but also with leaders of the Western Miners and officers of the United Mine Workers. The arrangement was made to allow ten representatives of each of the two unions along with company officials at the hearing of the Divisional Labor Board on Wednesday, April 18.[46]

As the hearing commenced in the Federal Office Building in Seattle two days later, leaders of the Western Miners movement—Hunter, Petrovich, Pasquan, Prescott, and six others—filed into the Customs Courtroom at 9:30 a.m. and came face to face, for the first time in months, with their opposition—Nicholls and Smethurst from the UMWA and Swem from the NWI. Most eyes kept forward, but some couldn't resist glancing across the aisle and wondering what was in the minds of their opponents and what lay ahead of them and their new union on that spring morning.

Hogan called the meeting to order. Reporters in the back row of the hearing room heard the chair repeat a qualifying remark he had uttered several times in the last few days to the press. Hogan reminded those present that his board had no jurisdiction in disputes where a valid contract was in effect. The crux of the matter before the board, then, was simply whether the contract with the United Mine Workers and operators that went into effect in October 1933, and which was extended in March 1934, validly represented workers in the district.

Hogan then took testimony from each of the Western Miners representatives. Andrew Hunter spoke first as president of the new union. He stated that his organization was formed in November 1933 after a number of miners found the October 1933 contract signed by the UMWA to be unsatisfactory. He disputed actions taken by the UMWA in revoking the district charter and instituting a provisional charter. After each Western Miner representative spoke, Hogan and Morgan questioned them carefully.

Representatives of the United Mine Workers of America were then invited to speak. Sam Nicholls, president of the provisional district, said that the actions of the UMWA international organization in revoking the district charter were taken in accordance with existing rules of the international organization, rules that local unions had agreed to when they became members. Nicholls said he had heard no complaints on wages or provisions of the agreement since it had come into effect.

Speaking on behalf of coal operators, D. R. Swem testified that his company had asked for the hearing after they had been forced to close the mines in the Roslyn-Cle Elum coal fields. Swem provided a history of agreements between the NWI and the UMWA dating back to 1905.[47]

After the first day's testimony, Swem summarized the events in a telegram to his boss in St. Paul: "Labor Board in session all day yesterday. Indications very good for favorable decision. Board questioned Western Miners very thoroughly and miners seemed quite discouraged when meeting adjourned."[48]

After another day of testimony in Seattle, the Division Labor Board rendered its decision on Friday, April 20, in an eight-page document. The decision stated that the United Mine Workers of America had represented miners across the state for nearly thirty years and that contracts had been made for the district as a whole and not for sub-districts. During that time, national leaders such as John L. Lewis had pushed for the best obtainable terms for coal miners in wages, hours, and working conditions.

The board found that the protracted contract negotiations at the state level and the subsequent recall of Sam Nicholls by the miners had forced John L. Lewis to take the action of revoking the district charter "in the best interests of the membership of the organization, including the members in the Roslyn-Cle Elum field. The mines had been closed for some three months and twenty-six days; the facts indicated that the resultant condition of unemployment and distress would continue indefinitely if the negotiations were permitted to continue in the manner in which they had been conducted up to this time."[49]

The report offered further proof of the wisdom of the course taken by the UMWA by stating: "nothing was gained by the disobedience of this [August 16 UMWA return to work] order, but on the other hand the men and their families suffered an additional two months and ten days of unemployment by reason of their refusal to obey said order."[50]

Miners who went to work under the UMWA contract in October 1933 received benefits from the contract and were thus bound by its obligations, the report stated, including the obligation to follow the decisions of union leaders regarding striking or working. The labor board made no mention of the fact that the vote of the Roslyn miners to return to work was made under protest of the eight-hour work day, and no mention was made as to whether that issue had been resolved.

The contract that was approved in October 1933 carried a provision for extension or renewal of the contract. Hogan and Morgan found that the UMWA had followed the stipulations of the contract appropriately in extending its terms beyond April 1.

Next was the tricky issue of membership. The board found evidence that the UMWA had a total bona fide membership in the entire state of 1,560 dues-paying or dues-exempt members, out of a total eligible membership of approximately 2,300. That meant that even if all the remaining miners were Western Miners, their number could not be greater than 740 in the state. Officials of the Western Miners Union claimed a membership of 608. The board described some of the irregularities in membership and recruiting that they found had occurred:

> If these figures are correct a considerable number of the men claimed by the Western Miners Union must also be members of the United Mine Workers. For instance, in the Roslyn-Cascade Coal Company's mines with a total of 131 men on the payroll who are eligible for union membership, 77 are on the United Mine Workers check-off and are so certified by an affidavit submitted to the Board by the operator of that mine. This would leave 54 who are not members of the United Mine Workers, and it is alleged that some eight or ten of this 54 do not belong to either organization. The Western Miners Union claim a membership in this company's mines of 86. At least a partial explanation of this duplication of membership may be found in some 80 to 100 affidavits filed with the Board at this hearing. A large number of these affiants have sworn before notary publics that after the strike was called at the Cle Elum-Roslyn field by the Western Miners Union, the parties making said affidavits were forced to sign the membership rolls of the Western Miners Union by threats, force and violence. In several cases the affiants swear that their homes were entered by groups of men and they were dragged therefrom and

abused and beaten until they signed said membership. Included in these affidavits are the affidavits of two doctors, who treated the victims of assault for injuries received as a result of this strike. The large number of these affidavits preclude the possibility that such assaults did not occur or that memberships were not obtained in this manner, and this Board cannot credit the Western Miners Union with members so obtained.[51]

With the numbers clearly indicating that the United Mine Workers constituted a majority of the miners in the state, the board determined that the demands of the Western Miners for an election were not warranted.

The decision mentioned several additional acts of violence supporting the claim that the leadership of the Western Miners was not operating in the best interest of the miners or the community. In one case, the report stated, "a courtroom was invaded and the judge prevented by violence and threats from proceeding with his official duties."[52]

The report also noted that a school teacher had been pelted with eggs and detained while on her way to school until a patrol officer had come to her rescue. She reported several additional instances of threats and abuse on subsequent trips to and from school. Several businessmen had also been threatened with boycott or with personal threats to family members, the report noted.

The decision of the board was, not surprisingly, a resounding endorsement of the validity of the United Mine Workers agreement as a valid contract for the miners of the Roslyn-Cle Elum fields.

"That by calling a strike in the Roslyn-Cle Elum mines on April 1st, 1934, the Western Miners Union and its members who participated therein violated the terms of the existing and valid contract and such action was not in conformity with the provisions or purposes of the Code of Fair Competition for the Bituminous Coal Industry,"[53] the report concluded.

Chapter 11

The Speed Cops

*H*erman *picked up his copy of the Ellensburg newspaper to read the banner headline again: "Coal Contract Upheld as Valid." The sub-headings in the paper provided a succinct if not premature death notice to the Western Miners movement: "Western Miners Lose Fight to Represent Field; Mines to Reopen Next Week, Probably Tuesday, Say Operators."*[1]

As Anna came into the living room, still wiping her hands on a dish towel, he looked up from his paper and said, "Anna, you'd better get those folks at your church to pray for me again. We're gonna need all we can get next week."

Herman had grown up in the Lutheran faith but had stopped attending church a decade before. Anna and the girls still went every week. Herman was among a large group of miners who felt their immigration to America represented a freedom "from" religion as well as a freedom "of" religion.

"Herman, you don't have to put yourself out there again. Why don't you just stay out for a while, until this all settles down?" Anna queried. "You know that's what a lot of them fellows are gonna do."

"Well, I'm gonna catch hell no matter what I do. If I stay home, Murphy will be all over my back saying I'm not supporting the company, and I've been with the NWI for more than twenty years, and they been good to me—always treated me fair." Herman sighed. "And if I go back to work, I don't know which'll be worse, the hell I'll catch from those women on the picket lines or the hell I'll catch from you."

"But you reported to work the day the strike started," Anna continued, ignoring Herman's slight. "You didn't have to go in that day. A lot of the other fellas didn't make it. That should count for something."

"We're not going to win this fight by staying home," Herman said. "We got to stick together and stand up for each other. The coal board made its decision, and the company says to get back to work, and it seems to me that we should get back to work."

"Herman, your skull is as hard as your miner's hat. How many rocks does it take to convince you that it's not worth it—threatening your life and your family like that—and for what?"

Herman did not report for work—at least not on the first day.

Andy Hunter was clearly stunned by the labor board's decision. All of his hopes and dreams of shorter working days, full employment for the miners, better pay—now even his future in the community—were coming apart around him. So stunned, in fact, was Hunter that for the first time in a long time he had little to say to the press when asked about the decision. He managed only that he would put the matter of going back to work in the hands of the members of his union for a vote.[2]

Northwestern Improvement Company representatives went into overdrive following the decision. Pressmen were rushed to put copies of the decision into the hands of miners in the district. Anxious to reopen the mines after nearly three weeks of inactivity, the company's Seattle legal representative, W. E. Coman, sent a coded telegram to Northern Pacific Railway vice president for legal affairs, B. W. Scandrett, about the situation:

> Have gone over labor board decision with daPonte [NWI Western Counsel] and Swem [NWI Manager Coal Operations] and we are agreed that it is a clear vindication of our position and is satisfactory. Swem and I are going to Olympia this morning and arrange for adequate protection by state highway police at opening of mine which Swem now plans for Tuesday or Wednesday. We believe that [with] the decision of the board and with ample protection we will be able to open and operate the mines successfully. Swem does not believe full force will report first day but will increase rapidly the following days and he does not plan to reemploy ringleaders of the strikers.[3]

After several weeks of Western Miners parades through Roslyn and Cle Elum, it was the United Mine Workers' turn for celebration. The organization called for a basket picnic to be held on Sunday, April 22, at a location about a mile above Bullfrog Bridge on the Cle Elum River. Invited to speak at the event were E. K. Brown, the Ellensburg lawyer who had fought the Western Miners through several legal battles, and UMWA representatives Walter Smethurst and William Dalrymple who had been working to settle the labor conflict for more than eight months. The event also featured sporting events for the adults and ice cream for the children.[4]

At the picnic, UMWA provisional district president Sam Nicholls called the decision of the labor board a "Victory for Americanism." E. K. Brown boomed out his praise for the decision, as the *Ellensburg Daily Record* reported the next day:

> "In 100 years from now the U. M. W. of A. will be the backbone of this country, but in two months from now the Western Miners will be nothing but a stinking memory," declared Attorney E. K. Brown, to a large group of United Miners picnicking at Bullfrog bridge west of the Cle Elum-Roslyn highway.
>
> "Eighty per cent of the new organization's membership has been coerced and intimidated or their families threatened in order to get them to affiliate with the Western Miners," he declared. "That 80 per cent is composed of citizens just as loyal as you, so let us extend to them the olive branch and permit them to return to the folds," he shouted amid a burst of applause. "I ask you to continue conducting yourselves above reproach. I don't anticipate any general uprising, but in any event, be prepared to meet anything," he concluded.[5]

UMWA international representative William Dalrymple continued by scoring Andrew Hunter for his role in leading the rival union, branding Hunter as:

> "Uncle Andrew, Little Moses and a selfish renegade leader. He admitted at the Seattle hearing that he could get no better wages nor better working conditions than had been obtained by the United Miners," Dalrymple stated. "Then what had they to offer by putting women and children on the picket lines and shoving the men so far behind them that they barely could be seen?" he asked.
>
> Dalrymple charged that for seven years while Hunter was secretary of the beneficial hospital he was trying to destroy the United Workers. "We do extend an open hand to the majority of the Western Miners, many of whom were forced into joining the organization, but to the renegades who led women and children to the picket lines, the door is closed," he said.[6]

Western Miners supporters held a rally of their own at the Roslyn ballpark that same Sunday. Speeches there branded the decision of the labor board as "unfair and the result of a raw deal." A committee was designated to appeal to President Roosevelt and to the state's federal representatives and senators for "fair treatment and a righting of the prejudiced decision."[7] A copy of that telegram appeared in the Ellensburg newspaper:

Dear President:

The Officers and members of the Western Miners Union of America appeal to you against a decision rendered by the Bituminous Coal Labor Board, division five, in which said decision is contrary to the rights of the Western Miners Union of America and its members as stated in section seven of the National Industrial Recovery Act, and section five of the Bituminous Coal Code.

The Western Miners Union contains a large majority of all miners in the Roslyn-Cle Elum field area, state of Washington, and on several occasions during the months of January, February and March requested the Coal Code Administration and the Bituminous Coal Labor Board to prevent John L. Lewis, U.M.W. of A. president, and any and all of his agents from renewing contract with the N.W.I. company, operators in Roslyn and Cle Elum field and requested that operators be required to recognize Western Miners Union of America, a majority organization.

General Manager D. R. Swem of the N.W.I. company agreed with representatives of the Western Miners Union on January 3, 1934, that he would recognize Western Miners Union if it had majority on or about April 1, 1934. Representatives of the Western Miners Union met Mr. Swem and he refused to recognize representatives of the Western union, stating he had agreed with representatives of the U.M.W. of A., a minority organization in the Roslyn-Cle Elum field, therefore violating section seven of the National Industrial Recovery Act.

We, the officers and members of the Western Miners Union of America, appeal to you against the decision of the Bituminous Coal Labor Board, division five, and ask your support to give us our rights under section seven of the National Industrial Recovery Act and the right to belong to an organization of our own choosing and the right to elect representatives of our own choosing for the purpose of collective bargaining.[8]

The three Western Miners Union locals in the Roslyn-Cle Elum field held votes on Tuesday to continue the strike. The final tally was reported as 509 to reject the labor board ruling and remain on strike with only 32 voting in favor of returning to work.[9] Hunter claimed that the number of votes proved that the Western Miners had a majority of the miners in the Roslyn-Cle Elum field, but NWI company officials questioned the validity of the vote count to newspaper reporters[10] as well as in company memos: "Mr. Swem advises that the statement of the vote of 509 to 32 taken by the Western Miners against going back to work is not correct as they do not have a membership of 541 coal miners and that the votes of the unemployed, communists and radicals who have been brought in from outside must also have been counted."[11]

The NWI legal team was now in regular contact with Governor Clarence D. Martin and Chief William Cole of the Washington State Patrol. Cole had requested forty-eight hours' notice before reopening the mines, and NWI representatives accommodated, agreeing to reopen the mines on Wednesday, April 25. In reply, Cole promised to bring the entire force of the state patrol, sixty-eight men, to the field by Tuesday.[12]

True to his word, Cole assembled his full force of available officers in Cle Elum just before noon on Tuesday, April 24: sixty-six uniformed officers, each mounted on a Harley-Davidson motorcycle with a sidecar. As their first official act in the troubled coal field, the patrolmen formed a motorcade, two abreast and using the entire roadway. In stately procession they rode, thirty-three rows of state law enforcement officers driving slowly through the main thoroughfares of Cle Elum, then down the three-mile stretch of highway into Roslyn, through the downtown area, past the school yard where children, out for recess, ran to the fence to catch a glimpse of the "speed cops" as they called them.[13] The patrol progressed out of Roslyn for another two miles into Ronald where they turned just past the Company Store and repeated their procession back toward Roslyn and Cle Elum.

In a few places, United Mine Workers supporters ran or drove along behind the motorcade, showing their support for the police presence. On one Roslyn street, a Western Miner supporter saw that his next-door neighbor, a UMWA loyalist, was headed out of his house to follow the state troopers. The Western Miner apparently would have none of it and chased the United Miner back into his house.[14]

The purpose of the motorcade, Cole said, was to familiarize his men with the coal district.[15] The show of force undoubtedly served a second purpose of informing every member of the community, from small children to the elderly, that the state intended to use its full force in supporting the rights of men attempting to work under a contract deemed by the government to be valid.

Wednesday morning, April 25, dawned with patches of rain, but most of the homes in the coal field were bustling long before sunrise. Picketers were roused again by cow bells and rallying calls from

Washington State Patrol File Photograph
Restored 1928 Harley-Davidson Motorcycle

In a show of strength, some 66 Washington State Patrolmen, each with a motorcycle and sidecar, rode through the streets of Cle Elum, Roslyn, and Ronald in late April 1934. The patrolmen were called to the area to restore order and assure that miners who wished to work under the valid UMWA contract could cross Western Miners picket lines safely. *Permission of Washington State Patrol*

the dark streets. Some joined the lines in high spirits, while others came more reluctantly. In Ronald, some mothers came to the picket lines dragging their young children along only because of threats of rocks being thrown through their windows if they failed to join the picketers.[16]

Several hundred picketers at each mine entrance were warned by state patrol officers to keep roadways clear and to allow workers to pass. A contingent of motorcycle-mounted officers led workers through the crowds and "shooed feminine picketers, crowding into the highways."[17] The only serious efforts to deter the state patrol officers on the first day that the mines reopened were tacks and roofing nails spread on some roadways in an attempt to puncture their motorcycle tires.[18]

All of the NWI mines resumed operation that morning, but with about one-third of their usual contingent of workers. Watching the situation closely, D. R. Swem, manager of coal operations, reported to NWI President J. M. Hughes on that first morning: "All mines resumed operations this morning but Western Miners decided to continue strike. Number of men at work No. 3 mine 47 [of 190], No. 5 mine 63 [out of 188], No. 7 mine 117 [out of 200], No. 9 mine 34 [out of 61], shop and miscellaneous 19 [out of 29]. Total 280 [out of 649]. Entire state patrol on duty and ample protection with no disturbance."[19]

Western Miners leaders contended that less than half that number actually reported for work.[20] Nonetheless, with the presence of the state patrol, enough men were reporting to work to produce nearly nine hundred tons of coal and to blunt the impetus of the strike. With the state's police force concentrated around mine entrances, the strikers took their protests in other directions.

On the evening of that first day that the mines reopened, Western Miners supporters began to show up again at the homes of miners who had crossed their picket lines. Swem reported the next day to the St. Paul office of the NWI: "several arrests made last night of Western Miners annoying homes of workers."[21]

While Western Miners tactics focused on miners who had gone to work that day, mine Superintendent Tom Murphy began the difficult challenge of filling his work roster with loyal miners. At the same time, Murphy was under orders from the NWI Company to reduce the size of his work force from more than nine hundred men to around five or six hundred. The company was using the strike to make strategic labor cuts.

NWI president J. M. Hughes had communicated in a letter to D. R. Swem even before the decision of the labor board had been announced that he was considering reducing the work force following resolution of the strike.

> We are all agreed that we are operating one too many mines, assuming No. 9 to be still in the development stage. We are employing too many men and meeting too heavy an overhead, and with a free hand could make a material reduction in operating costs by concentrating in two mines and continuing development work in Section 9 so that it may be fully ready to substitute for No. 7 when that is exhausted in the near future... With these matters in mind perhaps the present is not an appropriate time to consider a concentration of operation with consequent reduction in force, and yet again it may be that we would never have a better opportunity to dispense with the services of radicals who have kept the camp stirred up.[22]

After consulting with Swem, Murphy announced to the press that the company would close No. 5 because of the small number of men reporting to work there and switch those miners to No. 3 where he said there were enough men available to work two full levels out of five.[23]

The next strategy that the company employed to coax the remaining loyal workers out to the mines was to issue an ultimatum: Report to work within the next three days or lose your job.[24]

On day two of the reopening of the mines, Chief Cole stationed his state patrol contingent at the mine entrances before 6:00 a.m., but unlike the day before where the picketers had responded to police commands and allowed miners to pass, the crowds on this second day became more militant, throwing rocks and becoming unruly and abusive. "It was just a case of stopping the trouble before it got out of hand," Chief Cole said. "The yelling and talking was of a character likely to incite to violence, so we warned them to stop it and when they kept on, we stopped it ourselves."[25]

Cars loaded with coal emerge from No. 3 mine portal in Ronald while empty cars head back into the mine in this 1939 photo. After a four-month work stoppage over union contract disputes, 1933 was a record low year for coal production in the Roslyn field. The No. 3 mine continued coal production until 1956. *Courtesy of Roslyn Public Library, Roslyn Heritage Collection, by permission of Frank Schuchman*

Intent on completely dispersing the crowds from the mine entrances, the state police first swept over Mine No. 3 in Ronald, using smoke bombs and then tear gas canisters. Children at the scene recalled it vividly years later. "They were shooting out these canisters, and all these people they would start running," remembered one Roslyn resident. "When they start shooting, those people would start moving, and I did too, you know, because I would probably get sprayed. I mean, we were right there in our yard…I never seen anything like that before."[26]

Another recalled: "They had the State Patrol over here that one time trying to break it up—the fights here—and they would start throwing that tear gas around, you know, and I didn't know what that stuff would do to me, and boy, I would take off down that road and that old tear gas would be around there. Scarier than heck. But, it was pretty rough for a while. It's no fun when you have to fight for a job like that, you know."[27]

The state patrol continued their drive to clear out the picketers, moving from No. 3 in Ronald to No. 9 and No. 5 near Roslyn and finally to No. 7 in Cle Elum where a "heavy barrage of gas"[28] scattered the picketers. The tactic proved extremely effective at clearing the entrances. The *Seattle Daily Times* reported that picketers "were scattered over the hills like a horde of jack rabbits today by tear gas bombs."[29]

Those who could not outrun the gas suffered its effects. One resident who lived near No. 5 mine witnessed the effects of the state patrol's use of tear gas: "This older lady, they would throw tear gas at her. Well, she would pass out, and they'd put her in the side car and haul her home."[30]

Six arrests were made, mostly on drunk and vagrancy charges, but a seventh individual, sixteen-year-old Milton Kairis, was arrested on charges of agitation and lodged in county jail awaiting a juvenile hearing. As word of Kairis' arrest spread throughout the community, a crowd of up to two hundred, including a number of high school students gathered at the Cle Elum city hall in protest. Police again resorted to the use of smoke bombs to disperse them.[31]

The state patrol established a curfew, requiring lights out by 9:00 p.m. in homes around the mines. Workers were not allowed to be outside, even in their own yards, if their houses were near the mines. Children were rounded up and sent home.[32]

The number of miners reporting for work was up nearly one hundred from the day before, with 377 miners making their way through the smoke and tear gas into the mines.[33]

By Friday morning, the third day of the mines reopening, the crowds of picketers were becoming somewhat more subdued. No gas was needed to maintain order. Picketers were questioned by state patrol officers about their immigration and citizenship status and then ordered to return to their homes. But dispersing the crowds from the mine entrances only served to create more disturbances throughout the community. "When the pickets got home, the women started fighting with the wives of United Mine Workers who had reported for work," Chief Cole said, "necessitating heavy patrolling of residential sections."[34]

Meanwhile the mines continued to increase production, pushing over 1,100 tons of coal from the ground on Friday. Murphy stated the three-day production was sufficient to meet production demands for the week.[35]

On Saturday morning, a sign was posted at the mining office stating that all miners not currently employed by the company would need to reapply before being reinstated. The number of workers returning to their jobs continued to steadily climb.[36] Those who were rehired were asked to sign a statement renouncing their membership in the Western Miners Union, and rejoining the UMWA.[37]

From the Western Miners camp, Hunter sounded as though he was preparing to fight all summer if needed. "We are fighting for a legitimate cause," Hunter said, "and if we were not convinced of that, we would give up like men."[38]

The state patrol continued to flex its authority more visibly. Saturday morning, five miles outside Cle Elum, Communist organizer Mark Haller was arrested and taken to county jail on charges of agitation. That same day, Andrew Hunter led a delegation to Ellensburg to negotiate the release of Kairis, arrested two days earlier. While the boy's mother, Mrs. William Senuty, was visiting with her son, Chief Cole placed her under arrest on a charge of using abusive language while on the picket line at No. 3 mine the day before.[39]

Communist organizers in Seattle dispatched Revels Cayton, a twenty-six-year-old district secretary for the International Labor Defense (ILD), to arrange the legal defense of those arrested. The ILD was a Communist-supported organization that offered legal defense services for individuals arrested in labor disputes. The group had played a prominent role in the trial of anarchists Sacco and Vanzetti in the early 1920s,[40] and in the rape trial of nine southern blacks known as the Scottsboro Boys in 1933.[41]

Cayton worked as a seaman on Seattle's docks and was the son of a prominent black Seattle newspaper publisher. The month before, he had been defeated in a primary as a candidate for city council in Seattle. Campaigning in February he had spoken on "The Fight Against Lynch Law in the United States."[42] Later that month, he had led a group of frustrated blacks into a session of the Seattle City Council, disrupting the meeting and demanding that the council adopt laws that would make racial discrimination illegal in the city.[43]

But long before his political campaign or his disruption of the city council, Cayton attracted the attention of Washington State law enforcement officers. In March 1933, he organized and led a caravan of two hundred autos and trucks carrying some three thousand out-of-work citizens on a hunger march to the state capitol. As the group neared Olympia, more than two hundred policemen blocked the road, and the caravan was diverted to nearby Priest Point Park. There nearly one thousand members of a vigilante group had surrounded Cayton, shouting: "We got the nigger, we got the nigger!" With the quick assistance of friends, Cayton barely escaped the mob.[44]

When state patrolmen became aware of Cayton's presence in Roslyn on that Sunday morning, it didn't take them long to act.

Cayton arrived in Roslyn accompanied by Oxford economics professor E. M. Hugh-Jones and his wife, who were in the Northwest to study labor conditions in America. The three drove up to the union hall. Finding its doors locked, they were headed back to their vehicle when the state patrol rolled up and immediately placed all three under arrest. Cayton was packed into a motorcycle sidecar and driven two miles to Cle Elum's city jail.

One of the arresting officers was reported to have said to Cayton, "Remember Yakima and Boskaljon—that is what you are in for." Fresh in the minds of many in the central part of the state were labor struggles among Yakima hop growers and pickers who had clashed in the summer of 1933. A Communist organizer well-known to state patrolmen,[45] Casey M. Boskaljon had been taken into police custody during one of the clashes and then later released—directly into the waiting hands of local vigilantes who drove him several miles from town, beat him, and left him for dead.[46]

Sitting in a Cle Elum jail cell, Cayton grew concerned for his personal safety. The Communist newspaper, *Voice of Action*, described what happened next:

> In the jail, Cayton was grilled for five hours by authorities while Vigilantes peered in at the windows...
>
> Two vigilantes sat in front of the jail in a car which was without a license of any sort. When questioned by the police and again by Prosecutor [Spencer] Short, Cayton reminded them that he would hold them responsible for his safety and that they were not to turn him out to the Vigilantes in the middle of the night. They were very noncommittal in their responses. Short said, "You know I can't help it. Things are so bad here I wouldn't tell a traveling salesman to come in here. I can't help it. Things are out of my hands."[47]

A Cayton family biographer wrote of the incident: "The police grilled Revels for five hours, threatening to carve a swastika in his scalp and lynch him. Local vigilantes crowded around the jail cell. Only Hugh-Jones' persistent telephone calls to the British Consulate and the governor's office secured Revels' release."[48]

The May 30, 1934, edition of *New Republic* magazine carried an article by Hugh-Jones recounting his night at the Cle Elum jail titled "A Little Nest of Fascists." Hugh-Jones concluded in that article: "The lad...would certainly not have emerged undamaged, and, being a Negro, would have been lucky to emerge alive."[49]

Chief Cole reported to Governor Martin a few days later: "A negro communist, an Englishman and a lady reported to be his wife, were taken in on Saturday. The negro claimed to be from the communist party, but it was found he was sent from Seattle to Roslyn to arrange for the defense of all who were charged with any violation during the strike. The Englishman claimed to be a professor from Cornell and paid by the Rockefeller Foundation, but he didn't get a very pleasant reception. He was permitted to go to Seattle from where he came, and instructed not to return."[50]

That same Sunday, another altercation took place on the highway between Roslyn and Cle Elum. At about 9:00 p.m., reported the Cle Elum *Miner Echo,* two motorcycle-mounted state patrolmen were riding near the intersection of No. 5 Road when a sniper fired two shots at them from the heavy woods about thirty feet away.

> So close was one of the shots that [State Patrolman] Bruer heard the noise as it pierced the air past him. Chief Cole coming up 200 yards behind also heard the shots. In less than seven minutes as many as 50 patrolmen were at the spot. Combing thru [sic] the woods, they failed to find any trace of the person who fired but a close examination the next day revealed freshly broken branches making an opening so that he would not have to shoot thru the branches. The would-be assassin had also taken precautions to clear a retreat about four feet wide for several yards to the rear to permit him to make a quick get-away, showing the deed was premeditated.[51]

Just thirty minutes earlier, mine teamster Fred Bartol had been shot at while driving home with his wife, but the couple scurried home and did not report the incident until later.[52] State patrolmen were unable to identify a shooter.

On Monday, May 1, the NWI opted to concentrate its work force at No. 3 in Ronald and No. 7 in Cle Elum, idling No. 5 and No. 9. The move allowed the mining company to meet its orders by working smaller crews of around 150 to 200 men in each mine on a five-day per week schedule and to rehire selectively from those who had reapplied. The company was intentionally keeping the work force small, and many applicants were turned down. Company president J. M. Hughes was becoming concerned that leaving a number of men idle in the district might work to the benefit of the Western Miners ranks.[53]

The concentration of workers at two mines funneled the picketers to the entrances of those mines, with nearly five hundred rallying at No. 3. mine on Monday. State patrolmen again used large amounts of tear gas to deter crowds at both mines. Residents around No. 7 mine complained to the governor about the excessive use of gas.

When the complaint letters reached the governor's desk, each had an appended notation from the state patrol describing the writer's activities in relation to the Western Miners strike. William Ozanich wrote to the governor: "I protest against the State Highway Patrol throwing tear gas bombs at peaceful picketers. We voted for you and expect a better deal than that. They are getting brutal up here, and the N.R.A. says that we can picket. All we ask here is a square deal, and are looking to you to help give it to us."

Accompanying the note is this statement: "Very active on picket line."[54]

Mrs. Beatrice Davis, the former wife of the man who was shot and killed in Roslyn, wrote of the ill-effects of the gas in an impassioned letter to the governor:

> As you are fully aware of the situation in the Roslyn-Cle Elum coal fields, I need not go into detail concerning that matter, but I wish to protest the method that is being used, under your orders. That is the use of gas bombs around the residential districts, especially where a woman has just given birth to a child.
>
> The incident of which I write occurred on No. 7 hill in Cle Elum on the morning of Thursday, April 26—the day after your visit here. I was called at 5 a.m. to the home of Frank Subic, and found his wife and 2 day old infant, gasping for breath, the house filled with gas bomb fumes that the State Patrol had ignited around their home. I protested against these bombs being lit there, before entering the home, and knowing what was wrong in the house, and I told the Patrolmen of the circumstances. Then I went into the house and found the mother and babe gasping, and before I could attend to either of them, they lit another gas bomb just outside, within 8 or 10 feet of the house, and I went out and protested again, and the Patrolman told me to mind my own business lady—This is the Governor's orders.
>
> I proceeded to mind my own business by taking such action as any American citizen is entitled to take under these circumstances. As I am the nurse looking after this mother and child, I proceeded to look for the proper authorities, and again was stopped by a Patrolman, who said "Tell it to the Governor if you have something to say."
>
> Awaiting your opinion in regards to this matter, I remain yours truly, Mrs. Beatrice Davis.

Accompanying this letter was a note of explanation:

Mrs. Beatrice Davis was former wife of Robert Ruff who was shot and killed Dec. 23, 1933, by Sam Farrimond who was a member of the United Mine Workers of America. Ruff was a member of the Western Federation [sic] of Miners. Mrs. Davis was very active during the trial of Farrimond although she had been divorced from Ruff for a number of years and had frequently had him in court. P. S. Several persons living in neighborhood of Mrs. Subic state no gas came their way as wind was in opposite direction. The Dr. who attended her also stated she and the baby were not affected by gas.[55]

By mid-week, Mrs. William Senuty was brought before a Cle Elum jury, charged with using indecent and vile language while on the picket line. E. K. Brown acted as special prosecutor in the case alongside former courtroom rival and county prosecutor Spencer Short. Lawrence Seltzer, an ILD-funded Seattle lawyer, defended Mrs. Senuty. The Western Miner supporter was fined $50 plus court costs for her actions.[56] Her son was released at about that same time.

The application of a second wave of tear gas and the general dispersing of picketers by the state patrol seemed to have frustrated the movement and brought disagreement over how to proceed with the strike. The number of picketers dropped dramatically, while the number of men returning to work rose steadily.

One Western Miner decided to return to work, but he refused to sign on with or pay dues to the UMWA. The man worked one day, but the following morning, as he boarded the mantrip (shuttle) to enter the mines, 120 United Miners jumped off, refusing to ride with the disloyal miner. The man stepped off the car, and the miners reboarded. But when he attempted to join them, they left the cars again. This standoff was repeated several times until the humiliated Western miner was forced to go back home.[57]

One internal memo to NWI leaders painted the picture from the company's perspective:

I talked with Mr. Murphy about the Roslyn situation. He says that while for the past few days we have had no picketing or other disturbances, yet Hunter has had daily meetings with his gang and there is no evidence of any change in their general attitude and that just now we could expect further trouble from them if the State patrolmen were withdrawn. The help I mentioned as coming from the Longshoremen apparently is financial, as Mr. Murphy heard they sent Hunter $35. The State patrolmen and County authorities are assembling evidence on the principal agitators during the picketing, and from what Mr. Murphy can learn are planning to arrest from 25 to 40 of them about Wednesday, and Mr. Murphy thinks that may bring about a general change of attitude.[58]

The Communists, who actively supported the Western Miners, began to chafe at the direction that Hunter was taking in leading his cause. The *Voice of Action* newspaper castigated Hunter for leaving his leadership post for three critical days when he went to Seattle seeking relief for striking miners. The paper reported that John P. Pasquan, the secretary-treasurer of the organization and head of one of its locals, had failed to show up at meetings.[59]

Chief Cole of the Washington State Patrol promised to keep a sufficient force on the ground to handle the situation for as long as needed. Near the end of the first full week in the district, Cole had reduced the number of patrolmen from sixty-six to twenty-six with plans to draw down the number gradually to a handful within the following week.[60]

Governor Martin wrote a note to his father that included an assessment of the Roslyn situation: "[State Patrolman] Florence Morgan came back yesterday from the coal mine trouble. Says it is rather a hard one to handle, as they will be good while officers are around, but feels that there may be more trouble when the officers leave. Seems like most of the troublemakers are rather of an illiterate class."[61]

Concerns that Western Miners supporters were awaiting the withdrawal of the state patrol before reasserting their numbers at the mine entrances were apparently without merit. One incident, however, did demonstrate a seething undercurrent of frustration among some in the movement. On Sunday, May 13, mine superintendent Tom Murphy had made the rounds of the mines and returned to Roslyn at about 1:00 p.m. when he stopped in at "The Brick," a well-known watering hole considered a United Mine Workers stronghold at the time.

The Brick Saloon in Roslyn, pictured here around 1900, was a noted meeting spot for loyal United Mine Workers members. While in the tavern in May 1934, mine superintendent Tom Murphy became involved in a brawl that left him with a concussion. Murphy never sought retribution from the man who struck him, however, and eventually rehired him to work in the mines. *Courtesy of Ellensburg Public Library, WSU Digital Collections*

Murphy bought the three or four men there a round of drinks, and the men were talking quietly when Andrew "Duff" Schwab entered rather boisterously and made some pointed remarks to one of the miners. Murphy came to the man's defense, telling Schwab to leave the man alone. Schwab then reached across the bar and seized Murphy's beer. A general melee ensued, and the men fought for several minutes. None of the onlookers attempted to intervene until Murphy and Schwab were both on the floor. Finally the men were separated and Murphy was taken home.

The mine superintendent seemed to have taken most of the abuse, with both eyes blackened, cuts to his face, and a broken bone in his hand. Schwab stayed around town bragging of his part in the fight, but a highway patrolman arrested him later that day on a charge of being drunk and disorderly.

Tom Murphy (center), mine superintendent for the Northwestern Improvement Company in Roslyn, poses with (left to right) Frank Badda, Dick Caldwell, and Jack Caldwell by an NWI boring machine. Murphy developed an international reputation as an innovator in coping with challenges related to steep-pitch mining in the Roslyn-Cle Elum coal field. *Courtesy of Roslyn Public Library, Roslyn Heritage Collection, by permission of Frank Schuchman*

The next morning Murphy made the rounds of the mines, but when he spoke to Swem by phone, Swem noted that something was not right with him. Murphy headed back to bed for the day. Later one of Murphy's men called Dr. Orr to examine him. Orr said Murphy acted as though he had been given knock-out drops or had been drugged. He insisted that Murphy be taken to Seattle for further treatment. Murphy was driven to Seattle's Virginia Mason Hospital where further tests revealed that he had suffered brain concussions, and he remained in the hospital for several days.[62]

NWI company officials were anxious to press charges against Schwab over the incident, concerned that any show of weakness on their part might encourage further acts of aggression against company officials. Company men were ordered to keep away from bars and not to allow themselves to get into any position where they might be framed. Company leaders were sure that is what had happened to Murphy.

E. K. Brown offered to press charges on behalf of the NWI and Murphy, but the resilient mine superintendent would have no part of any legal recourse. He was convinced that the only way to hold the respect of tough miners was to take his licks in a fight and not cower behind the law. Holding no observable grudge, Murphy eventually rehired Schwab.[63]

Chapter 12

Into the Courts

*A*s Herman turned the soil in his garden plot on the first warm weekend *in May, his mind kept repeating a saying he had heard from his father, one that was popular among the farmers of Sweden during his boyhood:* När dalar är tomma, bita hästarna varandra. *It seemed particularly appropriate to the situation that he saw unraveling in Roslyn as neighbor turned against neighbor—"When the troughs are empty, the horses bite each other."*

Whether the threats were direct is not known, but the Roslyn miners who wanted Andrew Hunter dead had little need for subtlety. It had been a week since the state patrol had arrived, and already Hunter was becoming less talkative to the press, less of a presence at picketing sites. And when he did make an appearance in public, three or four bodyguards accompanied him.[1] "It's a wonder somebody didn't kill him," one resident recalled. "He hid a lot. He didn't go out in public."[2]

As worker rosters at the two active mine sites began to fill, and the NWI began to turn away new applicants, strikers became increasingly frustrated at their leaders. At a May 3 meeting of the Western Miners, they vented their feelings at a "hot meeting" in which Hunter was "severely criticized."[3]

Any fire remaining in the Western Miners movement was dampened six days later. On May 9, county prosecutor Spencer Short issued warrants for the arrest of sixty-two upper-county residents on charges of rioting and violence in a mob-like manner related to four incidents on April 3. None of the incidents took place on picket lines.[4]

Police made forty-four arrests within the first two days, transporting detainees to Ellensburg where several arranged for the $500 bail. The newspaper reported what happened to those unable to arrange bail: "The men are lodged in the county bastille and the women under the charge of Mrs. O. W. Pautzke, police matron and deputy are occupying quarters in the pest house."[5] Despite the inglorious terminology, the county pest house or poor farm, as it was called in those days, was a brick structure about five miles west of Ellensburg brought into emergency service to hold the female detainees.

A Ronald woman remembered when family members were incarcerated: "When I come home there was nobody home then. They took them down there to Ellensburg."[6]

The arrests frightened some, but perhaps for women used to a hard day's work of fixing meals, polishing floors, and washing clothes, life at the county farm may have seemed like a holiday. No toilets to clean. No husbands to feed. "Some of the women played the piano and sang. They thought it was a great break from cooking and cleaning,"[7] a resident recalled.

The arrests centered around four incidents on the first day of the Western Miners strike. Some twenty warrants charged that individuals had gathered and threatened violence and intimidated four Roslyn men in the Brookside section of the town. Another group of twenty-four was charged with similar activity against ten persons in South Roslyn in the Hoffmanville district. Thirteen arrests were made in connection with the confrontation with Ronald miner John Madzuma and his wife. Two women were charged with breaking an auto window by throwing rocks. And Mark Haller, already being held on agitation charges, was charged with loitering and having no visible means of support.[8]

Ellensburg attorney E. K. Brown was quick to offer his services to the county prosecutor in the forthcoming trials of the Western Miners supporters. Brown asked the NWI and the UMWA for money to cover his legal services, arguing that the company would benefit greatly from his prosecution of the cases. He reminded NWI officials that they had paid $500 for his representation in the Sam Farrimond murder trial in February, a sum that the UMWA had matched at the time.[9]

But given the circumstances now emerging, the NWI was not willing to take such direct intervention in the prosecution of strikers. NWI President J. M. Hughes stated, "[T]he National Recovery Act strictly prohibits employers interfering with the affairs of the employees, and we have very carefully refrained from any action which might be even remotely construed as interference. Furthermore, it seems to us that Major [E. K.] Brown's position as special prosecutor for the county would be materially weakened if he were not able to say that the Northwestern Improvement Co. had no connection with the prosecutions."[10]

The arrests definitely took steam out of the locomotive that for many months had been the Western Miners movement. But Andrew Hunter was not yet completely vanquished as leader of the cause. Rebuffed in attempts to gain relief at the county and state levels, Hunter had been lobbying U.S. Rep. Knute Hill, who represented Roslyn and the state's Fourth Congressional District in Congress. As a result of Hunter's efforts, on May 14 Hill brought the Western Miners complaint to Federal Relief Administrator Harry Hopkins, one of Roosevelt's closest advisers.[11]

Included in the complaint was a telegram from Hunter reporting that the state patrol had used tear gas on peaceful pickets, placed two bombs beside a sick woman sitting on a stump, and placed another bomb by the home of a sick three-day-old baby. A miners committee, Hunter said, was soliciting funds from citizens of the state since the county had refused to provide assistance. Hopkins replied to reporter queries that he had not studied the issue, but from a "hasty glance" it appeared to him that aid should be given.[12]

At about that same time, letters and telegrams went out from leaders in the Western Miners Women's Auxiliary to President and Mrs. Roosevelt for assistance. But these telegrams and letters were referred on to the NRA and finally found their way to the desk of Regional Labor Board chairman T. S. Hogan, the man who had written the final decision upholding the validity of the UMWA contract a month earlier. Hogan wrote letters of response to the women stating his belief that "most of their difficulties are due to the misguided leadership of their husbands and that there can be no peace in the community as long as Hunter assumes the position he does."[13] Hogan also reminded Harry Hopkins of the labor board decision against the striking miners and advised Hopkins not to provide the requested relief.

Hunter had been spending increasing time with miners in the western part of the state in hopes of strengthening his claim to represent miners statewide. Through his efforts he reportedly gained followers at mines in the towns of Bayne and Wilkeson.[14]

By May 21, the mine company had hired all the miners it intended to engage, with five hundred miners meeting the demand for coal while working just four days per week.[15] The Western Miners held a mass meeting and decided to renew peaceful picketing, hoping to join forces with a contingent of picketers from Seattle in a mass demonstration outside the mines on the morning of May 21. The Seattle group never materialized, but about 150 local men staged an orderly picketing of the mines that morning under close scrutiny of a beefed up state patrol squad. In the absence of other problems Chief William Cole planned to cut the watch to six by the end of the week.[16]

As the end of that week arrived, attention focused once again on Ellensburg where the citizenship hearings reopened for fourteen men with Western Miners connections whose hearings over questions of Communist associations were continued from the month before. After hearing testimony from such divergent perspectives as UMWA enforcer Bernard "Bun" Henry and Western Miners vice president Mike Petrovich, Judge Arthur McGuire determined that five of the applicants should be admitted for citizenship while five were denied, based on testimony showing: "They are not attached to the principles of the constitution of the United States and are not disposed to good order and happiness of the same."[17] The five applicants were rejected with prejudice for a period of five years. Four applications were postponed for other reasons.

The fabric of the grassroots movement began to unravel further in early June as the leaders of the Western Miners, confronted with defending the actions of the arrested strikers in court, took differing approaches to the challenge. Communist organizer Mark Haller had been released from jail on a $1,200 property bond, and he determined that the best way to promote the cause was to gather public support from around the state for his upcoming legal defense. The young communist organizer, along with sixteen-year-old Milton Kairis, also just released from jail, embarked in mid-June on a ten-day speaking tour of cities in the western part of the state, including Bellingham, Anacortes, Everett, Seattle, Tacoma, and Centralia.

Haller shared his perspective of the events in Roslyn in an article published in the *Voice of Action* on June 8.

> I was put in solitary confinement one week. Then in the "dark hole" two weeks in an attempt to break me down, but failed. The jail was "buggy" and the meals were not fit to feed hogs. The meals come from Antlers Hotels and we get scraps and left over's from the café.
>
> One morning oatmeal mush was served and I noticed spots in my mush which proved to be bugs. The worker next to me was luckier, he found a cooked mouse in his plate. Neither of us can look at mush any more. I was in jail three weeks before anyone was allowed to see me...I am charged with riot, inciting to riot, assault and vagrancy, out on $1,200 property bond. The ILD is taking up our defense, for only through mass pressure can we be saved from the big walls.[18]

A few days later, students at the University of Washington in Seattle found leaflets scattered about the campus commons promoting the two speakers from Roslyn. A student at the university, the daughter of NWI operations manager D.R. Swem, brought a leaflet home to her father. Swem shared its contents in a letter to the NWI president:

> MURDER
> MASS ARREST, SLUGGINGS
> FRAME UP, TEAR GAS
> Hear about the Terror in ROSLYN
> MARK HALLER, MILTON KAIRIS
> Young miners charged with "rioting," "assault," etc. will tell of the terror that was used by the State Police to break the strike of the Western Miners for recognition of their union.
> HAROLD BROCKWAY
> District Chairman of Unemployment Councils who is facing rioting charges for leading the strike in the Seattle Soup line.
> WEDNESDAY JUNE 20th, 8 P.M.
> MOOSE HALL
> Eighth and Union
> Admission 10 cents
> Auspices International Labor Defence [sic]
> Young Communist League
> (printed by volunteer labor)[19]

Andrew Hunter spurned offers of legal assistance from the ILD and instead retained prominent Seattle attorney George F. Vanderveer to defend the thirteen strikers charged with rioting in Ronald. Vanderveer had an impressive legal reputation, having gained national prominence as defense counsel for more than one hundred Industrial Workers of the World members accused of sedition during the World War. Vanderveer had also led the defense of IWW members charged with murder in the Everett massacre of 1916 and in labor battles in Centralia in the 1920s. His efforts in defense of unpopular defendants had earned him the moniker, "Counsel for the Damned."[20]

Five rioting cases were lined up on the June docket for Kittitas County Superior Court, and early reports suggested the cases could take nearly three weeks. But all eyes were on the first case: *State of Washington vs. Mike Sercesson, et al.*

The state had strengthened its "legal artillery" by wheeling "the E. K. Brown battery into a prosecution position," alongside county prosecutor Spencer Short.[21] For the defense, George F. Vanderveer was joined by Ellensburg attorney E. E. Wager.

The two contenders flexed their legal muscles in the early moments of jury selection for the trial. Vanderveer insisted on asking every juror about his or her understanding of an individual's right to join a union and to strike. Brown insisted just as strongly that the union issue was not relevant to the legal dispute. The Ellensburg *Evening Record* offered a glimpse into the proceedings:

> They clashed on the point during the examination of Edward Hill of Cle Elum, who told Vandeveer [sic] he knew no reason why he could not render a just verdict, except that "I belong to the United Miners and they (the defendants) are members of the Western Miners."
>
> "We are not interested in that controversy," interposed Brown.
> "Aren't we?" inquired Vandeveer.
> "No, we are not, and furthermore we are not going to get into it," said Brown.

McGuire Sustains

Judge McGuire, however, sustained the defense challenge of Hill for cause. The only other upper county resident called, Fred

Ashurst of Cle Elum, was excused for the same reason, as were Milton Flodman and James Shaw of Ellensburg. Harry Block of Ellensburg was excused on a preemptory challenge of the defense.[22]

The attorneys clashed again in the opening rounds of the trial as Vanderveer moved to separate the two charges brought against his clients.

> Judge McGuire ruled that they were crimes of a similar character, occurring during the one act of rioting, and that they could be joined into the single information.
>
> At another point, Vandeveer asked a juror if he believed in the golden rule. Given an affirmative answer, he asked the juror to keep it in mind during the progress of the trial.
>
> "We might stipulate," said Brown, "'that it be used throughout.'"[23]

The jury was finally seated, with eight men and four women, all from the lower county. Three prospective jurors from the upper county had been excused for cause, the judge perceiving that any upper county resident could not render an unbiased judgment in a case involving Western Miners.

The Ellensburg newspaper covered this clash of titans with language that might as easily have been found in coverage of the Max Baer boxing title match two weeks earlier.

Warrior Revived.

> A week ago E. K. Brown, veteran courtroom warrior, was at the point of death, suffering from his worst attack of asthma. Today he is ace sniper for the prosecution in a lively contest born of union warfare in the Roslyn-Cle Elum coal fields early in April.
>
> With his keen-edged horns firmly locked with those of the defense attorney, George Vanderveer, foxy Seattle lawyer of wide repute, Brown shows little indication of his recent illness.
>
> Courtroom railbirds who reserved seats in anticipation of something resembling a county classic in the Brown-Vanderveer engagement have not been disappointed. Little else than an impending tussle with a master tussler could have snared Mr. Brown from the portals of death in such a short time.

Signal Battle.

Signal for the battle was given at the outset of the trial yesterday when Mr. Vanderveer unsuccessfully moved to have Mr. Brown put out of the case because he was affiliated with the N.W.I. company.

Following the opening statement of the prosecution made by Prosecutor Spencer Short, Mr. Vanderveer moved that the two actions, unlawful assembly and assault, be segregated. Upon denial he warned the prosecution that he would move for dismissal of the action as soon as any one of the 16 defendants were shown to have left the scene.[24]

Tall and blonde, Tillie Madzuma made a striking impression as the first witness for the prosecution to outline her version of the events of April 3. She testified that she had met a group of picketers while driving into Ronald and had to drive off the pavement to avoid hitting one of them. She said she did not see the mob when she entered the company store, but she later began to hear a group outside shouting threats at her children unless she came outside.

"When you came out of the store, what did you see?" Brown asked. "About 150 to 200 men and women all hollerin' at me and calling my husband vile names."

"What did they say?"

"Do I have to tell you? I don't want to unless it is necessary because their language was too filthy for me to repeat."

A wave of laughter swept through the courtroom and Judge McGuire halted the proceedings to warn spectators that a recurrence would force him to clear the room.

Lock Horns

"I now renew my motion," said Mr. Brown, "to have all the defendants bunched together. That laughter was a deliberate attempt on the part of the defendants, scattered throughout the courtroom, to detract from the continuity of the testimony."

He had hardly finished with his motion when Vanderveer "exploded."

"I now renew my motion to have Mr. Brown put out of the case," he said. "Any private lawyer who don't [sic] know how to conduct himself as a public officer any better than to make such remarks should have no place in the prosecution of this case."[25]

Judge McGuire denied both motions.

Mrs. Madzuma continued her testimony, according to the *Ellensburg Evening Record*, stating that as she descended the stairs of the store, two women grabbed at her hands, and she threw the package of groceries at them to scare them away. The crowd started to close in around her when her husband appeared at the top of the stairs with the axe handle in hand.

"When my husband reached me, they let me go and went after him.

"I tried to pull the men off my husband. While we were scuffling, we gradually worked across the street to our yard.

"My husband went through our front gate and several men after him."[26]

On cross-examination, Attorney Vanderveer moved quietly through Mrs. Madzuma's testimony but then changed direction, flustering and revealing a more combative side of the demure witness.

"Now, you say, Mrs. Madzuma, that when the women grabbed hold of you, they twisted your thumb and hurt it?"

"Yes, I couldn't use it for some time."

"Now isn't it a fact that actually your husband broke your thumb?"

"That's a dirty lie," screamed Mrs. Madzuma, eyes flashing and crouching forward out of the witness chair.

"That's not a nice way to talk," replied Vanderveer.

"Well, that's not a nice question, either," replied the infuriated witness.

"I believe you're a little mad," Vanderveer provokingly smiled.

"Yes, you bet I'm mad. I'm twice as mad as I was during the rioting."[27]

The prosecution had produced a gunny sack which they said contained the pipes and debris that John Madzuma had collected from his front yard after the altercation on April 3. The bag was brought into court and marked for identification in one large bundle, but the state planned to introduce each piece and have it marked when identified. Vanderveer noticed that the sack was sitting unguarded under the prosecutor's table.

As soon as the judge called the noon recess, Vanderveer and his associate, John Geisness, raced to the B. J. Freeman Auto Company and the A. A. Bergan Plumbing Company, procuring two sections of lead pipe. Returning to the courtroom just as the noon recess ended, Vanderveer slipped one section of pipe into the burlap sack and placed another section in its folds.

Unaware of Vanderveer's devious act, E. K. Brown and Spencer Short called John Madzuma to the stand to start the afternoon session and proceeded to ask him to identify the contents of the sack. Madzuma inspected each section of pipe and testified that each piece had come from his yard. His wife, recalled to the stand, also said the pipes had come from the yard.

Vanderveer closed his clever trap by calling Jerome Mundy, an employee at the Bergan Plumbing shop, who identified one of the pipes as coming from his shop. Then came Cecil Newby of B. J. Freeman Auto, who testified that he had cleaned one of the pipes and marked it with a hacksaw.

The bailiff testified to returning the sack to the desk near the end of the recess. The Ellensburg newspaper reported the legal jousting that followed:

> To Bailiff Lee, Vanderveer said, "Do you remember kicking the sack under the desk when you brought in the exhibits?"
>
> "No," answered Lee.
>
> "Did you notice that I nearly had heart failure when you did?" queried Vanderveer.
>
> Vanderveer called Deputy Prosecutor Brown [to the witness stand], who said, "I am perfectly willing to take the stand, but I want it understood that I did not prejudice my right to argue this case to the jury by doing so."

Attorneys Tangle

Vanderveer agreed and asked his legal opponent: "When court adjourned yesterday noon did I say to you, 'Be careful how you identify those exhibits, because I've got an ace up my sleeve'?"

Brown leaped up and cried, "You've been trying to run a bluff on me ever since this trial started, and this is once that it won't stick."

"Your honor," began Vanderveer, "will you instruct the witness in his duty…"

Judge Arthur McGuire intervened to warn that the case was developing into a rumpus between the attorneys and Brown left the stand.[28]

John Madzuma was then given the opportunity to testify about his perceptions of the fracas.

"I was in the company store. They told me they were beating up my wife outside. I see a bunch of people, Hollerin'. I see some people pulling at my wife, calling her names. Big crowd to east and west, but more space in center. I see pick handle leaning against the porch. I pick it up. I got to have something to protect my wife."

"What was going on when you saw your wife out there?" asked Brown. "I don't know damn—I don't know nothin' about it," replied the witness.[29]

Madzuma said that Mike Sercesson, one of the defendants, grabbed the pick handle from his hand. "So I see I lost my help, so I ran for my gate. When I turned back, they jumped on my back."[30]

Madzuma said that he was hit across the back of the legs by one of the pipes. Then, he said, some of the men in the crowd yelled: "We've got him plenty boys, now turn him over and we'll give him some on the other side."

A number of witnesses testified of hearing Western Miners supporters gloating after the fighting, "We beat up on John and the women fought with Tillie." And a neighbor who came to her door when she heard the shouting said she heard shouts of "Kill the _____." She said she didn't hear anything more because she headed to the phone to call for help.[31]

Quite a different scene was painted by the defense in the case. Before taking up his defense before the jury, Vanderveer offered several motions including a motion for dismissal, a motion to force prosecution to choose between the two counts of information, and a motion to dismiss on behalf of each defendant to each count. Each motion was denied.

One woman, who others had testified as having an iron pipe in hand at the scene of the melee, said she had never seen the pipe before and that she was only at the scene looking for her children.

Others accused in the case corroborated a story of leaving the peaceful picket lines at No. 3 and Patrick's mines and coming together in Ronald to share their experiences from the morning's picketing. As the group met in front of the company store, they saw Tillie Madzuma and asked her why her husband had gone to work that day. She answered, they said, "My husband went to work today, and he's going back tomorrow, and no _____ is going to stop him!"

Mrs. Churchich, one of the accused ladies, testified through a translator: "I asked Mrs. Madzuma why, if her husband was a watchman, he sneaked around" (referring to the fact that Madzuma had entered the company store by the back door). Mrs. Churchich testified that Mrs. Madzuma came down from the store porch and threw the sack of groceries, striking her in the face. She said her son then took her away.[32]

Other witnesses came forward to report that John Madzuma then rushed into the scene, wildly swinging a pick handle. Joe X. Chopp, another defendant, said, "He just came running out and disappeared in the crowd." Later, they said, Madzuma emerged from the crowd on the ground after a concerted effort to remove the pick handle from his hands. No one was sure how Madzuma got to the ground since no one had hit him.

> Helen Briski, star defense witness, said she left the scene when Mrs. Madzuma threatened from her door to get a gun and shoot every _____ in the crowd. "Why did you leave?" inquired Deputy Prosecutor E. K. Brown.
>
> "I didn't want to get kilt!"
> "Did you hear the crowd cursing?"
> "No."
> "Are you positive?"
> "Well, you can't talk if you don't cuss a little," retorted Mrs. Briski.

As Attorney Brown started pressing the witness, Vanderveer picked up one of the two pieces of gas pipe he had planted in the collection of bludgeons identified by Madzuma and quietly placed it on the witness stand in front of Mrs. Briski, then smiled provokingly at Brown.

"Thank you, Mr. Vanderveer," said Brown.

The event eased the tenseness of the examination.[33]

Prosecutor Spencer Short offered the first closing argument for the prosecution, recounting the evidence in the case and asking the jury to do its duty and to return a guilty verdict. The prosecution team was holding the gifted oratory of E. K. Brown for the final defense rebuttal before the case went to the jury.

But the crafty Vanderveer had one more trick up his sleeve. He opted not to offer a closing argument to the jury. As the court's attention came to him for his final summation, he simply looked over at his co-counsel and said, "Mr. Wager and I believe that the evidence is clear and that nothing we can say will help the jury in their deliberations on the case."

The stunned Brown, who was poised to pick apart Vanderveer's arguments, had nothing left but to ask the court, "Your Honor, the action of the defense bars the state from further remarks, does it not?"

"It does, Mr. Brown."[34]

The jury began deliberations at 2:10 p.m. on Friday. Apparently the busy Seattle lawyer could not wait for the jury decision. Vanderveer told his clients, "Go home and don't worry," as the case went to the jury.

Heeding his own advice, Vanderveer and his associate headed over to Cle Elum and were having dinner at the Autorest Café. A miner and former prison guard by the name of Tom Wallace saw Vanderveer dining there and asked if he might join him. Wallace had apparently known Vanderveer some twenty years prior. During their conversation, Vanderveer asked what Wallace was doing for work. Wallace replied that he was working as foreman at a truck mine in the area. Vanderveer sneered, "Scabbing, eh? Well, I don't want to eat with a scab."[35]

Wallace apparently ate his meal elsewhere but waited for Vanderveer outside the café. When the lawyer emerged, Wallace had his sleeves rolled up ready for a fight. Vanderveer was wearing glasses, and Wallace was reluctant to throw the first blow. Vanderveer had no such inhibitions. He hit Wallace and had the much larger man on the sidewalk when a patrolman halted the fight.

Both men were taken to jail at about 6:30 p.m. for quarreling, fighting, and disturbing the peace. Vanderveer's associate posted a $100 bond for his freedom, and the case was heard at 9:30 p.m. before Judge Charles Connell. The judge fined both men $10. Both men appealed their cases to the superior court.[36]

An hour later, the jury in Ellensburg returned with its verdict in the first rioting case: Not guilty. Vanderveer had successfully defended the Ronald residents against the rioting charges and out-dueled the vaunted E. K. Brown.[37]

Prosecutor Spencer Short undoubtedly began to reevaluate his chances of getting guilty verdicts on the remaining rioting cases. Whatever the reasons may have been, Short asked to continue the cases until the October session of the court, with Judge McGuire citing the difficulty of seating jurors during the harvest.

NWI President J. M. Hughes was not unhappy with the postponements, as he reported to Northern Pacific Railway president Charles Donnelly: "This postponement would appear to be advantageous to us, inasmuch as the radical union is not likely to start anything while these cases are hanging over the heads of many of its prominent members."[38]

Epilogue

One of the most distressing aspects of an inter-union clash such as the Cle Elum-Roslyn coalfield is now experiencing is that of the arraying of various members of a family on opposing sides of the argument.

In several cases, father and son, man and wife, or brothers and sisters are found on opposite sides of the artificial fence of prejudice that separates the two groups, and heated arguments, even coming to blows, has resulted not only between what a few days ago was the best of neighbors, but members of the same family and living under the same roof.

Wounds like these leave scars that it takes years to heal. It is paying a dear price.

Editorial, *Miner Echo*, April 6, 1934

In October 1934, Prosecutor Spencer Short asked for a second continuance in the prosecution of the four rioting cases, and in December he filed papers officially dropping all charges.[1]

Stripped of any authority to represent miners in the district, torn apart by infighting from various factions within the group, with former members frightened away by UMWA loyalty oaths, by threats of litigation or challenges of citizenship, the Western Miners Union faded out of existence in the summer of 1934.

The power of John L. Lewis, his ability to control leadership at the state and local level, and his influence within the Roosevelt Administration and the National Labor Board, overwhelmed the upstart union. Law professor Jim Pope writes, "By early 1934, exit from the UMW was no longer a viable option for union miners. With the cooperation of employers and courts, the UMW had used its quasi-governmental position to withering effect against the alternative unions."[2]

Also crippling the Western Miners movement was the long history of successful agreements between the UMWA and the NWI. Certainly the coal producer desired a reliable source of labor, and its leaders found the demands of the new union leaders to be excessive and unsustainable. So NWI negotiators were strongly disinclined to work with the new union and used every resource, from their sizeable legal staff to their influential political contacts, to crush the movement.

A further factor working against the new union was the political climate of 1933-34. With the focus of the Roosevelt Administration keenly set on getting the economy moving again and negotiating stable wages and prices for energy production, organizations that deterred workers through agitation and strikes rather than acceding to the Recovery Administration's codes were viewed as greedy and unpatriotic at best, un-American and seditious at worst.

By the summer of 1934, gone was the fervor that had fueled the heated picket lines of April. Gone was the fighting spirit that had launched hopes for higher wages and shorter working days. In its place were the realities of life in a rural mountain community in America at the height of an economic depression.

Some Western Miners were hired back months or even years after the strike.[3] Mine superintendent Tom Murphy rehired selectively from among a group that included those who had remained loyal to the UMWA through the strike. But the work crews also included a fair number of men who had joined the ranks of the Western Miners.

Murphy valued loyalty highly and selected men he felt he could trust. He also valued effective labor, and he didn't ignore men who were able to produce. He was aided in his decisions by UMWA leaders who prepared a list of men it considered troublemakers. Years after the strike, community member Charles Rushton recalled the power of that list: "On the list, why, it said this man was okay and the other guy was okay and then there would be one now and then no good. So, it was actually the union that did the hiring back."[4]

Some of those who were not rehired to work for the NWI mines were able to locate work in independent mining operations in the area, but that number was limited. Other men found work in the area's timber industry. But one result of the strike and the NWI decision to downsize its work force was that many Roslyn residents, probably between two and three hundred families, were forced to relocate to jobs in the western part of the state and elsewhere in the months following the strike.

The actions taken on the picket lines and in neighborhoods throughout the upper county—the name-calling, the physical abuse, the threats and taunts—had taken an intense emotional toll in the community as well. Some families who had been close in the past stopped associating altogether. Some who had been good friends and neighbors became embittered enemies. Families who had lived in close proximity for years suddenly disappeared—some even moved out of their homes during the night and were never seen or heard of again in the community.[5]

Clubs that had for years served as meeting places for potlucks and dancing were forced to disband, their leaders unable or unwilling to work together with certain other members of the community.[6]

For other families the strike had less devastating impacts. Many in the community wanted nothing more than to put the whole ugly episode behind them and move on. The Cle Elum *Miner Echo* newspaper heralded the Labor Day 1934 celebration as a milestone that would mark a "brighter day for this field," and to represent a "marked contrast to the skipped celebration a year ago, when the mines of this field were standing still."[7]

The last reference to the Western Miners to be found suggests that some collection of men as well as women of its ladies' auxiliary may have held together for several months after the strike subsided. A political notice was published in an early October 1934 issue of the *Ellensburg Evening Record*: "All county and state political candidates are invited to be present at the next meeting of the Western Miners' union and its ladies' auxiliary at Druid Hall, Roslyn, Wednesday evening at 7:30 o'clock, Andrew Hunter, president, announced today."[8]

The role of women in supporting the strike marked a divergence from earlier labor actions in the district. Women were active in the Western Miners movement from its inception. One reason women may have taken such an aggressive role could be found in the experiences of the families who immigrated to the Northwest. Certainly a woman who was willing to uproot her family from the relative safety of kin and homeland, to travel not only across an ocean but then to embark on another journey across the country to the unknown wilds of the Northwest, would possess an unusual drive and desire for a better life for her family. Such a woman might have less inhibition in fighting for what she believed was necessary for her family's financial security.

The changing social and political climate of the nation was certainly another contributing factor. Women had been granted the right to vote with ratification of the Nineteenth Amendment in 1920. They began to recognize their political clout and influence over national policy with the vote on Prohibition that same year. And in many families, women controlled family finances and held a keen interest in their families' financial success.

John L. Lewis held to a traditional view for the role of women and did not wish to see them involved in the fight for miners' rights, so he avoided instituting a women's auxiliary for the UMWA.[9] Groups such as the Progressive Miners of America in Illinois and the Western Miners in Roslyn organized women's auxiliaries that became active participants in the actions of their associated organizations.[10]

The Western Miners leaders were coached in strike tactics by an adviser who had experience in both Illinois and Pennsylvania where strikers had placed women picketers strategically at the front of the picket lines.[11] This strategy placed women in the Western Miners strike at the epicenter of the hostilities. Part of the strategy undoubtedly was to avoid direct fighting as most men of the era might engage with another man but would resist hitting a woman. Women also may have had less to lose and more to gain from confrontational picketing methods. Their jobs were not as directly on the line. Their husbands could remain in back of the most intense fighting and avoid detection or at least deny direct involvement in hostile activities that would get them branded as "no good."

All of the leaders of the Western Miners movement were forced eventually to leave the community. Unable to find work of any kind in the Roslyn area, Western Miners president Andrew Hunter and his family relocated in 1935 to Renton, Washington, where he found employment with the Pacific Car Foundry as an iron worker. Hunter never lost his interest in standing up for worker rights and in later years spoke before state legislative committees representing individuals in worker rights issues.[12] He died in Renton in 1966 at age 83.[13]

Mike Petrovich, the Western Miners vice president, also moved away from the community. Nothing is known of his whereabouts, but state records indicate that he died in 1965. John P. Pasquan, Western Miners secretary-treasurer, worked in coal mines in the western part of the state after leaving Roslyn, and died in the mining community of Ravensdale, Washington, at age 80.[14]

Mark Haller, who had worked for an affiliation between the Western Miners and the Communist National Miners Union, and who had organized among high school students in the Roslyn area to form the Young Communists League, left Roslyn in May 1935 to go to his next assignment in Portland. Years later, Haller offered a bitter assessment of the Western Miners leader Andrew Hunter. "Hunter was a local opportunist who seized an opportunity to head a legitimate grievance. He had no understanding of leadership, solutions to problems and crises; no connections to get support outside of Roslyn, Ronald, and Cle Elum. He was a cardboard leader."[15]

Although Sam Farrimond avoided a prison term in the shooting death of Bob Ruff, his life in Roslyn was far from ideal. Some in the community shunned him for his actions and for what they felt was a travesty of justice.[16] Farrimond chose to use his other family name of Krahenbuhl after the shooting. He suffered the fate of many coal miners, dying of pneumonia just three years after the strike in 1937 at age 37.[17] He is buried in the Roslyn City Cemetery.

Life was not much kinder to Bernard "Bun" Henry. According to county death records, Henry died in 1940, also at age 37.

E. K. Brown continued his law practice in Ellensburg through the 1930s, but he lost a son in World War II, and the loss devastated him to the point that he was unable to continue his law practice after that time.[18] He died at age 76 in 1955.[19]

The damaging effects of the strike remained impressed in the minds of residents for years afterward. Those who remained loyal to the UMWA through the strike were seen by their Western Miners friends as having betrayed a friendship. Once opened, those wounds were slow to heal. It was said of one Croatian man, who had earlier held friendships on both sides of the dispute, that he died "without a friend."[20]

A brother and sister moved into Roslyn after the strike. The brother married into a family that had supported the UMWA and the sister married into a Western Miners family. Neither the brother nor the sister had experienced the strike directly, and they never talked about it through the years. But when the issue did come up nearly sixty years later, the sister was quick to call those who went through the picket lines "scabs," whereupon the brother took exception to the term and held up those miners as loyal to their union. The incident demonstrates how strongly held opinions became part of the thinking of the community, even for those who did not experience it directly.[21]

One wife suffered through the strike of 1934, but when her husband died nearly six years later, she couldn't wait to move from the community, claiming that she just couldn't stand Roslyn any longer. Certainly the strikes and divisions in the community contributed to her decision to leave, a family member believed.[22]

For many families in the Roslyn area, the strike was a forbidden topic of conversation in any social setting for years afterward—no less avoided than politics and religion as sure conversation spoilers. "They even now don't like me as much because I stick up for the miners, I mean the ones that went to work," one Ronald woman recalled. "A long time afterward, this one guy told me he thought the striking miners were right. Well, they thought they were so right, but I don't think they were using their heads."[23]

The selection of burial sites has been impacted by memories of the 1934 strike. Men are buried in Cle Elum because they didn't want to be buried in Roslyn next to a family who had been on the other side of the dispute.[24]

A Cle Elum man recalled the long-term effects of the strike, even after 50 years:

> [During the strike] my dad was going to work at No. 9, and old man Kladnik, he stopped my dad, and they were going to pull him out of the car. My dad had a gun in his seat, and he took a couple shots at 'em and they scattered.
>
> Well then, I was working at the county down here, this was probably about 1985 or so. Old man Kladnik, he was still alive, he come down there one day and he stopped me and he says, "Are you George Turner's son?" and I said, "Yeah." He told me about the deal, and he said that he'd [George Turner Sr.] a killed us. I said, "I don't blame him." I said, "I'd a killed you too."[25]

When citizens of Roslyn decided in 1996 to build a memorial to the area's coal miners, leaders of the project asked community members to purchase a plaque honoring their families to help pay for the memorial. One Roslyn man refused to take part in the project, reportedly because he was concerned that his name might be placed alongside the name of a family from the other side of the 1934 dispute.[26]

In developing this book, I have experienced firsthand some of the tension that has existed in the community for many years. Some of my sources have asked that individual names be withheld to avoid offending family members. I have attempted to use names only with permission or when the names are part of a public record or newspaper account.

A Seattle man who, in the 1990s, became interested in researching the strike, told me that a number of people had advised him against writing an account of the strike. "They told me it would be a no-win situation, that I would make enemies no matter what I wrote."

The Swanson family home on NW "B" Street in Roslyn as it appeared in the late 1950s. The author is building a snowman in the front yard. *Swanson family photo*

My experience has been much more positive. While feelings still exist for some who lived through those momentous events, much of the hostility and anger has given way to forgiveness and an attitude of helpfulness in preserving an accurate accounting of those events. And I am grateful to so many in the communities of Roslyn, Ronald, and Cle Elum who have helped immeasurably in this effort.

Herman Swanson continued to work at the No. 3 mine until his retirement in the late 1930s, and he worked for a short time after in the pensioners' mine—a section of the No. 5 mine reserved for NWI retirees that allowed miners to earn a small income while working at a slower pace. He died of lung cancer in 1948 at 73 years of age.

Anna Swanson survived her husband and lived with her son, Clarence, at the house on NW "B" Street until 1958. She then moved with him to Tacoma where she lived another four years. Her final three years were spent living in a mother-in-law apartment in Portland with my mother, Hannah, and our family. Anna died in 1965 at age 83. She and Herman are buried in the Masonic Cemetery in Roslyn.

Notes

Archives Consulted

NPRC. Corporate Records, 1872-1970, Special Assistant to the President. President's records. Northern Pacific Railway Company records. Minnesota Historical Society, St. Paul, MN.

NWI. Corporate records, 1896-1967, Northwestern Improvement Company. Northern Pacific Railway Company records (Subject Files, 1909-1966). Minnesota Historical Society, St. Paul, MN.

UMWA. United Mine Workers of America, President's Office correspondence with districts, 1898-1983, Pennsylvania State University Archives.

Prologue

1. Hiltzik, Michael A. *The New Deal: A Modern History* (New York: Free Press, 2011).
2. Schwantes, Carlos A. *Radical Heritage: Labor, Socialism, and Reform in Washington and British Columbia, 1885-1917* (Seattle: University of Washington Press, 1979), 29. Rogers, Meryl E. "The Labor Movement in Seattle, 1885-1905" (thesis, Pacific Lutheran University, 1970), 29. Clevinger, Woodrow R. "The Western Washington Cascades: A Study of Migration and Mountain Settlement." (PhD diss., University of Washington, 1955), 96.
3. Green, Stephen H. "Coal Production." *Coal and Coal Mining in Washington. Division of Mines and Geology, Report of Investigations No. 4R* (Olympia, WA: State Printing Plant, 1947), 19-20.
4. Morris, Homer Lawrence. *The Plight of the Bituminous Coal Miner* (Philadelphia: University of Pennsylvania Press, 1934), 1-2.
5. Johnson, James P. *A "New Deal" for Soft Coal: The Attempted Revitalization of the Bituminous Coal Industry under the New Deal* (New York: Arno Press, 1979), 3.
6. Moen, Wayne S. *The Mineral Industry of Washington—Highlights of its Development, 1853-1980* (Olympia, WA: State of Washington Department of Natural Resources, 1982), 18. www.dnr.wa.gov/publications/ger_ic74_min_industry_wa_devel.pdf.
7. Green, "Coal Production," 19-20.
8. Taylor, Edith L., Michael Krings, and Thomas N. Taylor. *Paleobotany: The Biology and Evolution of Fossil Plants* (London: Academic Press, 2009), 18.
9. "The Fireman from the Northern Pacific Railway," *Steamguy's Blog*. steamguy. wordpress.com/2013/07/16/the-fireman-from-the-northern-pacific-railway. The cooler-burning lignite required a larger firebox to generate heat for locomotive power. The Northern Pacific used nearly two dozen Belpaire engines with larger boilers on its rail lines between 1910 and 1940. See Schrenk, Lorenz P., and Robert L. Frey. *Northern Pacific Classic Steam Era* (Mukilteo, WA: Hundman Publishing, 1997). "The Belpaire Firebox." *American-Rails.com.* www.american-rails.

com/belpaire-firebox.html. Llanso, Steve. *Northern Pacific 2-6-6-2 Type Locomotives.* www.steamlocomotive.com/2-6-6-2/?page=np.

10. Green, "Coal Production," 19-20. USEIA, *State Coal Profiles*, 99.

11. Morris, *The Plight of the Bituminous Coal Miner*, 6.

12. Fishback, Price Van Meter. *Soft Coal, Hard Choices: The Economic Welfare of Bituminous Coal Miners, 1890-1930* (New York: Oxford University Press, 1992), 21.

13. Dix, Keith. *What's a Coal Miner to Do? The Mechanization of Coal Mining* (Pittsburgh, PA: University of Pittsburgh Press, 1988).

14. Fishback, *Soft Coal, Hard Choices*, 22.

15. Johnson, James P., *A "New Deal" for Soft Coal*, 4.

16. Fishback, *Soft Coal, Hard Choices*, 23.

17. Schwantes, *Radical Heritage*, 82.

18. LeWarne, Charles Pierce. *Utopias on Puget Sound, 1885-1915* (Seattle: University of Washington Press, 1995).

19. Shannon, David A. *The Socialist Party of America: A History* (New York: Macmillan, 1955), 39.

20. Schwantes, *Radical Heritage*, 89.

21. Debs, Eugene V. *The Left List: Eugene Debs*. www.leftlist.us/?page_id=21.

22. *The Cooperator*, (Burley, WA), July 6, 1901, 1; cited in Gary Seibel, *Squabbling Socialists in Washington State: A Guide to Factions and Newspapers 1900-1917*. Labor Press Project, 2003. depts.washington.edu/labhist/laborpress/squabbling.htm.

23. Dubofsky, Melvyn. *We Shall Be All: A History of the Industrial Workers of the World* (Chicago: Quadrangle Books, 1969), 81.

24. Seibel, *Squabbling Socialists*.

25. Weinstein, James. *The Decline of Socialism in America, 1912-1925* (New York: Monthly Review Press, 1967), 116-18.

26. Shannon, *The Socialist Party of America*, 122.

27. Quoted in Shannon, *The Socialist Party of America*, 122.

28. Ibid., 195-96.

29. Renshaw, Patrick. *The Wobblies: The Story of the IWW and Syndicalism in the United States* (Chicago: Ivan R. Dee, 1999), 21. Kimeldorf, Howard. *Battling for American Labor: Wobblies, Craft Workers, and the Making of the Union Movement* (Berkeley: University of California Press, 1999).

30. "Essay: The I.W.W. in Washington." Centralia Massacre Collection, University of Washington Digital Collections, content.lib.washington.edu/iwwweb/read-IWW.html.

31. Renshaw, *The Wobblies*, 23.

32. Foner, Philip Sheldon. *The Industrial Workers of the World, 1905-1917*. History of the Labor Movement in the United States, vol. 4. (New York: International Publishers, 1973), 147.

33. Rajala, Richard. "A Dandy Bunch of Wobblies: Pacific Northwest Loggers and the Industrial Workers of the World, 1900–1930," *Labor History* 37, no. 2 (1996): 205-34, 219.

34. Dubofsky, *We Shall Be All*.

35. Miller, Grace L. "The I.W.W. Free Speech Fight: San Diego, 1912," *Southern California Quarterly* 54, no. 3 (1972): 211-38.

36. "Riot Death Toll Now 7," *The Tacoma Times*, November 6, 1916, 1. (The report noted that twenty IWW and twenty Everett citizens were wounded.) "Essay: The I.W.W. in Washington."

37. "Essay: The I.W.W. in Washington."

38. Renshaw, *The Wobblies*, 23.

39. Reese, Michael. "The Cold War and Red Scare in Washington: Historical Context." University of Washington, Center for the Study of the Pacific Northwest. www.washington.edu/uwired/outreach/cspn/Website/Classroom Materials/ Curriculum Packets/Cold War & Red Scare/Cold War and Red Scare.html.

40. "Essay: The I.W.W. in Washington."

41. Renshaw, *The Wobblies*, 23.

42. Hathaway, Clarence. "For a Complete Mobilization of the Party for Real Mass Work in the Election Campaign," *Communist: Official Paper of the Communist Party of America* May (1932): 426.

43. Mullins, William H. *The Depression and the Urban West Coast: 1929-1933: Los Angeles, San Francisco, Seattle, and Portland* (Bloomington: Indiana University Press, 1991), 92.

44. Ko, Daeha. "Chapter 2: Rough Beginnings." Communism in Washington State History and Memory Project, 2002. depts.washington.edu/labhist/cpproject/ ko.shtml.

45. Klehr, Harvey. *The Heyday of American Communism: The Depression Decade* (New York: Basic Books, 1984), 6.

46. Lovestone, Jay. "Constitution of the Workers Party of America." *The Party Organization: Workers (Communist) Party of America.* (Chicago: Daily Workers Pub., 1925), 38-39.

47. Ko, *Rough Beginnings*. Dennett, Eugene V. *Agitprop: The Life of an American Working-class Radical: The Autobiography of Eugene V. Dennett*, SUNY Series in American Labor History (Albany: State University of New York Press, 1990).

48. "Red Suspects Jailed on Orders of Mayor Edwards," *Seattle Times*, November 12, 1929, 1.

49. Gunns, Albert F. *Civil Liberties in Crisis: The Status of Civil Liberties in the Pacific Northwest, 1917-1940.* (PhD diss., University of Washington, 1971), 95-96.

50. Black, Gordon. "Chapter 3: Organizing the Unemployed: The Early 1930s." Communism in Washington State History and Memory Project, 2002. depts. washington.edu/labhist/cpproject/black.shtml.

51. Gunns, *Civil Liberties in Crisis*, 123-62.

52. Klehr, *The Heyday of American Communism*, 7-9.

53. *Northern Pacific Railway Historical Association* (2012). www.nprha.org.

54. Johnson, Jeffrey A. *"They Are All Red Out Here": Socialist Politics in the Pacific Northwest, 1895-1925* (Norman: University of Oklahoma Press, 2008), 17.

55. An act to execute certain treaty stipulations relating to the Chinese, May 6, 1882; Enrolled Acts and Resolutions of Congress, 1789-1996; General Records of the United States Government; Record Group 11; National Archives.

56. Wynne, Robert E. "Reaction to the Chinese in the Pacific Northwest and British Columbia." (PhD diss., University of Washington, 1969). Karlin, Jules A. "Anti-Chinese Outbreaks in Seattle, 1885-1886." *Pacific Northwest Quarterly* 39 (1948): 103-30.

57. Foner, Eric, and John A. Garraty, editors. "Knights of Labor." *The Reader's Companion to American History* (Boston: Houghton Mifflin Harcourt, 1991). Cited at www.history.com/topics/knights-of-labor.

58. Taft, Philip. "The Knights of Labor." *Organized Labor in American History* (New York: Harper & Row, 1964), 84-92. Jeffrey A. Johnson, *"They Are All Red Out Here,"* 21. Foner and Garraty, "Knights of Labor."

59. Schwantes, *Radical Heritage*, 25.

60. "The Knights Will Fight: So Bailey Says of the Northern Pacific Company's Miners." *New York Times*, August 29, 1886.

61. Kershner, Jim. "Roslyn Coalminers Strike, Precipitating the Importation of Black Miners on August 17, 1888." Essay 9240, HistoryLink.org. historylink.org/index.cfm?DisplayPage=output.cfm&file_id=9240.

62. Nick Henderson, interview by author, August 25, 2010.

63. Kershner, "Roslyn Coalminers Strike."

64. Guide to the Northwestern Improvement Company, Field Survey Notebooks, MS 003, Ser. 06-03. Central Washington University Archives, n.d. www.lib.cwu.edu/static/manuscripts/MS003-06-03.htm. "North Pacific Cuts a Big Melon." *New York Times*, November 6, 1908.

65. Dubofsky, *We Shall Be All*, 36-56.

66. Jameson, Elizabeth. *All That Glitters: Class, Conflict, and Community in Cripple Creek* (Urbana: University of Illinois Press, 1998), 179.

67. Suggs, George G. *Colorado's War on Militant Unionism: James H. Peabody and the Western Federation of Miners* (Detroit: Wayne State University Press, 1972), 15.

68. Shideler, John C. *Coal Towns in the Cascades: A Centennial History of Roslyn and Cle Elum, Washington.* (Spokane, WA: Melior Publications, 1986), 80. On coal company fear of IWW organization, see also: Carlson, Linda. *Company Towns of the Pacific Northwest* (Seattle: University of Washington Press, 2003), 190.

69. Morris, James O. "The Acquisitive Spirit of John Mitchell, United Mine Workers President (1899-1908)." *Labor History* (Winter 1979): 5-24.

70. Walsh, Frank P. "Wages vs. Finances." *United Mine Workers Journal* (November 18, 1918): 15.

71. Draper, Theodore. *The Roots of American Communism* (Chicago: Ivan R. Dee, 1989), 61-79.

72. Singer, Alan, "Communists and Coal Miners: Rank-and-File Organizing in the United Mine Workers of America During the 1920s," *Science and Society* 55, no. 2 (1991): 132-57.

73. "John L. Lewis (1880-1969)." AFL-CIO. www.aflcio.org/About/Our-History/Key-People-in-Labor-History/John-L.-Lewis-1880-1969.

74. Nick Henderson.

75. Roberts, Ron. E. *John L. Lewis: Hard Labor and Wild Justice* (Dubuque, IA: Kendall/Hunt, 1994), 123.

76. See, for example, "Dual Unionists, Get an Earful of This." *United Mine Workers Journal* (May 15, 1933): 9.

77. Selekman, Sylvia K. *Rebellion in Labor Unions* (New York: Boni and Liveright, 1924).

78. Singer, "Communists and Coal Miners," 138.

79. Ibid., 146-49.
80. Klehr, *The Heyday of American Communism*, 38.
81. "National Miners Union: Communists and Miners in the Pennsylvania Anthracite, 1928-1931." *Pennsylvania Magazine of History and Biography* (2001).
82. Klehr, *The Heyday of American Communism*, 47, 132.
83. "The National Recovery Administration." Digital History. www.digitalhistory. uh.edu/disp_textbook.cfm?smtID=2&psid=3442.
84. Johnson, James P. *The Politics of Soft Coal: The Bituminous Industry from World War I through the New Deal* (Urbana: University of Illinois, 1979), 169.
85. Davis, Kenneth Sydney. *FDR, the New Deal Years: 1933-1937: A History* (New York: Random House, 1986), 249. Hiltzik, *The New Deal*, 130.
86. Davis, *FDR, the New Deal Years*, 250.
87. Hiltzik, *The New Deal*, 262.
88. *Schechter Poultry Corp. v. U.S.* 295 U.S. 495. 1935.
89. Hiltzik, *The New Deal*, 262.
90. Ibid., 275.
91. U.S. Department of Commerce. Bureau of the Census. *Historical Statistics of the United States: Colonial Times to 1970* (Washington, DC: Government Printing Office, 1975), 179.
92. Bernstein, Irving. *Turbulent Years: A History of the American Worker, 1933-1941* (Boston: Houghton Mifflin, 1970). Davin, Eric L. "The Very Last Hurrah? The Defeat of the Labor Party Idea, 1934-36" in *"We Are All Leaders": The Alternative Unionism of the Early 1930s*, ed. Staughton Lynd (Urbana: University of Illinois Press, 1996), 125.

Chapter 1. Unhappy Days

1. See Alter, Jonathan. *The Defining Moment: FDR's Hundred Days and the Triumph of Hope* (New York: Simon & Schuster, 2006).
2. Bird, Caroline. *The Invisible Scar* (New York: Longman, 1978), 59.
3. Lange, Greg. "Washington Governor Martin Closes Banks on March 3, 1933." Essay 2057, HistoryLink.org. www.historylink.org/index.cfm?DisplayPage= output.cfm&file_id=2057.
4. "Nation Moves To Issue Scrip for Quick Relief." *Ellensburg Evening Record*, March 6, 1933, 1.
5. Roosevelt, Franklin D. "Franklin D. Roosevelt's First Fireside Chat." www. infoplease.com/ipa/A0900146.html. American Rhetoric: Franklin Delano Roosevelt—First Fireside Chat ("The Banking Crisis"). www.americanrhetoric.com/ speeches/fdrfirstfiresidechat.html.
6. Green, Stephen H. *Coal and Coal Mining in Washington*. Division of Mines and Geology, Report of Investigations No. 4R (Olympia, WA: State Printing Plant, 1947), 5.
7. Dembo, Jonathan. *Unions and Politics in Washington State, 1885-1935.* (New York: Garland Publishing, 1983), 566. Browitt, David. "Roslyn History Lecture 7—Coal Mining." Roslyn History Lecture Series. Roslyn Public Library, Roslyn, Washington. January 27, 2002. www.washingtonruralheritage.org/cdm/singleitem/ collection/roslyn/id/474/rec/6.

8. Dembo, *Unions and Politics,* 566; "Miners Back On Job Today After Long Idle Period." *Ellensburg Evening Record*, October 26, 1933, 1.
9. "Grand Coulee Dam: Find Facts, History and Other Information about the Grand Coulee Dam." Grand Coulee Dam Motels & Vacation Information. grandcouleedam.com/gcda/GCD/grandcouleedam/grandcouleedam. htm.
10. Browitt, "Roslyn History Lecture 7."
11. Ibid.
12. Sign in the Roslyn Museum miners collection. Roslyn, WA.
13. Fishback, Price Van Meter. *Soft Coal, Hard Choices: The Economic Welfare of Bituminous Coal Miners, 1890-1930* (New York: Oxford University Press, 1992), 42-44.
14. 1930 U.S. Census, Kittitas County.
15. Shideler, John C. *Coal Towns in the Cascades: A Centennial History of Roslyn and Cle Elum, Washington* (Spokane, WA: Melior Publications, 1986).
16. Hunter, Andrew. "Open Forum—Hunter's Statement on Western Miners' Union of America." *Miner Echo* [Cle Elum, WA], December 22, 1933, 1.
17. UMWA Provisional District 10—Situation Report (October 1933). UMW Pres-Dist Dist 10, Box 47, Folder 39, District 10 Correspondence 1933 Re: Contract. UMWA.
18. Fishback, *Soft Coal, Hard Choices,* 23.
19. McDonald, David J., and Edward Anthony Lynch. *Coal and Unionism: A History of the American Coal Miners' Unions* (Silver Spring, MD: Cornelius Printing, 1939), 192.
20. "Six-hour Day and Five-Day Work Week Proposed in a Bill Introduced in United States Senate." *United Mine Workers Journal* 46, no. 3 (February 1, 1933): 3-5.
21. Newman, Roger K. *Hugo Black: A Biography* (New York: Pantheon, 1994), 159.

Chapter 2. Spring of Discontent

1. John Ferro, interview by author, June 26, 2009.
2. Joe Nieland, interview by author, June 26, 2009.
3. Robert Panerio, telephone interview by author, July 29, 2009. "Andrew Hunter Obituary," *Seattle Times,* March 22, 1966, 43.
4. Laslett, John H. M. "Swan Song or New Social Movement? Socialism and Illinois District 12, United Mine Workers of America, 1919-1926," in *Socialism in the Heartland: The Midwestern Experience, 1900-1925,* ed. Donald T. Critchlow (Notre Dame, IN: University of Notre Dame, 1986), 167-214, 170.
5. Fivek, Karl W. "From Company Town to Miners Town, Spring Valley: 1885-1905" (Certificate of Advanced Study thesis, Northern Illinois University, 1976), 34.
6. Laslett, John H. M. "Swan Song or New Social Movement?," 171.
7. See Mark Haller, letter to Richard Major, January 15, 1992, personal property of Richard L. Major, Seattle, WA. Haller states that Hunter favored the Progressive Miners' Union of southern Illinois. See also William Cole, letter to Clarence Martin, Washington State Governor, May 4, 1934, Washington State Archives, Olympia, WA, where Cole states that strikers in Roslyn followed methods used in Illinois and Pennsylvania and had one of the Pennsylvania organizers dictating the methods to be used in the strike.

8. Zieger, Robert H. *John L. Lewis: Labor Leader* (Boston: Twayne, 1988), 50.
9. Roberts, Ron E. *John L. Lewis: Hard Labor and Wild Justice* (Dubuque, IA: Kendall/Hunt, 1994), 127.
10. "Four Minor Parties Go Through Motion; Nominate and Adopt." *Seattle Daily Times,* September 12, 1928, 8. "Burch, Seattle, Liberty Party's Senate Nominee." *Seattle Daily Times,* September 14, 1932, 5.
11. "District 10 Active: Gets New Mining Laws and Fuel Statute for Washington." *United Mine Workers Journal* 46, no. 7 (April 1, 1933): 7.
12. Washington State Hospital Association. "A Century of Service: 1858-1958." 1958. Seattle, WA. www.wsha.org/files/62/CenturyofService.pdf.
13. "District 10 Active."
14. *UMWA Provisional District 10 Situation Report. October 1933.* Rep. UMW Pres-Dist Dist 10, Box 47, Folder 39, District 10 Correspondence 1933 Re: Contract. UMWA.
15. McAuliffe, Eugene, President, Union Pacific Coal Co., Omaha, NE. Letter to John L. Lewis, September 25, 1933. UMW Pres-Dist Dist 10, Box 47, Folder 39, District 10 Correspondence 1933 Re: Contract. UMWA.
16. Wilma, David. "Hunger Marchers Demand Relief from the Washington State Legislature on January 17, 1933." HistoryLink.org. January 24, 2003. www.historylink.org/index.cfm?DisplayPage=output.cfm&file_id=5106.
17. Session Laws of the State of Washington, 23rd Session, January 9 to March 9, 1933. books.google.com.
18. Photo Archives, Roslyn Museum. Roslyn, WA.
19. Murray, Charles A., letter to L. B. daPonte, March 13, 1933. Northern Pacific Railway Archives. Minnesota History Center, St. Paul, MN.
20. Murphy, Thomas, letter to Clarence D. Martin, March 14, 1933. Northern Pacific Railway Archives. Minnesota History Center, St. Paul, MN.
21. Session Laws of the State of Washington, 23rd Session, January 9 to March 9, 1933. books.google.com.
22. Zieger, *John L. Lewis*, 63.
23. Clemente, Joe, letter to John L. Lewis, May 2, 1933. UMW Pres-Dist Dist 10, Box 47, Folder 36, District 10 Correspondence Oct-Dec 1933. UMWA.
24. Hughes, J. M., letter to Charles Donnelly, June 10, 1933. NWI.
25. *UMWA Provisional District 10 Situation Report. October 1933.* Rep. UMW Pres-Dist Dist 10, Box 47, Folder 39, District 10 Correspondence 1933 Re: Contract. UMWA.
26. Ibid.
27. Cohen, Adam. *Nothing to Fear: FDR's Inner Circle and the Hundred Days That Created Modern America* (New York: Penguin, 2009), 281.
28. Section 7a, National Industrial Recovery Act.
29. Kennedy, David M. *Freedom from Fear: The American People in Depression and War, 1929-1945* (New York: Oxford University Press, 1999), 296.
30. Dix, Keith. *What's a Coal Miner to Do? The Mechanization of Coal Mining* (Pittsburgh, PA: University of Pittsburgh, 1988).
31. McDonald, David J., and Edward Anthony Lynch. *Coal and Unionism: A History of the American Coal Miners' Unions* (Silver Spring, MD: Cornelius Printing, 1939), 196.
32. McDonald and Lynch, *Coal and Unionism*, 200.

33. Later to become Central Washington University.
34. Browitt, David. "Roslyn History Lecture 7: Coal Mining." Roslyn History Lecture Series. Roslyn Public Library, Roslyn, WA. January 27, 2002. www.washingtonruralheritage.org/cdm/singleitem/collection/roslyn/id/474/rec/6.
35. Dubofsky, Melvyn. *John L. Lewis: A Biography*. (New York: Quadrangle/The New York Times Book Co., 1977, 187.
36. "Idle Miners Greet State Labor Envoys." *Ellensburg Evening Record*, July 10, 1933, 1.
37. "Soft Coal Operators Threatened With 'Big Stick' Unless Code Agreement Is Reached." *United Mine Workers Journal* 46, no. 14 (July 15, 1933): 3.
38. "Mine Delegation Seek County Aid During Wage Talk." *Ellensburg Evening Record*, July 19, 1933, 1.
39. "Coal Miners Ask New Hearing on Relief Question." *Ellensburg Evening Record*, August 4, 1933, 1.
40. "Cut Off All Jobless Aid." *Voice of Action* [Seattle], August 28, 1933, 3.
41. "Highlights in the Coal Codes Hearing." *United Mine Workers Journal* 46, no. 16 (August 15, 1933): 3.
42. Kennedy, *Freedom from Fear*, 183.
43. "Fireside Chats of Franklin D. Roosevelt." *On the Purposes and Foundations of the Recovery Program*. July 24, 1933. www.mhric.org/fdr/fdr.html.
44. Hughes, J. M., letter to D. R. Swem. August 7, 1933. NWI.
45. Dubofsky, *John L. Lewis*, 188; "Highlights in the Coal Codes Hearing," 3.
46. Carnes, Cecil. *John L. Lewis: Leader of Labor* (New York: Robert Speller Publishing, 1936), 141-42.
47. Dubofsky, *John L. Lewis*, 187; Kennedy, *Freedom from Fear*, 297.
48. Quoted in Dubofsky, *John L. Lewis*, 188.
49. "Coal Miners Ask 30-Hour Week, $5 Basic Daily Wage," *Ellensburg Evening Record*, August 9, 1933, 1.
50. "U.S. Will Boycott Firms Refusing to Support NRA Code." *Ellensburg Evening Record*, August 9, 1933, 1.
51. "NRA About Ready to Use More Than Gentle Persuasion." *Ellensburg Evening Record*, August 12, 1933, 1.
52. "F.D.R. Wants Blue Eagle on Coal and Steel by Saturday." *Ellensburg Evening Record*, August 18, 1933, 1.
53. Nicholls, Sam, telegram to John Bator, Secretary, Local Union No. 2583, August 12, 1933. Property of author.

Chapter 3. Battle of Ideologies

1. "Strike Hits Mines, Mill, Orchards." *Voice of Action* [Seattle], August 28, 1933, 1.
2. UMWA Provisional District 10—Situation Report (October 1933). UMW Pres-Dist Dist 10, Box 47, Folder 39, District 10 Correspondence 1933 Re: Contract. UMWA.
3. "NMU Organizes in New Mexico." *Mining Notes* (August 1933): 5.
4. See *United Mine Workers Journal* 46, no. 10 (May 15, 1933): 1.

5. "Dual Unionists, Get an Earful of This." *United Mine Workers Journal* 46, no. 10 (May 15, 1933): 9.
6. "Communist Party USA." *Communist Party of Washington State Brief History.* www.cpusa.org/communist-party-of-washington-state-brief-history.
7. Klehr, Harvey. *The Heyday of American Communism: The Depression Decade* (New York: Basic, 1984), 4.
8. Ibid., see chapter 7.
9. "Companies Made Millions: Miners Starved." *Mining Notes* (August 1933): 4.
10. Wilma, David. "Hunger Marchers Demand Relief from the Washington State Legislature on January 17, 1933." HistoryLink.org.
11. Dubofsky, Melvyn. *We Shall Be All: A History of the Industrial Workers of the World* (Chicago: Quadrangle Books, 1969).
12. Anderson, C. C., letter to Thomas Cooper, August 16, 1919. Northern Pacific Railway Records, Corporate Records 1861-1970. Minnesota History Center, St. Paul, MN.
13. Ibid.
14. "LAWS Digital Collection—The I.W.W. in the Pacific Northwest." UW Libraries Digital Collections. content.lib.washington.edu/lawsweb/iww.html.
15. Cole, William, letter to Clarence Martin, May 13, 1933. Washington State Patrol, Washington State Archives, Olympia, WA.
16. "And as soon as equality is achieved for all members of society in relation to ownership of the means of production, that is, equality of labor and wages, humanity will inevitably be confronted with the question of advancing further, from formal equality to actual equality, i.e., to the operation of the rule 'from each according to his ability, to each according to his needs.'" Lenin, Vladimir I. "Introduction." *State and Revolution* (Washington, DC: Regnery Publishing, 2009).
17. Hughes, J. M., letter to Charles Donnelly. November 20, 1933. NWI.
18. "Washington Miners Strike!" *Voice of Action* [Seattle], August 21, 1933, 1.
19. Ibid.
20. Steele, Sr., Walter, letter to John L. Lewis, September 9, 1933. UMW Pres-Dist Dist 10, Box 47, Folder 38, District 10 Correspondence 1933 Re: Dual Union Matters. UMWA.
21. "Dobbins Offers Support of Organized Unemployed." *Voice of Action* [Seattle], August 21, 1933, 3.

Chapter 4. Fevered Pitch

1. "Eyes of Nation on State Today—Wash Is 24th State to Vote on Repeal of 18th Amendment Prohibiting Alcohol." *Ellensburg Evening Record*, August 29, 1933, 1.
2. "F.D.R. Wants Blue Eagle on Coal and Steel by Saturday." *Ellensburg Evening Record*, August 18, 1933, 1.
3. Nicholls, Sam, telegram to John L. Lewis, August 19, 1933. UMW Pres-Dist Dist 10, Box 47, Folder 35, District 10 Correspondence Aug-Sep 1933. UMWA.
4. Smethurst, Walter, letter to John L. Lewis, August 27, 1933. UMW Pres-Dist Dist 10, Box 47, Folder 35, District 10 Correspondence Aug-Sep 1933. UMWA.

5. Nicholls, Sam, telegram to John L. Lewis, August 26, 1933. UMW Pres-Dist Dist 10, Box 47, Folder 35, District 10 Correspondence Aug-Sep 1933. UMWA.

6. Lewis, John L., telegram to Roslyn Cascade Coal Co., South Bellingham, WA, August 22, 1933. UMW Pres-Dist Dist 10, Box 47, Folder 35, District 10 Correspondence Aug-Sep 1933. UMWA.

7. www.genealogy.com.

8. Smethurst, Walter, letter to John L. Lewis, September 10, 1933. UMW Pres-Dist Dist 10, Box 47, Folder 39, District 10 Correspondence 1933 Re: Contract. UMWA.

9. "Mires and Hunter Named Delegates for State Repeal." *Ellensburg Evening Record*, August 31, 1933, 1.

10. Swem, D. R., telegram to John L. Lewis, September 1, 1933. UMW Pres-Dist Dist 10, Box 47, Folder 35, District 10 Correspondence, Aug-Sep 1933. UMWA.

11. McDonald, David J., and Edward Anthony Lynch. *Coal and Unionism: A History of the American Coal Miners' Unions* (Silver Spring, MD: Cornelius Printing, 1939), 198.

12. "NRA Works to Cinch Coal Code; Push Retail Pact." *Ellensburg Evening Record*, August 29, 1933, 1. "Coal Code Nears Accord Today in Final Conference." *Ellensburg Evening Record*, September 7, 1933, 1. "Reaction of Coal Industry to Code is Watched Today." *Ellensburg Evening Record*, September 8, 1933, 1. "Thousands March in NRA Parade." *Ellensburg Evening Record*, September 13, 1933, 1. "Coal Code Accord Deadline is Set by Roosevelt Today." *Ellensburg Evening Record*, September 15, 1933, 1. "Johnson Seeks Roosevelt Stick in Coal Squabble." *Ellensburg Evening Record*, September 16, 1933, 1. "Roosevelt Acts to End Deadlock on Coal Code." *Miner Echo* [Cle Elum, WA], September 8, 1933, 1.

13. "Mine Strike is Protest to Delay in Signing Code." *Ellensburg Evening Record*, September 13, 1933, 1.

14. District No. 10 United Mine Workers of America. September 5, 1933. Minutes, Exec. Board Meeting. UMW Pres-Dist Dist 10, Box 47, Folder 35, District 10 Correspondence Aug-Sep 1933. UMWA.

15. Hughes, J. M., letter to Charles Donnelly, September 2, 1933. NWI.

16. Kennedy, David M. *Freedom from Fear: The American People in Depression and War, 1929-1945* (New York: Oxford University Press, 1999), 150-51.

17. Lewis, John L., telegram to Walter Smethurst, September 25, 1933. UMW Pres-Dist Dist 10, Box 47, Folder 39, District 10 Correspondence 1933 Re: Contract. UMWA.

18. "Roosevelt Signs Soft Coal Code; Labor is Favored." *Ellensburg Evening Record*, September 19, 1933, 1.

19. This imagined conversation is based on facts discussed in a teletype conversation between L. B. daPonte and B. W. Scandrett, September 11, 1933. NWI.

20. daPonte, L. B., letter to W. E. Coman, April 25, 1933. Hughes, J. M., letter to B. W. Scandrett. May 27, 1933. Both in NWI.

21. Teletype conversation between L. B. daPonte and B. W. Scandrett.

22. The event is described in: "Roslyn Miners Defy National Board Big Shot." *Voice of Action* [Seattle], September 25, 1933, 1.

23. Ibid.

24. Smethurst, Walter, letter to John L. Lewis, September 20, 1933. UMW Pres-Dist Dist 10, Box 47, Folder 39, District 10 Correspondence 1933 Re: Contract. UMWA.

25. "Mine Firm Wins Law Injunction." *Ellensburg Evening Record,* September 26, 1933, 1+.

26. Ibid., 4.

27. "Court Passes Death Sentence on Wn. Miners." *Voice of Action* [Seattle], October 9, 1933, 1.

28. "Background of Labor Disputes Fought in Trial." *Ellensburg Evening Record,* February 17, 1934, 1.

29. "Assault Roslyn Girl." *Ellensburg Capital,* July 23, 1925, 1. "Bun Henry, Fighter, Wanted by Police." *Ellensburg Evening Record,* July 25, 1925, 1.

30. "Trial of Roslyn Trio Nears End; To Jury By 5 P.M." *Ellensburg Evening Record,* December 5, 1925, 1.

31. *State v. Henry,* 143 Wash. 39, 254 Pac. 460 (1927). Bernard Henry, Corrections Department, Penitentiary Commitment Registers, 1887-1945. Washington State Archives. www.digitalarchives.wa.gov.

32. "Bud Henry Wins Decision Over Calder in Roslyn." *Ellensburg Evening Record,* January 21, 1933, 1. "Bun Henry Boxer." *BoxRec Boxing Records.* boxrec.com/ list_bouts.php?human_id=90525&cat=boxer.

33. Clyde Fisher, transcribed interview in "Mining Union Disputes in Roslyn, 1934." *Voices of Washington State: Discussion Guides,* Ed. Judith C. Espinola (Seattle, WA: Metrocenter YWCA, 1980.

34. "Background of Labor Disputes Fought in Trial." *Ellensburg Evening Record,* February 17, 1934, 1. It should be noted that this version of the encounter is based solely on testimony given by Henry at the Sam Farrimond murder trial. Ruff did not have the opportunity to present his version of these accounts.

35. "Defense Witness Gives 'Surprise' Story of Killing." *Ellensburg Evening Record,* February 19, 1934, 2.

36. Ibid.

Chapter 5. Tapping the Ceiling

1. Nick Henderson, interview by author, August 25, 2010.

2. Smethurst, Walter, letter to John L. Lewis, October 4, 1933. UMW Pres-Dist Dist 10, Box 47, Folder 39, District 10 Correspondence 1933 Re: Contract. UMWA.

3. Ibid.

4. Smethurst, Walter, letter "To Officers and Members of Local Unions in Roslyn Field," September 30, 1933. UMW Pres-Dist Dist 10, Box 47, Folder 39, District 10 Correspondence 1933 Re: Contract. UMWA.

5. Smethurst, Walter, letter to John L. Lewis, October 10, 1933. UMW Pres-Dist Dist 10, Box 47, Folder 39, District 10 Correspondence 1933 Re: Contract. UMWA.

6. "An Economic Loss" [Editorial]. *Miner Echo* [Cle Elum, WA], October 6, 1933, 4.

7. "Roosevelt Demands Coal Peace." *Seattle Times,* October 8, 1933, 1; "Roosevelt Warns Capital, Labor to Cease Quarreling." *Seattle Times,* October 8, 1933, 3. "Roosevelt Scans Coal Field; Asks Work Resumed." *Seattle Times,* October 9, 1933, 1. "Anti-Strike Law Threat is Made to Curb Unions." *Seattle Times,* October

11, 1933, 1. "Strikes Lose Federal Relief if Unjustified." *Seattle Times,* October 14, 1933, 3.

8. Swem, D. R., telegram to J. M. Hughes, October 10, 1933. NPRC.
9. Swem, D. R., telegram to J. M. Hughes, October 14, 1933. NPRC.
10. Nicholls, S., telegram to John L. Lewis, October 13, 1933. Lewis, John L., telegram to Sam Nicholls, UMWA Dist. 10 President, October 13, 1933. Lewis, John L., telegram to Walter Smethurst. October 13, 1933. All in UMW Pres-Dist Dist 10, Box 47, Folder 39, District 10 Correspondence 1933 Re: Contract. UMWA.
11. Smethurst, Walter, letter to John L. Lewis, October 13, 1933. UMW Pres-Dist Dist 10, Box 47, Folder 39, District 10 Correspondence 1933 Re: Contract. UMWA.
12. Lewis, John L. UMWA Revocation of District 10 Charter. October 18, 1933. UMW Pres-Dist Dist 10, Box 47, Folder 36, District 10 Correspondence Oct-Dec 1933. UMWA.
13. Smethurst, Walter. Situation Report. Undated. UMW Pres-Dist Dist 10, Box 47, Folder 39, District 10 Correspondence 1933 Re: Contract. UMWA.
14. Lewis, John L., letter to Walter Smethurst, October 21, 1933. UMW Pres-Dist Dist 10, Box 47, Folder 38, District 10 Correspondence 1933 Re: Dual Union Matters, UMWA.
15. "President United Mine Workers Decrees Provisional District." *Miner Echo* [Cle Elum, WA], October 20, 1933, 1.
16. "Strike Monday, Oct 30!" *Voice of Action* [Seattle], October 23, 1933, 1.
17. Smethurst, Walter. Situation Report. Undated. UMW Pres-Dist Dist 10, Box 47, Folder 39, District 10 Correspondence 1933 Re: Contract. UMWA.
18. Swem, D. R., telegram to John L. Lewis, October 23, 1933. UMW Pres-Dist Dist 10, Box 47, Folder 39, District 10 Correspondence 1933 Re: Contract. UMWA.
19. "550 Roslyn Miners Vote to Work; Cle Elum Will Ballot on Issue Tonight." *Ellensburg Evening Record,* October 25, 1933, 1.
20. Hughes, J. M., telegram to D. R. Swem. October 24, 1933. NWI.
21. Swem, D. R., telegram to J. M. Hughes., October 24, 1933. NPRC.
22. "Roslyn Miners Back at Work—Defy Lewis." *Voice of Action* [Seattle], October 30, 1933, 1.
23. "Miners Back on Job Today After Long Idle Period." *Ellensburg Evening Record,* October 26, 1933, 1.
24. Hughes, J. M., letter to Charles Donnelly, October 27, 1933. NPRC.

Chapter 6. Go West

1. A meeting of members from a larger convention who secede and organize their own convention elsewhere.
2. "Call Miners Meeting to Fight Lewis." *Voice of Action* [Seattle], November 6, 1933, 1.
3. Haller, Mark, letter to Richard Major, January 15, 1992. Personal property of Richard L. Major, Seattle, WA.

4. Cole, William, letter to Clarence D. Martin, September 23, 1933. Washington State Patrol, Communist Activities—1933-34, Washington State Archives, Olympia, WA.
5. Haller, Mark. "Miners Split Away from Corrupted UMWA Machine." *Voice of Action* [Seattle], November 20, 1933, 1.
6. Smethurst, Walter, letter to John L. Lewis, November 16, 1933. UMW Pres-Dist Dist 10, Box 47, Folder 38, District 10 Correspondence 1933 Re: Dual Union Matters. UMWA.
7. "Recovery Act Carnival Will Open Tuesday." *Seattle Times*, November 12, 1933, 8.
8. "'Great Black Blizzard' 1st Great Dust Storm in Great Plains." November 11 in History. www.brainyhistory.com/events/1933/november_11_1933_92412.html.
9. Haller, "Miners Split Away."
10. Smethurst, Walter, letter to John L. Lewis, November 16, 1933. UMW Pres-Dist Dist 10, Box 47, Folder 38, District 10 Correspondence 1933 Re: Dual Union Matters. UMWA.
11. The *Voice of Action* identified the speaker as A. Booth. But the *Industrial Worker*, November 22, 1932, p. 3, identifies an Arthur Boose as a Portland orator and IWW organizer who had visited the Roslyn area in 1932.
12. Haller, letter to Richard Major.
13. "Red Scare in Washington State." Communism in Washington State History and Memory Project. depts.washington.edu/labhist/cpproject/redscare.shtml.
14. Digital History. www.digitalhistory.uh.edu/database/article_display.cfm?HHID =228.
15. Hughes, J. M., letter to Charles Donnelly, November 20, 1933. NWI.
16. Smethurst, Walter, telegram to John L. Lewis, November 14, 1933. UMW Pres-Dist Dist 10, Box 47, Folder 38, District 10 Correspondence 1933 Re: Dual Union Matters. UMWA.
17. McAuliffe, Eugene, telephone message to John L. Lewis, November 14, 1933. UMW Pres-Dist Dist 10, Box 47, Folder 38, District 10 Correspondence 1933 Re: Dual Union Matters. UMWA.
18. Lewis, John L., telegram to Walter Smethurst, November 14, 1933. UMW Pres-Dist Dist 10, Box 47, Folder 38, District 10 Correspondence 1933 Re: Dual Union Matters. UMWA.
19. George Turner, interview by author, June 18, 2011.
20. Angie Briski, interview by author, May 28, 2011. Lea Beardsley, interview by author, June 16, 2011.
21. Charles Rushton, transcribed interview in *Voices of Washington State: Discussion Guides*, Ed. Judith C. Espinola (Seattle, WA: Metrocenter YWCA, 1980).
22. "Mine Workers Union Absolves Men of Charges." *Miner Echo* [Cle Elum, WA], December 1, 1933, 1.
23. Ferns, J. R., letter to Philip Murray, UMWA Vice President. December 19, 1933. UMW Pres-Dist Dist 10, Box 47, Folder 38, District 10 Correspondence 1933 Re: Dual Union Matters. UMWA.
24. Ferns, J. R., letter to Philip Murray, UMWA Vice President, December 22, 1933. UMW Pres-Dist Dist 10, Box 47, Folder 38, District 10 Correspondence 1933 Re: Dual Union Matters. UMWA.

25. "Mine Union Hall Dispute Settled." *Ellensburg Evening Record,* December 20, 1933, 1.
26. "Open Forum—Hunter's Statement on Western Miners' Union of America." *Miner Echo* [Cle Elum, WA], December 22, 1933, 1.
27. "Open Forum—Fontecchio Makes Public Statement on Mine Status." *Miner Echo* [Cle Elum, WA], December 22, 1933, 1.
28. Nick Henderson, interview by author, August 26, 2010.
29. "Cle Elum Man Fatally Shot." *Ellensburg Evening Record,* December 26, 1933, 1.

Chapter 7. Murder at Christmas

1. "Obituary—Robert Ruff." *Ellensburg Evening Record,* December 29, 1933, 3.
2. Farrimond was an adopted child and used both the name Farrimond and Krahenbuhl at various times in his life. He is buried in the Roslyn Cemetery with the name "Sam Jack Krahenbuhl" on his gravestone.
3. "Cle Elum Man Fatally Shot." *Ellensburg Evening Record,* December 26, 1933, 1.
4. "Funeral Services—Robert Ruff." *Ellensburg Evening Record,* January 2, 1934, 3.
5. "Lewis Thug Kills Militant Wn. Miner." *Voice of Action* [Seattle], January 1, 1934, 1.
6. Ibid.
7. Joe Neiland, interview by author, June 26, 2009.
8. Clyde Fisher, transcribed interview in "Mining Union Disputes in Roslyn—1934." *Voices of Washington State: Discussion Guides.* Ed. Judith C. Espinola (Seattle, WA: Metrocenter YWCA, 1980).
9. "Witnesses State Farrimond Drunk When Shot Fired." *Ellensburg Evening Record,* February 16, 1934, 1.
10. McAuliffe, Eugene, letter to John L. Lewis, UMW President, January 27, 1934. UMW Pres-Dist Dist 10, Box 47, Folder 43, District 10 Correspondence 1934 Re: Contract Matters. UMWA.
11. "Washington Rural Heritage: Ellensburg Heritage Collection." Washington State Library. washingtonruralheritage.org.
12. "Spencer Short Enters Race for Co. Prosecutor." *Ellensburg Evening Record,* July 11, 1930, 1.
13. Barto, Harold E., and Catharine Bullard. *History of the State of Washington.* Vol. 3. (Boston: C.C. Heath and Co, 1947), 19.
14. Sam Talerico, telephone interview by author, November 18, 2010.
15. "Mining Union Disputes in Roslyn—1934," 4.
16. Hughes, J. M., letter to Charles Donnelly, January 10, 1934. NWI.
17. Camilla Saivetto, interview by Steve Addington, June 22, 1976, Frederick Krueger Collection, Central Washington University Archives, Ellensburg, WA.
18. "Lewis Thug Kills Militant Wn. Miner," 1.
19. McAuliffe, Eugene, letter to John L. Lewis. January 27, 1934. UMW Pres-Dist Dist 10, Box 47, Folder 43, District 10 Correspondence 1934 Re: Contract Matters. UMWA.
20. "Labor Troubles Sees Background for Murder Trial [sic]." *Ellensburg Evening Record,* February 14, 1934, 1.
21. *State v. Farrimond,* Kittitas County Superior Court, February 21, 1934. Washington State Archives, Ellensburg, WA.

22. "Witnesses State Farrimond Drunk When Shot Fired." *Ellensburg Evening Record*, February 16, 1934, 4.
23. Ibid.
24. "Witnesses State Farrimond Drunk When Shot Fired," 1.
25. "Background of Labor Disputes Fought in Trial." *Ellensburg Evening Record*, February 17, 1934, 3.
26. Ibid.
27. "Court Cleared of Spectators Till Morning." *Ellensburg Evening Record*, February 16, 1934, 1.
28. "Gangster Beats Haller!" *Voice of Action* [Seattle, WA], February 27, 1934, 4.
29. "Assault Charges Are Dismissed at Hearing." *Miner Echo* [Cle Elum, WA], March 16, 1934, 1.
30. "Background of Labor Disputes Fought in Trial," 3.
31. "Bud [sic] Henry Wins Decision Over Calder in Roslyn." *Ellensburg Evening Record*, January 21, 1933, 1.
32. "Defense Witness Gives 'Surprise' Story of Killing." *Ellensburg Evening Record*, February 19, 1934, 2.
33. "Background of Labor Disputes Fought in Trial," 3.
34. "Defense Witness Gives 'Surprise' Story of Killing," 2.
35. Ibid.
36. "Defense Witness Gives 'Surprise' Story of Killing," 1.
37. Ibid.
38. Ibid.
39. "Defense Witness Gives 'Surprise' Story of Killing," 2.
40. Ibid.
41. "Statement Given Officers Hurled Into Murder Trial." *Ellensburg Evening Record*, February 20, 1934, 3.
42. "Farrimond Freed By Jurors Today in Roslyn Slaying." *Ellensburg Evening Record*, February 21, 1934, 1.
43. "Statement Given Officers Hurled Into Murder Trial," 1.
44. Ibid.
45. Ibid.
46. "Farrimond Freed By Jurors Today in Roslyn Slaying," 1.
47. Ibid.
48. "Farrimond Freed By Jurors Today in Roslyn Slaying," 2.
49. *State v. Farrimond*. Kittitas County Superior Court, February 21, 1934. Washington State Archives, Ellensburg, WA.
50. "Farrimond Freed By Jurors Today in Roslyn Slaying." 1.
51. Ibid.

Chapter 8. Prelude to the Storm

1. "John McGraw, Manager (New York Giants), Dies at 60." February 25 in History. www.brainyhistory.com/events/1934/february_25_1934_92682.html.

2. *Fight the Terror in Roslyn*. Government Exhibit A, Hearing held May 25, 1934. Washington State Archives, Ellensburg, WA.

3. Donnelly, Charles, letter to J. M. Hughes, February 24, 1934. Hughes, J. M., Memorandum, March 20, 1934. NWI.

4. Hunter, Andrew, letter to T. S. Hogan. March 1934. UMW Pres-Dist Dist 10, Box 47, Folder 45, District 10 Correspondence 1934 Re: Contract Matters. UMWA.

5. Ibid.

6. "Radical Responses to the Great Depression—The Case of the Scottsboro Boys." University of Michigan Special Collections Library. www.lib.umich.edu/radical-responses-great-depression/work_page_644.html.

7. "Farrimond Trial Arrouses [sic] Ire of Mine Communists." *Ellensburg Evening Record*, February 27, 1934, 1+.

8. Ibid., 3.

9. *Fight the Terror in Roslyn*.

10. "Miners Ask Secret Ballot on Union Recognition." *Voice of Action* [Seattle], January 1, 1934, 3.

11. Hughes, Ed, Local 2512; A. P. Grimast, Local 1706; Ted Morgan, Local 2510; John Bator, Local 2583; James Thompson, Local 2269, letter to John L. Lewis, November 21, 1934. UMW Pres-Dist Dist 10, Box 47, Folder 43, District 10 Correspondence 1934 Re: Contract Matters. UMWA.

12. Crook, Neal, and Robert Livett, letter to John L. Lewis, January 15, 1934. UMW Pres-Dist Dist 10, Box 47, Folder 43, District 10 Correspondence 1934 Re: Contract Matters. UMWA.

13. Hunter, Andrew [signed by Richard Prescott, Mike Petrovich, Jack Boose, George Gasparich, Joe Lenac, George Mitchell, John P. Pasquan], letter to John L. Lewis, January 5, 1934. UMW Pres-Dist Dist 10, Box 47, Folder 43, District 10 Correspondence 1934 Re: Contract Matters. UMWA.

14. Lewis, John L., letter to Andrew Hunter, February 14, 1934. UMW Pres-Dist Dist 10, Box 47, Folder 43, District 10 Correspondence 1934 Re: Contract Matters. UMWA.

15. Hughes, J. M., "Memorandum" letter, March 20, 1934. NWI.

16. McAuliffe, Eugene, letter to John L. Lewis. January 8, 1934. UMW Pres-Dist Dist 10, Box 47, Folder 43, District 10 Correspondence 1934 Re: Contract Matters. UMWA.

17. McAuliffe, Eugene, letter to John L. Lewis, January 13, 1934. UMW Pres-Dist Dist 10, Box 47, Folder 43, District 10 Correspondence 1934 Re: Contract Matters. UMWA.

18. McAuliffe, Eugene, letter to John L. Lewis, January 27, 1934. UMW Pres-Dist Dist 10, Box 47, Folder 43, District 10 Correspondence 1934 Re: Contract Matters. UMWA.

19. Hughes, J. M., letter to D. R. Swem, January 8, 1934. NWI.

20. Hughes, J. M., letter to D. R. Swem, January 20, 1934. NWI.

21. McAuliffe, Eugene, letter to John L. Lewis, January 25, 1934. UMW Pres-Dist Dist 10, Box 47, Folder 43, District 10 Correspondence 1934 Re: Contract Matters. UMWA.

22. Hughes, J. M., letter to Charles Donnelly, February 12, 1934. NWI.

23. Hughes. J. M., letter to H. E. Stevens, March 21, 1934. NWI.
24. Nicholls, Sam, telegram to John L. Lewis, March 1, 1934. UMW Pres-Dist Dist 10, Box 47, Folder 45, District 10 Correspondence 1934 Re: Contract Matters. UMWA. Lewis, John L., telegram to Sam Nicholls. March 2, 1934. UMW Pres-Dist Dist 10, Box 47, Folder 45, District 10 Correspondence 1934 Re: Contract Matters. UMWA.
25. Nicholls, S., letter to John L. Lewis, March 6, 1934. UMW Pres-Dist Dist 10, Box 47, Folder 43, District Correspondence 1934 Re: Contract Matters. UMWA.
26. "Cole Leads Patrol To Mine Area," *Ellensburg Evening Record*, April 4, 1934, 4.
27. Hughes, J. M., Memorandum, March 5, 1934. NWI.
28. Ibid.
29. Hogan, T. S., telegram to Charles Donnelly, March 14, 1934. Hughes, J. M., telegram to D. R. Swem, March 14, 1934. Both in NWI.
30. Hughes, J. M., Memorandum, March 20, 1934. NWI.
31. Hunter, A., letter to T. S. Hogan, March 6, 1934; W. A. Smethurst letter to T. S. Hogan, March 1934. Both in UMW Pres-Dist Dist 10, Box 47, Folder 45, District 10 Correspondence 1934 Re: Contract Matters. Pennsylvania State University Archives, University Park, PA.
32. Swem, D. R., letter to J. M. Hughes, President NWI, March 24, 1934. NPRC.
33. "District Officers Authorized to Extend Present Contract." *Miner Echo* [Cle Elum, WA], March 23, 1934. 1. "Coal Men Heads Extend Present Union Contract." *Miner Echo* [Cle Elum, WA], March 30, 1934. 1.
34. Swem, D. R., telegram to J. M. Hughes, President NWI, March 24, 1934. NPRC.
35. Hughes, J. M., telegram to D. R. Swem, March 28, 1934. NWI.
36. Hughes, J. M., letter to B. W. Scandrett, March 21, 1934. NWI.
37. "7-Hour Day, Wage Raise Are Ordered for Miners." *Seattle Times*, April 1, 1934, 1.
38. Hughes, J. M., letter to Charles Donnelly, April 2, 1934. NWI.

Chapter 9. The Gauntlet

1. "Miners Nervous As Strike Nears." *Ellensburg Evening Record,* April 2, 1934, 1.
2. Nick Henderson, interview by author, June 26, 2009.
3. Darwin Kanyer, interview by author, August 25, 2010.
4. Angie Briski, interview by author, May 28, 2011.
5. "Mine Strike Starts—Field Quiet." *Ellensburg Evening Record*, April 3, 1934, 1.
6. John and Agnes Ferro, interview by author, June 26, 2009.
7. Angie Briski.
8. "Cole Leads Patrol To Mine Area." *Ellensburg Evening Record,* April 4, 1934, 1, 4.
9. Ibid.
10. "Mine Strike Starts—Field Quiet." *Ellensburg Evening Record*, April 3, 1934, 1.
11. Nick Henderson.
12. Darwin Kanyer.
13. Clyde Fisher, transcribed interview in "Mining Union Disputes in Roslyn—1934." *Voices of Washington State: Discussion Guides*. Ed. Judith C. Espinola (Seattle, WA: Metrocenter YWCA, 1980), 6.
14. "Cole Leads Patrol To Mine Area," 4.

15. "Mine Strike Starts—Field Quiet," 1.
16. Bob Bell, interview by Steve Addington, June 28, 1972, Frederick Krueger Collection, Central Washington University, Ellensburg, WA.
17. "Union Warfare Shuts All Mines in Cle Elum Area." *Seattle Times,* April 4, 1934, 1.
18. "Cle Elum-Roslyn Miners' Unions Lock Horns." *Spokane Spokesman Review,* April 4, 1934, 1.
19. Camilla Saivetto, interview by Steve Addington, June 22, 1976, Frederick Krueger Collection, Central Washington University, Ellensburg, WA.
20. Gus Jaderlund, interview by Steve Addington, October 21, 1975, Frederick Krueger Collection, Central Washington University, Ellensburg, WA.
21. Clyde Fisher, 7.
22. "Mine Strike Starts—Field Quiet," 1.
23. "Coal Fields See Quietest Day in Turbulent Week." *Ellensburg Evening Record,* April 6, 1934, 1.
24. David Browitt, interview by author, August 24, 2010.
25. "Coal Fields See Quietest Day in Turbulent Week," 1.
26. "Cle Elum-Roslyn Miners' Unions Lock Horns," 1.
27. "Mine Strike Starts—Field Quiet," 6.
28. "Mine Strike Starts—Field Quiet," 1.
29. Swem, D. R., letter to J. M. Hughes. April 4, 1934. NPRC.
30. "Seek Roosevelt Aid in Coal Flare; Martin Promises Mine Protection." *Ellensburg Evening Record,* April 7, 1934, 1.
31. "Cole Leads Patrol To Mine Area," 1, 4.
32. John and Agnes Ferro.
33. "State Forces Move to Mine Battle Areas." *Seattle Star,* April 4, 1934, 1.
34. "Relief For Idle Miners Looms." *Ellensburg Evening Record,* April 5, 1934, 1.
35. Darwin Kanyer.
36. "Lead Pipe, Clubs Feature State's Rioting Evidence." *Ellensburg Evening Record,* June 26, 1934, 1. "Jury To Get Riot Case Today; Four Others on Docket." *Ellensburg Evening Record,* June 28, 1934, 1.
37. Swem, D. R., letter to J. M. Hughes, April 4, 1934. NPRC.
38. Swem, D. R., telegram to J. M. Hughes. April 4, 1934. NPRC.

Chapter 10. Tense Waiting

1. "Miners Strike for Recognition." *Voice of Action* [Seattle], April 10, 1934, 1. This reference stated separate buses and classrooms were being provided, but locals in school during the strike could recall no such action.
2. John and Agnes Ferro, interview by author, June 26, 2009.
3. Darwin Kanyer, interview by author, August 25, 2010.
4. "Mine Strike Starts—Field Quiet." *Ellensburg Evening Record,* April 3, 1934, 1, 6.
5. "State Forces Move to Mine Battle Areas." *Seattle Star,* April 4, 1934, 1.
6. "Miners Strike for Recognition," 1.
7. Robert Lawson, telephone interview by author, March 25, 2011.
8. Julia Wallgren, interview by author, June 17, 2011.
9. George Turner Jr., interview by author, June 18, 2011.

10. Lea Beardsley, interview by author, June 16, 2011.
11. "State Police Withdrawn; Mines Close Down." *Miner Echo* [Cle Elum, Wash.], April 6, 1934, 1. "Relief for Idle Miners Looms." *Ellensburg Evening Record,* April 5, 1934, 1.
12. "Relief for Idle Miners Looms," 1.
13. Ibid.
14. "Cle Elum Strife Rouses Fear of Serious Clashes." *Seattle Times,* April 6, 1934, 4.
15. Angie Briski, interview by author, May 28, 2011.
16. "Coal Fields See Quietest Day in Turbulent Week." *Ellensburg Evening Record,* April 6, 1934, 1.
17. Ibid.
18. *State of Washington v. Jane Doe Pasquan.* Kittitas County Superior Court. April 5, 1934. Washington State Archives, Ellensburg, WA.
19. "Coal Fields See Quietest Day in Turbulent Week," 1, 3.
20. *State of Washington v. Helen Pasquan.* April 6, 1934. Bail Bond. Washington State Archives, Ellensburg, WA.
21. "State Police Withdrawn; Mines Closed Down," 1.
22. "Relief for Idle Miners Looms," 1.
23. "Coal Fields See Quietest Day in Turbulent Week," 1.
24. "Code Mediator on Way to Coal Field." *Ellensburg Evening Record,* April 9, 1934, 1.
25. "Cle Elum-Roslyn Miners' Unions Lock Horns." *Spokane Spokesman-Review,* April 4, 1934, 1.
26. "Seek Roosevelt Aid in Coal Flare; Martin Promises Mine Protection." *Ellensburg Evening Record,* April 7, 1934, 1.
27. Swem, D. R., telegram to J. M. Hughes, April 10, 1934. NPRC.
28. Swem, D. R., telegram to J. M. Hughes, April 7, 1934. NPRC.
29. Hogan, T. S., telegram to D. R. Swem, April 8, 1934. NPRC.
30. Scandrett, B. W., telegram to W. E. Coman, April 9, 1934. NWI.
31. "Relief Denied Coal Miners in Cle Elum Area; Mediator on Way to Scene." *Seattle Times,* April 9, 1934, 4. "Code Mediator on Way to Coal Field." *Ellensburg Evening Record,* April 9, 1934, 1. "Coal Fields Await Mediator; Other Chiefs Expected." *Ellensburg Evening Record,* April 10, 1934, 1. "Code Mediator to Advise in Coal Strike." *Ellensburg Capital,* April 13, 1934, 1.
32. "Code Mediator on Way to Coal Field," 1.
33. "Western Miners Parade City in Demonstration." *Miner Echo* [Cle Elum, WA], April 13, 1934, 1.
34. "Code Mediator on Way to Coal Field," 1.
35. Ibid.
36. "E" telegram to W. E. Coman, April 9, 1934. NWI.
37. "Relief Denied Coal Miners in Cle Elum Area." *Seattle Times,* April 9, 1934, 4.
38. Ibid.
39. "State Refuses Relief to Men on Coal Strike." *Seattle Post-Intelligencer,* April 11, 1934, 3.
40. Mires, Austin. Personal diary, April 12, 1934. Austin Mires Papers 1876-1936. Washington State University Archives, Pullman, WA.

41. "Strike Affects Citizenship Test; Judge Holds Up Paper To Probe Mine Activities." *Ellensburg Evening Record,* April 11, 1934, 1-2.
42. Ibid.
43. Swem, D. R., Memorandum, April 16, 1934. NPRC.
44. Ibid.
45. Swem, D. R., letter to J. M. Hughes. April 16, 1934. NPRC.
46. "Coal Factions to Meet Mediator in Seattle Parley." *Ellensburg Evening Record,* April 17, 1934, 1. The *Miner Echo* reported the number of representatives at the meeting as seven. "Coal Labor Board Arrives to Decide Union Jurisdiction." *Miner Echo* [Cle Elum, WA], April 20, 1934, 1. Other documents support the number as ten. D. R. Swem, telegram to J. M. Hughes, April 18, 1934. NPRC. "Report of the Hearing Held by the Bituminous Coal Labor Board Division V," April 20, 1934. NWI.
47. "Cle Elum Mine Decision Will Be Made Here." *Seattle Times,* April 18, 1934, 9.
48. Swem, D. R., telegram to J. M. Hughes, April 19, 1934. NPRC.
49. "Report of the Hearing held by the Bituminous Coal Labor Board Division V," April 20, 1934, 5. NWI.
50. Ibid.
51. Ibid.
52. Ibid.
53. Ibid.

Chapter 11. The Speed Cops

1. "Coal Contract Upheld as Valid." *Ellensburg Evening Record,* April 20, 1934, 1.
2. "New Mine Union Loses; Old Pact is Found Valid." *Seattle Times,* April 20, 1934, 4.
3. Coman, W. E., telegram to B. W. Scandrett, April 21, 1934. NWI.
4. "Coal Mines to Open Wednesday Says NWI Chief." *Ellensburg Evening Record,* April 21, 1934, 1.
5. "Western Miners to Vote on Coal Decision Tuesday." *Ellensburg Evening Record,* April 23, 1934, 1.
6. Ibid.
7. Ibid.
8. "Mines Reopen Under Guard of Highway Patrol." *Ellensburg Evening Record,* April 25, 1934, 1, 4.
9. "Miners Resume Cle Elum Work Without Clash." *Seattle Times,* April 25, 1934, 11.
10. "Majority Union Still Off Job." *Spokane Spokesman-Review,* April 26, 1934, 9.
11. Coman, W. E., letter to B. W. Scandrett, April 27, 1934. NWI.
12. Coman, W. E., telegram to B. W. Scandrett, April 21, 1934. NWI.
13. Aggie Ferro, interview by author, June 26, 2009. Lea Beardsley, interview by author, June 15, 2011.
14. Sam Talarico, interview by author, October 26, 2010.
15. "State Patrol Assembles in Cle Elum as Mines Prepare to Reopen Tomorrow Morning." *Ellensburg Evening Record,* April 24, 1934, 1. "State Patrol Here to Maintain Order." *Miner Echo* [Cle Elum, WA], April 27, 1934, 1.

16. Angie Briski, interview by author, May 28, 2011.
17. "Mines Reopen Under Guard of Highway Patrol," 1.
18. Ibid.; Harry Georgeson, interview by author, May 28, 2011. Georgeson recalled that miners would often take nails from the mines in their lunch pails for personal use.
19. Swem, D. R., telegram to J. M. Hughes, April 25, 1934. NPRC.
20. "Mines Reopen Under Guard of Highway Patrol," 1.
21. Swem, D. R., telegram to J. M. Hughes, April 26, 1934. NPRC.
22. Hughes, J. M., letter to D. R. Swem, April 20, 1934. NWI.
23. "Mines Reopen Under Guard of Highway Patrol," 1.
24. Sam Talarico.
25. "Gas Bombs Route Mine Pickets." *Ellensburg Evening Record*, April 26, 1934, 1.
26. Julia Wallgren, interview by author, June 17, 2011.
27. George Gasparich, interview by Steve Addington, January 6, 1976. Frederick Krueger Collection, Central Washington University, Ellensburg, WA.
28. "Gas Bombs Route Mine Pickets," 1.
29. "Tear Gas Used to Scatter Mob at Cle Elum." *Seattle Daily Times,* April 26, 1934, 8.
30. George Turner Jr., interview by author, June 18, 2011.
31. "Gas Bombs Route Mine Pickets," 1.
32. "Gallagher Defies Roslyn Terror; Committee of Liberals to Enter Field; Strike Cracking Thru Misleadership." *Voice of Action* [Seattle], May 8, 1934, 1.
33. "Tear Gas Used on Picketers." *Seattle Post-Intelligencer,* April 27, 1934, 2.
34. "Battling Wives Keeping Patrol Busy at Mines." *Seattle Times,* April 27, 1934, 13.
35. "2 More Arrests Made in Roslyn Mine Disorders." *Ellensburg Evening Record,* April 28, 1934, 1.
36. Swem, D. R., letter to J. M. Hughes, April 30, 1934. NPRC.
37. UMWA Document of Membership. May 28, 1934. Statement of Joe Glondo renouncing membership in Western Miners Union and rejoining UMWA. Copy in personal collection of author.
38. "2 More Arrests Made in Roslyn Mine Disorders," 3.
39. Ibid., 1.
40. See Digital History. www.digitalhistory.uh.edu/database/article_display.dfm?HHID=445.
41. See "The Trials of The Scottsboro Boys." UMKC School of Law. law2.umkc.edu/faculty/projects/FTrials/scottsboro/scottsb.htm.
42. "Cayton Speaks Tonight." *Seattle Times,* February 2, 1934, 2.
43. Falconer, Sarah. "Seattle Civil Rights and Labor History Project." Communism in Washington State History and Memory Project, 2005. depts.washington.edu/revels-cayton.htm.
44. Hobbs, Richard S. "Chapter 6: The Torch Is Passed." *The Cayton Legacy: An African American Family* (Pullman: Washington State University Press, 2002), 91.
45. See Cole, William. Letter to Clarence D. Martin. October 14, 1933. Washington State Patrol, "Communist Activities—1933-34," Washington State Archives, Olympia, WA.
46. DiBernardo, Mike. "1933 Yakima Valley Trial." The Great Depression in Washington State Project, 2009. depts.washington.edu/depress/yakima_valley.shtml.

47. "Cayton Describes Roslyn Jailing, Lynch Threats; Grilled by Police, Thugs." *Voice of Action* [Seattle], May 8, 1943, 4.
48. Hobbs, Richard S., *Cayton Legacy*, 92.
49. Hugh-Jones, E. M. "A Little Nest of Fascists." *New Republic*, May 30, 1934, 68-69.
50. Cole, William, letter to Clarence Martin, May 4, 1934. Washington State Patrol "Labor Troubles 1934" Washington State Archives, Olympia, WA.
51. "Two Patrolmen are Fired Upon From Ambush." *Miner Echo* [Cle Elum, WA], May 4, 1934, 1.
52. "Coal Area Tense After 2 Ambush Shots at Officers." *Ellensburg Evening Record*, May 1, 1934, 1. "Labor Trouble Is Diminishing." *Ellensburg Capitol*, May 4, 1934, 1.
53. Hughes, J. M., telegram to D. R. Swem, May 3, 1934. NWI.
54. Cole, William, letter to Frank B. Rennie, May 10, 1934. Washington State Patrol, "Labor Troubles Roslyn," Washington State Archives, Olympia, WA.
55. Ibid.
56. "Western Miners Protest Closed Shop Mine Policy." *Ellensburg Evening Record*, May 4, 1934, 1. "Defendant Fined in Justice Court." *Miner Echo* [Cle Elum, WA], May 4, 1934, 1.
57. "Western Miners Protest Closed Shop Mine Policy," 1.
58. Hoke, A. M., letter to W. E. Coman, May 7, 1934. NWI.
59. "Gallagher Defies Roslyn Terror; Committee of Liberals to Enter Field; Strike Cracking Thru Misleadership." *Voice of Action* [Seattle], May 8, 1934, 1.
60. Cole, William, letter to Clarence Martin, May 4, 1934. Washington State Patrol, "Labor Troubles 1934," Washington State Archives, Olympia, WA.
61. Martin, Clarence D., letter to F. M. Martin, May 4, 1934. Gov. Clarence Martin, Personal Correspondence, 1934, Washington State Archives, Pullman, WA.
62. Swem, D. R., letter to J. M. Hughes, May 17, 1934. NPRC.
63. Sam Talerico. George Turner.

Chapter 12. Into the Courts

1. Swem, D. R., letter to J. M. Hughes, May 3, 1934. NPRC.
2. George Turner Jr., interview by author, June 18, 2011.
3. Swem, D. R., telegram to J. M. Hughes, May 4, 1934. NPRC.
4. "Charged With Rioting in Mine Strike Disorders." *Ellensburg Evening Record*, May 9, 1934, 1.
5. "Arrest Many For Rioting." *Ellensburg Capitol*, May 11, 1934, 1.
6. Mrs. George Gasparich, interview by Steve Addington, January 6, 1976, Frederick Krueger Collection, Central Washington University, Ellensburg, WA.
7. Nick Henderson, interview by author, June 26, 2009.
8. "62 Charged With Rioting in Mine Strike." *Miner Echo* [Cle Elum, WA], May 11, 1934, 1. *State of Washington v. Vera Valakovich and Anna Sercesson; State of Washington v. Eino Johnson, et al.; State of Washington v. Mark Haller; State of Washington v. Frances Plesha*. All in Kittitas County Superior Court. May 19, 1934, Washington State Archives, Ellensburg, WA.

9. Brown, E. K., letter to L. B. daPonte, May 11, 1934. NWI.
10. Hughes, J. M. Letter to D. R. Swem. May 25, 1934. NWI.
11. "Striking Coal Miners Accuse State Patrol." *Seattle Daily Times,* May 14, 1934, 3.
12. "Miners Plea for Relief Carried to Hopkins at Capital." *Ellensburg Evening Record,* May 14, 1934, 1.
13. Swem, D. R., letter to J. M. Hughes, May 23, 1934. NPRC.
14. Ibid.
15. Note dated May 21, 1934. NWI.
16. Cole, William, letter to Clarence Martin. May 22, 1934. Washington State Patrol, "Labor Troubles 1934," Washington State Archives, Olympia, WA.
17. "Miners Records Closely Probed in Citizenship Test." *Ellensburg Evening Record,* May 26, 1934, 1.
18. "Dead Mouse in Jail House Mush Charges Roslyn Terror Victim." *Voice of Action* [Seattle], June 8, 1934, 4.
19. Swem, D. R., letter to J. M. Hughes, June 22, 1934. NPRC.
20. Crowley, Walt. "Five IWW Members and Two Deputies Die in a Gunbattle Dubbed the Everett Massacre on November 5, 1916." HistoryLink.org. March 1, 2003. www.historylink.org/index.cfm?DisplayPage=output.cfm&File_Id=5326.
21. "Mine Disorders to Be Aired in Long Court Fight." *Ellensburg Evening Record,* June 25, 1934, 1.
22. Ibid., 1, 2.
23. Ibid., 2.
24. "Lead Pipe, Clubs Feature State's Rioting Evidence." *Ellensburg Evening Record,* June 26, 1934, 2.
25. Ibid.
26. Ibid.
27. Ibid.
28. "Attorney Spends Profitable Noon Hour; Finds Pipe." *Ellensburg Evening Record* June 27, 1934, 1, 3.
29. "Lead Pipe, Clubs Feature State's Rioting Evidence," 1.
30. Ibid.
31. "Attorney Spends Profitable Noon Hour; Finds Pipe," 3.
32. "Jury to Get Riot Case Today; Four Others on Docket." *Ellensburg Evening Record,* June 28, 1934, 1.
33. Ibid., 6.
34. "Vanderveer Waives Plea; Jury Gets Ronald Riot Case." *Ellensburg Evening Record,* June 29, 1934, 1.
35. "Vanderveer Fined $10 for Cle Elum Fist Fight." *Ellensburg Evening Record,* June 30, 1934, 1. "Street Fight Aftermath of Rioting Trial." *Miner Echo* [Cle Elum, WA], July 6, 1934, 1.
36. "Vanderveer Fined $10 for Cle Elum Fist Fight," 1.
37. "Jury Acquits 13 Ronald Residents on Riot Charge." *Ellensburg Evening Record,* June 30, 1934, 1.
38. Hughes, J. M., letter to Charles Donnelly, July 16, 1934. NWI.

Epilogue

1. Kittitas County Superior Court Records. Washington State Archives. Ellensburg, WA.
2. Pope, James Gray. "The Western Pennsylvania Coal Strike of 1933, Part II: Lawmaking from Above and the Demise of Democracy in the United Mine Workers." *Labor History* 44, no. 2 (2003): 259.
3. Robert Bell, Sr. interview by Steve Addington, June 28, 1972, Frederick Krueger Collection, Central Washington University, Ellensburg, WA.
4. Charles Rushton, interview, "Mining Union Disputes in Roslyn—1934." *Voices of Washington State: Discussion Guides*. Ed. Judith C. Espinola (Seattle, WA: Metrocenter YWCA, 1980).
5. Browitt, David. "Roslyn History Lecture 7—Coal Mining." Roslyn History Lecture Series. Roslyn Public Library, Roslyn, Washington. January 27, 2002. www.washingtonruralheritage.org/cdm/ref/collection/roslyn/id/474.
6. Camilla Saivetto, interview by Steve Addington, June 22, 1976, Frederick Krueger Collection, Central Washington University, Ellensburg, WA.
7. "Celebration Will Mark Brighter Day for This Field." *Miner Echo* [Cle Elum, WA], August 31, 1934, 1.
8. "Politicians' Invitation." *Ellensburg Evening Record*, October 9, 1934, 1.
9. Dubofsky, Melvyn. "Rebirth of a Union, 1933-1934." *John L. Lewis: A Biography.* (New York: Quadrangle/The New York Times Book Co., 1977), 201.
10. Laslett, John H. M. "Swan Song or New Social Movement? Socialism and Illinois District 12, United Mine Workers of America, 1919-1926." *Socialism in the Heartland: the Midwestern Experience, 1900-1925.* (Notre Dame, IN: University of Notre Dame, 1986), 182-83.
11. Cole, William, letter to Clarence Martin, May 4, 1934. Washington State Patrol, "Labor Troubles 1934," Washington State Archives, Olympia, WA.
12. Robert Panerio, telephone interview by author, July 29, 2009.
13. "Andrew T. Hunter Obituary." *Seattle Times*, March 22, 1966, 43.
14. Washington State Digital Archives. www.digitalarchives.wa.gov.
15. Haller, Mark, letter to Richard Major, January 15, 1992, personal property of Richard L. Major, Seattle, WA.
16. Camilla Saivetto.
17. Baich, Molly. "Joseph Pasquan (1873-1963)." *From Old Country to Coal Country.* (Cle Elum, WA: Roslyn-Ronald-Cle Elum Heritage Club, 2005), 20.
18. Sam Talerico, interview by author, October 26, 2010.
19. "Death Takes E. K. Brown Here Today." Ellensburg Daily Record, October 28, 1955, 1.
20. David Browitt, interview by author, June 18, 2011.
21. Ibid.
22. Darwin Kanyer, interview by author, August 25, 2010.
23. Julia Wallgren, interview by author, June 17, 2011.
24. Nick Henderson, interview by author, August 25, 2010.
25. George Turner Jr., interview by author, June 18, 2011.
26. Nick Henderson.

Bibliography

Alter, Jonathan. *The Defining Moment: FDR's Hundred Days and the Triumph of Hope.* New York: Simon & Schuster, 2006.

Barto, Harold E., and Bullard, Catharine. *History of the State of Washington.* Vol. 3. Boston: C.C. Heath and Co, 1947.

Bernstein, Irving. *Turbulent Years: A History of the American Worker, 1933-1941.* Boston: Houghton Mifflin, 1970.

Bird, Caroline. *The Invisible Scar.* New York: Longman, 1978.

Black, Gordon. *Communism in Washington State: Organizing the Unemployed: The Early 1930s.* Communism in Washington State History and Memory Project, 2002. depts.washington.edu/labhist/cpproject/black.shtml.

Carlson, Linda. *Company Towns of the Pacific Northwest.* Seattle: University of Washington Press, 2003.

Carnes, Cecil. *John L. Lewis: Leader of Labor.* New York: Robert Speller, 1936.

Cohen, Adam. *Nothing to Fear: FDR's Inner Circle and the Hundred Days That Created Modern America.* New York: Penguin, 2009.

Davis, Kenneth Sydney. *FDR, the New Deal Years, 1933-1937: A History.* New York: Random House, 1986.

Dembo, Jonathan. *Unions and Politics in Washington State, 1885-1935.* New York: Garland Pub., 1983.

Dennett, Eugene V. *Agitprop: The Life of an American Working-class Radical: The Autobiography of Eugene V. Dennett.* Albany: State University of New York Press, 1990.

Dix, Keith. *What's a Coal Miner to Do?: The Mechanization of Coal Mining.* Pittsburgh, PA: University of Pittsburgh Press, 1988.

Draper, Theodore. *The Roots of American Communism.* Chicago, IL: Dee, 1989.

Dubofsky, Melvyn. *John L. Lewis: A Biography.* New York: Quadrangle/New York Times Book Co., 1977.

_____. *We Shall Be All: A History of the Industrial Workers of the World.* Chicago: Quadrangle, 1969.

Espinola, Judith, ed. *Voices of Washington State: Discussion Guides.* Seattle, WA: Metrocenter YWCA, 1980.

Fishback, Price V. *Soft Coal, Hard Choices: The Economic Welfare of Bituminous Coal Miners, 1890-1930.* New York: Oxford University Press, 1992.

Foner, Philip S. *History of the Labor Movement in the United States.* Vol. 4. New York: International, 1973.

Green, Stephen H. *Coal and Coal Mining in Washington. Division of Mines and Geology, Report of Investigations No. 4R.* Olympia, WA: State Printing Plant, 1947.

Hiltzik, Michael A. *The New Deal: A Modern History.* New York: Free Press, 2011.

Hobbs, Richard S. *The Cayton Legacy: An African American Family.* Pullman: Washington State University Press, 2002.

Jameson, Elizabeth. *All That Glitters: Class, Conflict, and Community in Cripple Creek.* Urbana: University of Illinois Press, 1998.

Johnson, James P. *A "New Deal" for Soft Coal: The Attempted Revitalization of the Bituminous Coal Industry under the New Deal*. New York: Arno, 1979.

———. *The Politics of Soft Coal: The Bituminous Industry from World War I through the New Deal*. Urbana: University of Illinois Press, 1979.

Johnson, Jeffrey A. *"They Are All Red Out Here": Socialist Politics in the Pacific Northwest, 1895-1925*. Norman: University of Oklahoma Press, 2008.

Karlin, Jules A. "Anti-Chinese Outbreaks in Seattle, 1885-1886." *Pacific Northwest Quarterly* 39 (1948): 103-30.

Kennedy, David M. *Freedom from Fear: The American People in Depression and War, 1929-1945*. New York: Oxford University Press, 1999.

Kimeldorf, Howard. *Battling for American Labor: Wobblies, Craft Workers, and the Making of the Union Movement*. Berkeley: University of California Press, 1999.

Klehr, Harvey. *The Heyday of American Communism: The Depression Decade*. New York: Basic Books, 1984.

Ko, Daeha. *Communism in Washington State: Rough Beginnings: The 1920s*. Communism in Washington State History and Memory Project, 2002. depts.washington.edu/labhist/cpproject/ko.shtml.

Laslett, John H. M. "Swan Song or New Social Movement? Socialism and Illinois District 12, United Mine Workers of America, 1919-1926." *Socialism in the Heartland: The Midwestern Experience, 1900-1925*. Ed. Donald T. Critchlow. Notre Dame: University of Notre Dame Press, 1986.

LeWarne, Charles P. *Utopias on Puget Sound, 1885-1915*. Seattle: University of Washington Press, 1995.

Lynd, Staughton. *"We Are All Leaders": The Alternative Unionism of the Early 1930s*. Urbana: University of Illinois Press, 1996.

McDonald, David J., and Lynch, Edward A. *Coal and Unionism: A History of the American Coal Miners' Unions*. Silver Spring, MD: Cornelius Printing, 1939.

Morris, Homer L. *The Plight of the Bituminous Coal Miner*. Philadelphia: University of Pennsylvania Press, 1934.

Morris, James O. "The Acquisitive Spirit of John Mitchell, United Mine Workers President (1899-1908)." *Labor History*, Winter (1979): 5-24.

Mullins, William H. *The Depression and the Urban West Coast, 1929-1933: Los Angeles, San Francisco, Seattle, and Portland*. Bloomington: Indiana University Press, 1991.

Newman, Roger K. *Hugo Black: A Biography*. New York: Pantheon, 1994.

Northern Pacific Railway Historical Association. 2012. www.nprha.org.

Pope, James G. "The Western Pennsylvania Coal Strike of 1933, Part II: Lawmaking from Above and the Demise of Democracy in the United Mine Workers." *Labor History* 44.2 (2003).

Rajala, Richard. "A Dandy Bunch of Wobblies: Pacific Northwest Loggers and the Industrial Workers of the World, 1900–1930." *Labor History* 37.2 (1996): 205-34.

Renshaw, Patrick. *The Wobblies: The Story of the IWW and Syndicalism in the United States*. Chicago: Ivan R. Dee, 1999.

Roberts, Ron E. *John L. Lewis: Hard Labor and Wild Justice*. Dubuque, IA: Kendall/Hunt, 1994.

Roslyn-Ronald-Cle Elum Heritage Club. *From Old Country to Coal Country*. Cle Elum, WA: Roslyn-Ronald-Cle Elum Heritage Club, 2005.

Schwantes, Carlos A. *Radical Heritage: Labor, Socialism, and Reform in Washington and British Columbia, 1885-1917*. Seattle: University of Washington Press, 1979.

Selekman, Sylvia K. *Rebellion in Labor Unions*. New York: Boni and Liveright, 1924.

Shannon, David A. *The Socialist Party of America: A History*. New York: Macmillan, 1955.

Shideler, John C. *Coal Towns in the Cascades: A Centennial History of Roslyn and Cle Elum, Washington*. Spokane, WA: Melior Publications, 1986.

Singer, Alan. "Communists and Coal Miners: Rank-and-File Organizing in the United Mine Workers of America During the 1920s." *Science and Society*, 55.2 (1991): 132-57.

Suggs, George G. *Colorado's War on Militant Unionism: James H. Peabody and the Western Federation of Miners*. Detroit: Wayne State University Press, 1972.

Taft, Philip. *Organized Labor in American History*. New York: Harper & Row, 1964.

Weinstein, James. *The Decline of Socialism in America, 1912-1925*. New York: Monthly Review, 1967.

Zieger, Robert H. *John L. Lewis: Labor Leader*. Boston: Twayne, 1988.

Acknowledgments

The author gratefully acknowledges the generous assistance provided by the following individuals in the preparation of this book.

Reference assistance: Thelma Blount, United Mine Workers of America, Triangle, Virginia; Brigid Clift, Washington State Archives, Central Branch, Ellensburg, Washington; Nick Henderson, Roslyn Museum, Roslyn, Washington; Gerard Hogan, Central Washington University Library, Ellensburg, Washington; Barry Kernfeld, Historical Collections and Labor Archives, The Pennsylvania State University, University Park, Pennsylvania; Frederick Krueger, historian, Ellensburg, Washington; Alison Purgiel, Minnesota History Center, St. Paul, Minnesota; Kim Renfro, Suncadia Cultural Archive, Roslyn, Washington; Milton Wagy, Ellensburg Public Library, Ellensburg, Washington; Lauren Walton, Kittitas County Historical Museum, Ellensburg, Washington; and Erin Whitesel-Jones, Washington State Archives, Western Branch, Olympia, Washington.

Roslyn history: Angie Briski, John and Agnes Ferro, Harry Georgeson, Pete Horsch, Darwin Kanyer, Sam and Margy Talerico, George Turner, and Julia Wallgren.

Documents: Richard Major (letter of Mark Haller), Robert Panerio Sr. (photo of Andrew Hunter), and Barbara Ruff Strem (newspaper clippings of Bob Ruff).

Editorial assistance on early drafts: Lea Beardsley, David Browitt, Montgomery Buell, Mary Lou Ham, Erin Krake, Frederick Krueger, Lee Myers, Sam Talerico, and Ron Torland.

Funding: Walla Walla University Faculty Development Grant.

206

Index

About the Author

David Bullock is a professor of communication at Walla Walla University with interests in political communication, media law and ethics, and media cultural and social influence. He holds a Ph.D. from the University of Arizona, and served as lecturer for the Humanities Washington Speakers Bureau. He was honored as distinguished faculty lecturer at Walla Walla University in 2013.

Bullock's interest in Roslyn history stems from frequent childhood visits. His family roots in the community go back to his grandfather who worked as a coal miner in Roslyn from the 1920s to the 1940s. Bullock lives with his wife, Anne, in Walla Walla, Washington.